SOCIAL PROBLEMS

SOCIAL PROBLEMS

An Introduction
to Critical Constructionism

ROBERT HEINER

Plymouth State College

New York   Oxford
OXFORD UNIVERSITY PRESS
2002

Oxford University Press

Oxford   New York
Athens   Auckland   Bangkok   Bogotá   Buenos Aires   Calcutta
Cape Town   Chennai   Dar es Salaam   Delhi   Florence   Hong Kong   Istanbul
Karachi   Kuala Lumpur   Madrid   Melbourne   Mexico City   Mumbai
Nairobi   Paris   São Paulo   Shanghai   Singapore   Taipei   Tokyo   Toronto   Warsaw

and associated companies in
Berlin   Ibadan

Published by Oxford University Press, Inc.
198 Madison Avenue, New York, New York, 10016
http://www.oup-usa.org

Oxford is a registered trademark of Oxford University Press

Library of Congress Cataloging-in-Publication Data

Heiner, Robert, 1956–
   Social problems : an introduction to critical constructionism/Robert Heiner.
      p. cm.
   Includes bibliographical references and index.
   ISBN 0-19-512992-X (pbk. : alk. paper)
      1. Social problems. 2. Social problems—United States. 3. United States—Social
   conditions—1945– I. Title.

HN17.5 .H42 2001
361.1′0973—dc21

                                                                    2001021132

Printing number: 9 8 7 6 5 4 3 2 1
Printed in the United States of America
on acid-free paper

*For Judy, Steve,
Edith, and Boo*

CONTENTS

PREFACE

Six billion people in the world and all around us are social phenomena that could possibly be seen as problematic; yet, only a few capture the public's attention for a brief period of time and these are replaced by another few in a subsequent period. The problems that capture our attention are not necessarily the worst ones and they are not replaced because they have gotten better. There must, therefore, be forces, other than the seriousness of these problems, that explain their procession through the public imagination. This book employs a synthesis of conflict theory and social constructionism (herein called "critical constructionism") to the understanding of the forces that influence the public's understanding of social problems.

This book would not have been possible without the help and support of numerous people. Two of them come immediately to mind. The concept of this book, especially its format, is largely the brainchild of Dana Dunn at the University of Texas at Arlington. Thanks, Dana, for entrusting this project to me. I hope you like the final product. Special thanks go also to Jeffrey Hadden. When I started my doctoral studies, I served as a teaching assistant in Jeff's Social Problems course at the University of Virginia. His definition of a "social problem" lent much to the paradigm used throughout this book. Jeff, it was an honor working for you; thanks for the inspiration and for the material.

I also want to thank Karita dos Santos, Lisa Grzan, and Jeffrey Broesche, my editors at Oxford University Press, for believing in this project and for making its completion as painless as possible. And my deepest appreciation goes to Judith McDonnell at Bryant College and others who reviewed earlier drafts of this book. Your suggestions and criticisms were most welcome and I hope you will find that they contributed to making this a better text.

An incomplete list of others I want to thank for their assistance, expertise, and moral support includes Ginny Barry, Robin Bowers, Joyce Bruce, Kate Donahue, Mike Fischler, Bob Fitzpatrick, Grace Fraser, Gary Goodnough, Anne Kulig, Gary McCool, Kathy Melanson, Katherine Min, Sandy Ramsay, Alice Staples, David Switzer, Terry Timmins, and Stacey Yap.

Lastly, I want to thank my wife, friend, and colleague, Sheryl Shirley. Her training in political science and international relations complements my training in sociology and her compassion for the disenfranchised has always been an inspiration. I hope Sheryl's influence can be seen throughout this book.

SOCIAL PROBLEMS

An Introduction to the Sociology of Social Problems

T
o begin our study in the sociology of social problems, we should note that "Social Problems" is a subdiscipline of sociology. Sociology is a very broad field, encompassing such subdisciplines as the sociology of the family, of crime and delinquency, of race relations, of the environment, of education, of law, of medicine, of science, of knowledge, and yes, even the sociology of sociology. Sociology is so broad that most sociologists specialize in just one or two subdisciplines. The point is that the sociology of social problems is a subdiscipline; it is *not* simply a current events course. The sociologist who specializes in social problems is not a news journalist, nor simply a social commentator; he or she brings to the analysis of current events the perspective, tools, and theories specific to their sociological training.

THE SOCIOLOGICAL PERSPECTIVE

Sociology is a social science and, as a science, it attempts to approach its subject matter objectively. The social sciences include such disciplines as sociology, psychology, and anthropology. The natural sciences include such disciplines as biology, chemistry, and physics. The social sciences are often called "soft" sciences, or are accused of being mere "fluff," referring to the fact that they are less scientific, or less objective than the natural or "hard" sciences. Indeed, there is truth to these charges. Value judgments do come into play more often in the social sciences than in the natural sciences. The social sciences are more subjective because humans are conducting the research and humans are the *subject* of the research. One cannot study oneself objectively. However, the natural sciences are not totally objective either. Implicit judgments underlie the conduct of research in the natural sciences; judgments such as: What is important to know? What is the best way to study it? What constitutes sufficient evidence? *Important, best, sufficient*— these are all value judgments.

We can, then, conclude that the social sciences are less scientific than the natural sciences because they are less objective. However, we cannot conclude that the social sciences are not truly sciences on the basis of their lack of objectivity (as the term "fluff" implies), because if we use objectivity as our primary criterion, then the natural sciences are not sciences either; in fact, there would be no such thing as science. What the natural sciences and the social sciences have in common is that they systematically strive for objective understanding.

This is an important point in the sociological study of social problems because most people assume that "social problems" are bad and need to be eliminated. Indeed, the very use of the word "problem" promotes such connotations. However, if we approach the study of social problems assuming that they are bad, we are not being objective, and we will not achieve a sociological understanding.

Let's take crime, for example. Most students of social problems and of criminology begin their study of crime presuming that it is bad and needs to be eliminated. "Bad" is a value judgment, and it impedes our objective understanding of the phenomenon of crime. One who presumes crime is bad is likely to overlook many of the "good" aspects of crime. For example, crime provides us with nearly three million jobs in local, state, and federal criminal justice, and in private security.[1] Perhaps it could be argued that without crime these people could find other jobs. But we should note that a lot of people who work in these areas like their jobs, so for them crime is good. As will be discussed later in this book, Emile Durkheim[2] and Kai Erikson[3] both argued that crime plays an essential role in uniting a society against common enemies and in establishing the moral boundaries of a community. To the extent that crime performs these functions, crime is good. Further, sociologists have pointed out the role organized crime has played in American history in terms of providing ethnic minorities with a ladder to the middle class.[4] Through organized crime, minority members have acquired wealth, and with that wealth they established legitimate businesses; they hired others of their own kind who were previously excluded from the workplace. This process began with the Irish in the late nineteenth century, then the Jews at the turn of the century, then the Italians and Sicilians, and now Hispanic and African Americans. If you are of Jewish, Irish, or Italian descent, perhaps you or someone you know can afford to be in college because your or their grandparent was hawking drugs in the 1920s (i.e., alcohol during Prohibition). Likewise, twenty or thirty years from now, more Hispanic and African American kids may be able to afford to go to college because their parent or grandparent was hawking crack in the 1980s. Consequently, crime has been good for millions of immigrants and minorities in American history. Only a small proportion of them participated in organized crime; but millions more were helped into legitimate business by the participation of a few.

To suggest that crime has its positive aspects is not to argue that the United States' relatively high crime rates are reason to rejoice, nor is it to suggest that crime should be encouraged; but it does suggest that the layperson's assumption that crime is bad and needs to be eliminated is a limited and limiting view. One who takes this perspective will not likely be open to a more complete understanding of the phenomenon. The same can be said of all social problems. Thus, as social scientists, it is important that we suspend some of our moral beliefs and value judgments as we pursue a fuller, more objective understanding of social problems. Unfortunately, the word "problem" is a value-laden term; to the layperson, it connotes an element of undesirability. The sociologist striving for some degree of objectivity, therefore, defines the phrase "social problem" very carefully. Sociologically, *a social problem is a phenomenon regarded as bad or undesirable by a significant number of people, or a number of significant people who mobilize to eliminate it*. To understand the scientific advantages of this definition, it is important to understand the concept of *social structure*.

In a society, there are individuals, groups, and institutions. These individuals, groups, and institutions are all related to one another. These relationships may be very strong or very weak, very direct or very indirect. The totality of these individuals, groups, institutions and the relationships between them make up the social structure. It is presumed that there are rules governing these relationships. Sociology is the study of these rules; and a sociological theory is an attempt to describe such a rule.

Now let us get a little abstract and graphically depict a social structure as illustrated in Figure 1.1. The social structure is arbitrarily represented below as a grid [A], a set of intersecting rules and relationships. Contained within this social structure is a phenomenon [B] that is a *potential* social problem. According to our sociological definition, this phenomenon does not become an *actual* social problem until it is defined as such by a group [C]. To repeat our definition, a social problem is a phenomenon regarded as bad or undesirable (B in the diagram) by a significant number of people, or a number of significant people (C in the diagram) who mobilize to eliminate it. The group [C], which is either significant in size or significant in composi-

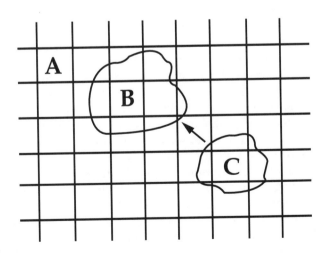

Figure 1.1

tion, is often called a *social movement organization*. To understand why this group forms, one must understand the social structure [A]. The point of this conceptualization is that a phenomenon [B] does not become a social problem because of its inherent badness; it becomes a social problem because of factors *external* to the problem itself—namely, the social structure [A] and the social movement organization [C]. Here's the scientific advantage of this conceptualization: the sociologist cannot objectively say that phenomenon B is bad; but he or she *can* objectively say that group C says phenomenon B is bad. Hence, the sociologist is able to establish a degree of objectivity over the otherwise value-laden phrase "social problem." We will call this conceptualization *the social problems perspective*.

To illustrate the social problems perspective, let's take the example of child abuse. Children have been physically abused by the millions for hundreds or thousands of years. There were brief periods in history when a group would organize on behalf of abused children; but for the most part, what we call "child abuse" was overlooked or tolerated by most of Western civilization throughout most of its history.[5] That is, it did not meet our definition of a social problem. One might be inclined to argue that child abuse was a social problem, even though it was not recognized as such, because countless children were being hurt, even killed, at the hands of their parents, and that is bad. But "bad" is a value judgment. How badly do the children have to have been hurt, and how many have to have been hurt, for child abuse to constitute a social problem? We cannot objectively say. Where do we draw the line in terms of injury or numbers of injuries before we can call something a social problem? This is a matter of opinion, and science cannot answer this question.

It was not until the early 1960s that physicians began to organize, opposing the previous medical practice of overlooking evidence of child abuse. According to Pfohl[6] there were a number of features of the medical profession that help to explain this timing. First, in the late 1950s, pediatric radiology had advanced to the point where long bone fractures could be identified. Long bone fractures travel up and down the bone, and are almost certainly the result of periodic trauma occurring over a long period of time, fitting the pattern of child abuse. Before this advance in pediatric radiology, emergency room doctors encountering injuries resulting from abuse could be pretty certain that abuse was the cause; but they generally refrained from reporting their suspicions to the authorities. They were inclined to overlook child abuse because, at the time, what went on between family members was considered a family matter; parents had almost absolute property rights over their children. Furthermore, norms of doctor-patient confidentiality made the reporting of child abuse a difficult ethical decision. At the time, it was not clear exactly who was the patient: the child, or the parents who "owned" the child and were paying for the doctor. On the other hand, pediatric radiologists acted largely as consultants, having little or no direct contact with either the child or the parents. They also received little or no respect within the medical profession because they were *merely* consultants; they did not perform surgery; and their connection to life-or-death decisions was indirect. They, therefore, had something to gain by their "discovery" of child abuse. So they became the "experts," and they were often called into court to testify about life-and-death decisions involving children. Their prestige increased within the profession as a result of the discovery of child abuse. Soon, psychiatrists joined in the mobilization against child abuse. They, too, had previously enjoyed little prestige in the medical profession and could only stand to elevate themselves by aligning themselves with what was becoming a popular cause. Then, with the help of the media, the police, and various political leaders, child abuse became a full-blown social problem.

Note that we just explained how child abuse became a social problem without stating or implying that it is bad, without making a subjective evaluation of the harm that it causes. Instead, we explained how the phenomenon (B in Figure 1.1) became a social problem because a group [C], made up of pediatric radiologists and psychiatrists, mobilized against it. This group came about because of features and changes in the social structure [A]. Remember that the social structure is made up of individuals, groups, institutions, and the relationships between them. That is what we described: the relationships between parents and their children, between doctors and parents, between doctors and children, between pediatric radiologists and the rest of the medical profession. Child abuse became a social problem *not* because of the harm done by the phenomenon, but because of features *external* to the phenomenon.

A Few Drawbacks

While sociology is a social science, and while we strive to control our subjectivity, it must be noted that objectivity is an impossible goal. All of us are products of our society and, as such, we cannot study society objectively. We are *subject* to the same rules of society that we are trying to study. The social problems perspective should be recognized as merely *a device*, a flawed device, that enables us to achieve *some degree* of objectivity. Now let us take a look at the flaws in this device.

Our definition of a "social problem" is a good deal less than purely objective. According to this definition, a social problem is a phenomenon regarded as bad or undesirable by a significant number of people, or a number of significant people who mobilize to eliminate it. The problem with this definition is, of course, the word "significant." Significance is a value judgment. How many people make up a significant number? Or, how significant do the people involved have to be? Having this word in the definition allows the researcher to identify virtually any phenomenon he or she wants and to justify this identification by calling the group opposed to it "significant."

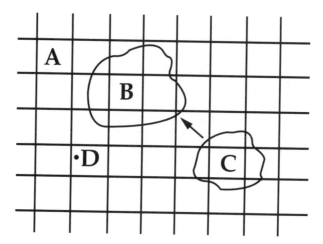

Figure 1.2

Let us take a look at the diagram again. It has been redrawn in Figure 1.2. Another flaw in the social problems perspective is that the sociologist lives, breathes, and conducts her or his research *in* that social structure. (The sociologist is now represented by the little speck [D] marked on the diagram.) In other words, the sociologist is not looking at the social structure from above, as you are looking at the diagram on this page. The sociologist is part of the social structure that she or he is trying to study, subject to the same norms, values, and beliefs that characterize that social structure. Consequently, his or her objectivity is compromised.

A Few Advantages

These flaws notwithstanding, there are certain advantages to this perspective for the sociologist interested in social problems. The social problems perspective emphasizes that it is not the objective harm done by a phenomenon that makes it a "social problem"; instead, it is the activities of parties external to the phenomenon that give it the status of a "social problem," and those activities must be understood in terms of their social structural context. Therefore, this perspective allows us to ask two very important questions: (1) Why does a seemingly harmful phenomenon that has been around for a long time suddenly achieve the status of social problem? (for example, child abuse), and (2) Why are some seemingly harmful phenomena considered social problems while other seemingly harmful phenomena are not? (For example, why is street crime so often defined as a social problem, while corporate crime is not?) These two questions ("why all of a sudden?" and "why this and not that?") are of fundamental concern from the sociological perspective referred to in this book as "critical constructionism." From the social problems perspective and from the critical constructionist perspective, the answers to these questions do not have to do with the relative harm done by the phenomenon.

CRITICAL CONSTRUCTIONISM

Critical constructionism is largely a synthesis of two very influential theories in sociology, namely, conflict theory and symbolic interactionism. It will be useful to review these theories before turning to our discussion of critical constructionism.

Conflict Theory

Conflict theory is derived largely from the works of Karl Marx. Writing at the time of the Industrial Revolution, Marx was concerned with the struggle between the *bourgeoisie* and the *proletariat*. The bourgeoisie owned the factories and the proletariat worked in them. The relationship between the two classes, according to Marx, was one of exploitation. With the state representing the interests of the bourgeoisie, the social structure itself favored the interests of the bourgeoisie; the proletariat were unable to do anything but work for them. All terms of employment favored the employers, and they worked their advantage to the hilt, underpaying their workers and treating them like replaceable parts. Modern conflict theory is concerned not only with the struggle between employers and employees, but with the struggle between all interest groups: rich and poor, white and black, men and women, etc.

Conflict theorists are concerned mostly with inequality. Those interested in social problems usually attribute them to inequality and the use and abuse of power. *Power is the ability to influence the social structure.* Those with power—the elite—influence the social structure in ways that will enhance their power. Generally, the elite tend to use their power to prevent change and maintain the *status quo*. It is, after all, contemporary social arrangements—the present social structure, the status quo—that allow them their power. Those with relatively little power tend to accept the status quo, not necessarily because they are forced to, but more often because they believe in it. Our norms, values, and beliefs are the product of the social structure. Therefore, the ability to influence the social structure is the ability to influence the way people think. People are socialized by society's basic institutions—government, education, religion, and the media—to think that those in power should be in power.

Like their predecessor, Marx, modern conflict theorists tend to be very critical of capitalism. Contrary to what most people think, the people in power, referred to above, are not the nation's political or military leaders. The real power in the United States, they argue, is in the hands of the capitalists, specifically, the nation's corporate leaders. Controlling as much money and resources as they do, they are able to influence legislation and policy for their own interests. The free market economy of the United States, with its relative lack of regulations, benefits American corporations often at the expense of the American people. According to the neo-Marxists, the American people, on the other hand, often tend to believe that anything that is good for corporate America is good for them, not because this is true, but because that is what they have been socialized to believe.

It is not surprising, then, that conflict theory often comes across as a very terse critique of capitalism. Americans tend to be far less receptive to such ideas than their European counterparts. During the thirty-plus years of the cold war, everything Marxist was considered bad, and most things capitalist were considered good. Besides being ideologically unpopular, conflict theory also suffers in that it is easily interpreted to suggest that the elite make up a united, all-powerful conspiracy. This, however, is not the intention of the conflict theorist. First of all, the elite are not all-powerful. Their ability to influence the social structure is not boundless. There is a certain give and take. All legislation and policy does not favor their interests; but their influence is such that the totality of legislation and policy, at least slightly, favors their interests. Second, few conflict theorists would suggest that the elite conspire to subjugate the rest of society. Instead, the elite have a *unity of interests* that makes it seem *as if* they conspire. That is, on average, the same policies that would benefit one powerful person will also benefit most powerful people; when they each pursue their individual self-interest, it produces the same effect as a conspiracy.

Another feature of conflict theory that may or may not be problematic is the primacy it gives to the value of equality. There is an inherent value judgment implicit to most conflict theory. The pain and suffering that are the result of inequality are viewed negatively. Objectivity is often willingly suspended in the name of equality. In fact, many conflict theorists often take an activist role, feeling it is their moral duty to promote social and political change. Even though its objectivity may be compromised, conflict theory is generally highly regarded among sociologists. Many would argue that the human rights that conflict theorists study and promote are universal or inherent rights and, therefore, do not constitute subjective values. Whether this is true or not is a philosophical matter, but their perspective remains sociological because their emphasis is on the social structure and the inequality built into the relationships between individuals, groups, and institutions. Conflict theory's emphasis on social justice has added the elements of liberalism and humanitarianism for which sociology is renowned, and for which it is sometimes reviled.

Symbolic Interactionism

Unlike conflict theory, which focuses on the broader social structure, symbolic interactionism focuses on the day to day interactions between people. Symbolic interactionism is considered a branch of social psychology because it focuses on the ways people think and give meaning to the world. Virtually all human interaction involves the act of interpretation. George Herbert Mead argued that human beings are different from animals because our communication is based on language. The communication of animals is genetically programmed, and therefore, their utterances have inherent meaning. Human communication, on the other hand, is based on language; language is based on words; and words are *symbols*. A symbol, by definition, is something that signifies something else. Symbols, then, have no inherent meaning and, therefore, require interpretation.[7]

The act of interpretation is critical to all of our social experiences, not just the processing of language. Between us and our environment is our interpretation of the environment. People do not respond directly to the environment, instead they respond to their *interpretation* of the environment. The way we interpret the environment depends upon our past experiences. Since no two people have the same history of experiences, no two people interpret the same event or object exactly the same way. Hence, the word "college," for example, has at least slightly different meanings for everyone who uses it. Likewise, any given social problem will mean something different to all who conceive of it. Based on their different histories of experience, people will interpret and prioritize social problems differently.

Though no two people's experiences can be the same, members of different groups within the social structure will have experiences more similar to each other than they will to members of other groups. Their interpretations of the environment, therefore, will be more similar to each other than to members of other groups. For example, members of the upper class have more experiences in common with one another than they do with members of the lower class. Therefore, upper class and lower class individuals are likely to label or define social problems differently.

We have already been introduced to the logic of symbolic interactionism in our discussion of the social problems perspective, illustrated in Figure 1.1. In this diagram, the *potential* social problem [B] does not become an *actual* social problem until it is defined, or *labeled* as such by a significant number of people or a number of significant people [C]. Like a symbol, the potential social problem [B] has no inherent meaning. Before it can become a social problem, it has to be interpreted as such by a significant group [C]. Symbolic interactionism, then, directs our attention *not* to the social problem itself, but to meanings that are assigned to it. This leads us directly to a discussion of critical constructionism.

Critical Constructionism

Some seemingly harmful phenomena meet our definition of a social problem, while other seemingly *more* harmful phenomena do *not* meet this definition. Put another way, some phenomena come to be interpreted by a significant number of people or a number of significant people as social problems that need to be addressed and some do not, irrespective of the amount of harm done by these phenomena. *Social constructionism* is concerned with how the meanings of social problems are constructed. Problem construction involves the following processes: the identification of a phenomenon as problematic, the providing of explanations for the causes of that phenomenon, and the persuasion of the public that the phenomenon is problematic and needs to be dealt with. The social constructionist examines these processes. *Critical constructionism* is different from social constructionism only in that it emphasizes the role of elite interests in the process of problem construction. Borrowing from conflict theory, the critical constructionist argues that the way social problems are constructed, conceived, and presented to the public, more often than not, reflects the interests of society's elite more than those of the mainstream and often at the expense of those with the least power in our society.

It was suggested above that the social problems perspective allows us to ask the question: Why are some seemingly harmful phenomena considered social problems and not other seemingly harmful phenomena? The example of street crime versus corporate crime was given. Most Americans would consider it common sense that street crime is more "dangerous" than corporate crime. The critical constructionist might argue that street crime is considered more of a social problem than corporate crime because the groups that have the power to frame social problems have an interest in diverting public attention away from crimes committed by the upper class and directing it to the crimes committed by members of the lower class. Thus, the way the crime problem is constructed reflects the interests of the elite (whose crimes do more harm) to the detriment of the poor (who are punished more severely for their crimes).

Symbolic interactionists argue that all interpretations of reality are influenced by our experiences. To put it more strongly, all knowledge is socially constructed. All constructions of social problems are, therefore, worthy of constructionist analysis. Without denying this position, however, the critical constructionist is most concerned with those constructions of social problems that are in the popular domain—namely, those that receive a great deal of media attention—and how those constructions are influenced by elite interests. Popular constructions of social problems are those that sway social policy, and elite interests are most in need of critical scrutiny because they are so often obscured or confused with societal interests. Consistent with conflict theory from which it is derived, critical constructionism strives to give voice to the less powerful groups in society, a voice that is typically overwhelmed in public debate by the resources of those groups with more power.

Though the term "critical constructionism" may be unfamiliar, this type of analysis is not new to sociology. Many of its components were described by Marx and later developed further by Antonio Gramsci. Gramsci, a socialist, was incarcerated by the Fascist government in Italy in the 1920s, in the words of the prosecutor, "to stop that brain from working for twenty years."[8] Gramsci wrote many of his ideas down in what have come to be known as "the prison notebooks." Gramsci addressed what many have argued is a critical flaw in the work of Marx, the question of "inevitability."

Marx argued that it was inevitable that the workers would rise up in revolution and overthrow their capitalist oppressors. Such a revolution did not take place in a great many countries, including the United States. In these countries, Gramsci argued, the capitalist elite have been able to thwart a revolution through its influence on institutions associated with the production of knowledge and culture. Gramsci called this influence "hegemony;" and through their hegemony, the elite are able to shape what the public considers "common sense."[9] For example, in the United States, it is considered common sense that the U.S. is both the "the land of the free" and "the land of opportunity" despite, as we shall see, evidence to the contrary. But as long as Americans believe these to be matters of common sense, they feel no need to change the status quo, let alone revolt against the capitalists. Thus, Gramsci and critical constructionists are in agreement that, through their influence on the production of cultural knowledge, the elite are able to influence the public's perceptions of social problems to their own advantage.

Critical constructionists do not argue that the social problems that are successfully constructed are inconsequential and harmless. Instead, they argue that our view of the problems that exist in society has been distorted by the power relations involved in the construction of social problems. In this regard, critical constructionism is not very useful in terms of providing solutions to problems. But it is useful in terms of providing a perspective that allows us to decipher what the real problems are in society and to prioritize them on a rational basis, a basis that is concerned with the societal welfare and that does not weigh more heavily in favor of society's elite.

NON-SOCIOLOGICAL PHILOSOPHIES

Very often, non-sociological philosophies dominate the public debate about social problems. The most popular of these is the notion of *free will*. Sociology, as well as the other social sciences, is based on the principle of *determinism*, arguing that human behavior and the choices we make are largely determined by forces that can be empirically studied. The principle of free will, on the other hand, asserts that our choices are voluntary and not determined by such forces. Philosophers have been debating these two points for millennia. But perhaps we should see the issue as being a matter of degree. The question is how free or how determined are the choices we make?

Americans tend to favor a free will style of explanation for social problems. American religious life is dominated by the Judeo-Christian ethic; the United States is the most capitalistic society in the world; Americans place a high value on individualism. Free will is the ideology that ties all these features of being "American" together. Whether or not a person goes to heaven or hell is a matter of the free choices that the individual makes (the Judeo-Christian ethic); whether one becomes rich or poor is a matter of the free choices that one makes (capitalism); we, as individuals, have a right to make our choices freely and to be judged accordingly (individualism). On the determinism-free will continuum, debates in the United States concerning social problems tend strongly to favor free will, and sociological explanations often face a good deal of resistance.

Here are some examples of the types of arguments put forth by free will advocates: if you cut welfare recipients from the welfare roles, poverty will decline, because people will make the rational choice and go to work; if we toughen sentencing, crime will decline, because people will make the rational choice and not commit crime. Compelling as it may be in American culture, the free will explanation for social problems does have a serious drawback. One problem with free will is that it fails to explain some of the *patterns* that characterize these problems. For example, why are African Americans more likely to be poor in this country than white Americans? To say that blacks are more likely to be poor because they are less likely to make the decisions necessary to move out of poverty amounts to a non-explanation. It leaves out *why* blacks are less likely to make those decisions. Obviously, there are forces that influence (or "determine") the choices we have to make, that influence the choices we have available, and that influence the way we derive our decisions.

Another non-sociological philosophy that enjoys considerable popularity in relation to social problems is the *human nature* argument. Like sociology, it is a form of determinism, but it is quite the opposite of sociology. Human nature proponents argue that we are the way we are because that is the way nature (or God) has ordained us. Sociology, on the other hand, holds that we are the way we are because of our culture and our experiences within the social structure. Human nature is a form of biological determinism; sociology employs a form of social or cultural determinism. Again, philosophers have been debating these two points for thousands of years; the debate is often referred to as "nature versus nurture." Human nature, thus, has its legitimacy; however, with regard to social problems, it shares a serious flaw with the free will argument. Both philosophies often fall short when it comes to explaining cross-cultural patterns. Free choice and human nature explanations for crime, poverty, and other social problems fail to account for cross-cultural variations.

THE CROSS-CULTURAL AND GLOBAL PERSPECTIVES

One of the first things that sociologists and anthropologists learn from their studies of other cultures is that statements about human nature are usually ethnocentric, or culturally biased. That is, we think that it is human nature to be the way our culture has made us. Virtually from the time we are born, we are exposed to the norms, values, and beliefs of our culture. They are omnipresent, and we learn to take them for granted. We do not question them, we live by them; we have no basis for questioning them. We come to think of them as "natural." This is ethnocentrism. People all over the world are ethnocentric, believing their culture to be superior to the "strange" ways of other cultures.

The problem with ethnocentrism is that it is limiting. It does not just limit our ability to understand other countries, their people, and their practices; it also limits our ability to understand our own country, our policies, and ourselves. Understanding requires perspective; the kind of perspective we seek in this book is a *cross-cultural* (or a "comparative") perspective. Comparisons are an essential element of the scientific process. Paleontologists may compare fossils over time. Medical researchers may compare the relative effects of different drugs. Behaviorists may compare the ability of mice who have been exposed to different stimuli to get through a maze. Likewise, an essential tool of the sociologist is cross-cultural comparison. Through comparisons, we can gain new insight into social problems in the United States. For example, if another country has considerably less violent crime than we have in the United States, an explanation for their lower rates will help us to understand our high rates of violent crime. If another country is able to avoid the problem of poverty, then an understanding of its culture and practices may provide us with insight into our own problem of poverty. And so it goes with other social problems.

We must be wary, however, when we engage in comparative sociology. Cultures are very complex and not easily compared. For example, just because another country executes its robbers *and* has a lower robbery rate than the United States does not mean that it has a lower robbery rate *because* it executes its robbers. There are many more factors that may affect robbery rates that need to be considered, such as religion, family structure, media, distribution of wealth, unemployment, urbanization, the availability of guns, etc.

Though we may be tempted to look to other countries for solutions to our social problems, the complexity of cultures makes this problematic. One country's solutions may not be applicable in another country. This should not, however, deter us from comparative inquiry. While an examination of other countries may not provide us with all of the answers to all of our problems, we can acquire insight from these other countries; and it would be the height of ethnocentrism to believe that we have nothing to learn from them.

A cross-cultural perspective allows us to see the variety of possible ways of looking at and solving different social problems, while a *global* perspective allows us to look at the interrelations between countries and their social problems. For better or worse, the world is becoming increasingly globalized. Current economic trends and telecommunications are making the world smaller and smaller. Countries throughout the world are becoming more and more interdependent. Geopolitical boundaries are becoming less relevant. One country's social problems may well impact problems in other countries. One country's refugees flood into another country, threatening its political stability. Another country's population is exploding, which may cause mass starvation, or it may motivate its leaders to expand its borders beyond their present position. Another country expends far more resources per capita than any other country, causing it to look to other countries to exploit their assets, and contributing to a disproportionate depletion of the earth's natural resources. There is no question that more and more social problems will be global in their scope, and a global perspective will be necessary to confront them. It is time we shed some of our provincialism and look at social problems and social solutions throughout the world.

CORPORATE AMERICA

As we examine our neighbors, it becomes apparent that the United States is unique among the modern nations of the world. The U.S. has a short history, and that makes it somewhat easier to characterize it in a few words. American culture is highly individualistic and places a great deal of emphasis on freedom. This notion of "freedom," however, is quite elusive. Freedom of religion was suppressed by our ancestors who persecuted the pagan Native Americans. Freedom of speech was suppressed by the Alien and Sedition Act of World War I, later during the McCarthy Era, and at various other points in our history. The sexual freedom of homosexuals continues to be suppressed in many parts of the country today. The degree to which we enjoy such freedoms as those of the press, speech, religion, and sexuality do not distinguish us from many other countries in the world. What does distinguish the United States, however, is the degree of emphasis that we place on freedom of the market. Though not absolute, the one freedom that we have historically enjoyed more than any other country is freedom of the market. Market freedom is the linchpin of capitalist ideology, and this explains why the United States is often characterized as the most capitalist society in the world.

Consistent with critical constructionism, it is the opinion of this author that many of the social problems we experience in the United States stem from our capitalist extremes, that many of our social problems would be amenable to improvement were we not so individualistic in our personal affairs and in the economic affairs of our country. Community and compassion are often sacrificed in the name of individualism and the free market. It is not that the values of individualism and free market are inherently bad; in fact, they are often good. It is the extreme to which these values are expressed in the United States that results in a good many of our social problems.

What is worse is that these extreme values are rapidly spreading throughout the world. Deregulation has benefited American corporations so much that other countries are being forced to deregulate their markets in order to compete. The result has been the momentous and incredibly rapid restructuring and deregulation of the world market through programs and treaties such as GATT (General Agreement on Tariffs and Trade), NAFTA (North American Free Trade Agreement), the WTO (World Trade Organization), and the EU (European Union). The American style of capitalism that is now spreading across the globe glorifies efficiency and profit at any cost. Large corporations stand to gain considerably from the freedom of the world market; that would not be bad if their profits did indeed "trickle down" to the workers and improve the general standard of living in the societies involved. This, as we shall see, has not been and is not likely to be the case. Instead, millions of American workers are being—or face the threat of being—"downsized." Because corporations seek to "trim the fat," American workers and workers all over the world are facing cuts in their benefits. Environments throughout the world are being devastated as transnational corporations (TNCs) set up shop wherever the labor is cheap and environmental regulations will not interfere with their quest for profit. As the world economy is being restructured and as corporations throughout the world are racing to get "leaner and meaner," we need to consider seriously what the phrase "leaner and meaner" means, with all of its implications.

THE MEDIA

The critical constructionist is very sensitive to the role of the news media in defining social problems. The chance that a problem will receive much attention—or have societal resources mobilized against it—are almost nil without media coverage. Politicians often manipulate and/or criticize the media to highlight social problems that fit their own political agenda. The media have their own agenda, as well. In recent years, the media have merged into huge conglomerates. In the early days of television, providing the news was largely considered a public service; profits were to be made from other programming, and news bureaus were less concerned with "the bottom line."[10] Today's network news has become a huge moneymaker. The network executives are responsible to their shareholders, and their principal concern is profit. The way to make a profit is to sell commercial advertising; the way to sell commercial advertising is to attract a large audience; the way to attract a large audience is to entertain. While a democracy depends upon an informed citizenry, the goal of today's media is to entertain, not to inform.[11] Unfortunately, we depend upon the media for much of our information about contemporary social problems, and the media have found that certain problems sell advertising better than others.

Most of the television networks and major newspapers now belong to some of the largest corporations in the world. These corporations make most of their profits from sources other than their news agencies. Large corporations are large investors in other large corporations. They share the unity of interest discussed earlier in this chapter. As investors in other corporations, they have an incentive *not* to provide information through their news agencies that might cast a negative light on the companies in which they are invested. For example, if a corporation is invested in the timber industry, their news agency will face a conflict of interests in deciding whether or not to report the devastation of our forests caused by clear-cutting. They face similar conflicts deciding whether or not to report transgressions committed by the TNCs with whom they have multimillion dollar advertising accounts. This is not to say that the news agencies will never make such reports, but that there is tremendous incentive not to make too many of such reports. In other words, news agencies cannot objectively report the effects of corporatization because they themselves are corporations, invested in other corporations, and profiting from still other corporations by broadcasting their commercial advertising. They have an interest in portraying the country's social problems in some ways and not in others.

Americans have a choice: They can choose to have society run by "Big Government," or they can choose to have it run by "Big Business." "Big Government" is run by people who are elected by the citizenry, serving specific terms of office, and, to be reelected, they must, at least, present the image of concern for the society's welfare. "Big Business" is run by CEOs not elected by the citizenry, whose goal is to increase profits and who are under little or no pressure to attend to society's welfare. "Big Government" means regulation. "Big Business" means deregulation.

In 1996, ABC's prime-time newscast featured a segment, usually several times every week, called "Your Money," showing how the government squandered *your* tax dollars. This segment clearly was designed to foster a distrust of "Big Government," and this clearly served the interests of "Big Business." ABC could just as easily have presented a nightly segment on the abuses and negative effects of American corporate capitalism, but this clearly would not have been in its corporate interest. This is just one example of the media's pro-corporate bias. What is remarkable about it, though, is that this segment was broadcast almost every night for about a year, yet few people seemed to recognize it as antigovernment or pro-capitalist propaganda. Segments such as this, financial affairs programming on all the major networks (including "public" television), and the hundreds of thousands of television commercials that most people have seen by the time they graduate high school—all of these represent instances of pro-business propaganda that are rarely if ever recognized as such. Instead, they have become so much a part of the media landscape that they are taken for granted and never questioned.

THE HOMOGENIZATION OF CULTURE

As American corporate capitalism spreads around the globe, so do our products: our tennis shoes, our cars, our music, our films, our television programming, our tastes, our language, and our values—especially our consumerist values. The American value of consumption used to be distinctively American. Today, people, government representatives, and pundits from around the world are complaining that the citizens of their countries are becoming too wrapped up in American culture; they are abandoning their own culture, striving to be like Americans, and striving to consume what Americans consume. If you have done some traveling outside the United States, you have probably observed different aspects of this trend.

Cultures throughout the world are being homogenized to the American model. This can be seen in both a positive and a negative light. On the one hand, it is good for American exports, and that is good for American workers. It also has its advantages for American travelers. It is sometimes comforting to find a McDonald's or to hear your favorite music in foreign lands. On the other hand, this trend makes some of these other countries susceptible to the same social problems we face in America. That is why people, government representatives, and pundits around the world are complaining; they realize that they will soon face the same problems that we face because of our glorification of free markets and individualism.

A related problem that arises when other countries adopt American values lies in the fact that the "American Dream" is not a realistic goal for most of their citizens—just as it is not for many American citizens, given the nature of inequality in our society—and intense frustration will be the result. Further, the "homogenization of culture" threatens to end millennia of cultural diversity. People throughout the world are concerned that their traditional cultures are giving way to modern American culture. Some people strive to be "modern" like Americans, others are virtually forced to be. For example, when rainforests are cut down, their inhabitants are forced out so the wood can be provided to the Americans or the Japanese. Once in the cities, these former forest dwellers are exposed to the same American values as their urban neighbors. Whether voluntary or forced, much of the cultural richness of the globe is being absorbed into one extended American culture. Though this may somewhat exaggerate the situation—cultures generally change slowly—it still concerns many; certainly foreign travel is becoming less and less exotic. "Like sand castles on a beach," David Crotean and William Hynes write, local cultures are being eroded and flattened by the gradual impact of the endless tide of U.S. and other Western media products."[12]

It is arguable whether or not the restructuring and deregulation of the world market and the homogenization of culture constitute a social problem as we have defined it. Surely there are a number of significant people (a diverse number of people, ranging from Ralph Nader to Pat Buchanan) who have identified them as such, and there are significant numbers of people (from Islamic fundamentalists to environmentalists) who have mobilized against these trends. However, in the United States, political leaders and the mainstream media have made very little of these issues. If these issues do not fit our definition of a social problem, they do suggest alternative constructions of social problems, and they do impact other social problems that will be discussed in this book.

SUMMARY

Sociology is a social science, and the sociology of social problems is a sub-discipline within that science, not simply a study of current events. One important goal of social scientists is to minimize the influence of values in their research endeavors. While the layperson is inclined to view social problems as inherently bad, this is a value judgment, and the sociologist tries to avoid making such an assumption. The sociologist, instead, seeks to understand the complexity of the social problem and its interrelatedness to the social structure. Consequently, it is not the inherent badness of a phenomenon that makes it a social problem, but the fact that it has been defined as such by a particular group, a social movement organization. Features and changes in the social structure explain the emergence of that social movement organization.

Throughout this book, social problems will be addressed from the perspective of critical constructionism, which is largely a synthesis of two classical sociological perspectives: conflict theory and symbolic interactionism. Conflict theorists are concerned primarily with inequality and the use and abuse of power. Those in power have the ability to influence the social structure, and they do so to promote their own interests. It is not that the elite conspire to maintain their power and subjugate the rest of society, but a unity of interests makes it seem as if they conspire. This is the more liberal branch of sociology; conflict theorists often implicitly or explicitly advocate change, with the goal of reducing inequality. Symbolic interactionists are concerned with the process of interpretation that goes on in human interaction. Accordingly, people do not respond to their environment, but to their interpretation of that environment. The same can be said of social problems; people do not respond to the problem itself, but to the meaning the phenomenon has for them.

Critical constructionists examine how the meanings of various social problems are constructed and how these constructions often favor the interests of the elite at the expense of the middle and lower classes. The critical constructionist does not argue that all social problems are merely fabrications of the elite, but that the attention accorded to a given problem often does not correspond to the objective conditions associated with that problem *vis à vis* other potential problems. Critical constructionism provides a perspective that facilitates the prioritization of social problems rationally and equitably.

Competing with sociological theories in the public arena are the philosophies of free will and human nature (or "biological determinism"). Free will, especially, plays an important role in the American psyche because of American religious, capitalist, and individualist traditions. Both philosophies are antisociological in that they downplay or ignore the role of the environment in determining human behavior. They also suffer in their inability to explain the patterned characteristics of various social problems within a country as well as between countries.

A cross-cultural analysis of social problems calls into question the validity of free will and human nature as explanations for social problems. Cross-cultural analyses are necessary to overcome our ethnocentric views of social problems and their solutions. In addition to a cross-cultural perspective, a global perspective is important because the world is becoming increasingly interdependent, and problems in one country often impact other countries.

One pronounced global trend has been the restructuring and deregulation of the world market. Though certainly not limited to American corporations, this represents an extension of American corporate capitalism to the rest of the world market. Individualism and the quest for profit in an unregulated world market portend well for the large TNCs, but not necessarily for American citizens or their counterparts throughout the world. The TNCs are becoming exceedingly powerful, but their interests are in profit and not in the welfare of the people in the countries in which they operate. An informed world public could slow down or shape this process into something more beneficial, but the media that are responsible for informing them are part of the process itself. As a result, the world's diverse cultural landscape is being transformed into a consumerist monoculture, vulnerable to the TNCs unfettered pursuit of profit.

THE PLAN OF THIS BOOK

Unlike many social problems texts that deal with a dozen or more social problems, this short text will deal with only a few problems commonly addressed in most texts. We will analyze how these problems have been constructed and why they have been constructed the way they have; alternative theories (whether sociological or not) will often be presented; cross-cultural data will be provided. In the "Applications" section of each subsequent chapter, specific alternative constructions will be supplied. The goal of this book is to impart to the reader a different, more sociological, cross-cultural, and global manner of conceiving social problems than he or she had before approaching the sociology of social problems.

Inequality

THE "BOOMING" ECONOMY

J ust as "problems" in society are socially constructed, so too is the "health" of a society socially constructed. When I began writing this book, Americans were being bombarded with "news" of the booming economy. True to the concerns of the critical constructionist, the popular construction of a booming economy served the interests of the upper class at the expense of the middle and lower classes, and it bore little resemblance to the data. During the "boom" of the latter half of the 1990s and into the turn of the new century, a great preponderance of the resulting wealth poured into the coffers of the upper class, economic inequality grew, the incomes of the working and middle classes remained virtually stagnant, despite the fact that they were working harder, and the poor continued to suffer as they always had, some even more so than before. Before we examine these phenomena in detail, a basic primer in critical economics will help us to understand how they came about.

On a national scale, "economics" refers to a system employed by a nation to produce and distribute goods and services. There are two basic types of economic systems: capitalism and socialism. In a capitalist economy, the means of producing and distributing goods and services are privately owned; in a socialist economy, they are publicly owned. But there are no purely capitalist societies in the world and no purely socialist societies. Generally speaking, the United States is considered the most capitalist society in the world; and North Korea is the most socialist. The United States is not purely capitalist because certain services are publicly owned (e.g., public schools, the police, fire departments, welfare agencies), and there are restraints on what private owners can do with their property, or their businesses, or their employees (e.g., antitrust laws, minimum wage laws, rent control). North Korea is not purely socialist because people can conduct certain business transactions free from public regulation. Thus, we might conceive of different nations as falling on a continuum, somewhere between pure capitalism and pure socialism, as depicted in Figure 2.1. Now, let us put these terms in present-day vernacular. Note that socialism is on the left, as it is associated with the political left (or liberalism), and capitalism is on the right, as it is associated with the political right (or conservatism). In a socialist society, the government is much more involved in running the econ-

Socialism ← - → Capitalism

Figure 2.1

omy and, hence, socialism in the American vernacular is associated with "Big Government." From the critical perspective, the fewer restraints on businesses in a capitalist society, the more the economy will be run by large corporations, so maintaining the same vernacular, we will say "Big Corporations." Governments have a tendency to regulate; corporations tend to eschew regulations.

Keep in mind that "socialism" and "capitalism" are economic and *not* political terms. This is an important distinction because Americans are socialized into associating socialism with totalitarianism as seen in the former Soviet Union and in North Korea. Totalitarianism, however, is a political system and not an economic system. Socialism, at least in its moderate forms, does not have to be enforced by a totalitarian government. This is apparent in most of the Western European economies. They have an economic system that can be located toward the center of the continuum, known as "democratic socialism." In these economies, the state owns strategic industries and services such as mining, steel, banking, airlines, television stations, and health care systems. Further, these economies provide extensive welfare services paid for by public taxes, including higher education, retirement pensions, family leave, and health care. Note that these societies are democratic societies; the governments that enact these policies are freely and popularly elected in democratic political systems. A more detailed diagram is seen below in Figure 2.2. As we will see throughout this book, contrary to popular constructions of "Big Government" in the United States, both American political and economic policy—from tax laws to labor laws to environmental laws—strongly favor "Big Corporations" and their wealthy investors. While the United States does not have a purely capitalist economy, as we have mentioned, it falls on the extreme end of the continuum. It is not surprising, then, that its extreme form of capitalism is supported by very powerful ideological systems that influence social problem construction. The mainstream media, for example, while often accused of being "liberal," are components of very large multinational corporations and, therefore, have an

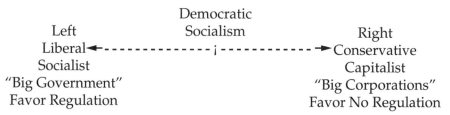

Left	Democratic Socialism	Right
Liberal ← - - - - - - - - - - - - - ¡ - - - - - - - - - - - → Conservative		
Socialist		Capitalist
"Big Government"		"Big Corporations"
Favor Regulation		Favor No Regulation

Figure 2.2

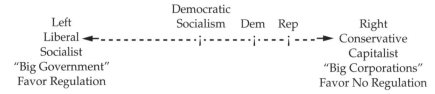

Figure 2.3

interest in deregulation. Since the media belong to such corporations, it should be expected that, more often than not, they will represent the interests of these corporations. We must, therefore, develop a degree of circumspection when reading or viewing their coverage of various social problems.

If an American is asked why he or she is proud to be an American, the word most likely contained in their answer is "freedom." Yet when it comes to the most important of freedoms, political freedom, the United States' record is less than remarkable. While we have been socialized to equate "democracy" with "freedom," Americans only have the freedom to choose between two political parties, both of which are capitalist. There are only two political parties in the American democratic system that can raise enough money to run viable campaigns: the Democrats and the Republicans. While the Democrats are considered liberals in the American political system, in the world scheme of things, they fall considerably to the right of center. Bill Clinton, for example, a Democratic president, championed the North American Free Trade Agreement (NAFTA) and other free trade agreements that have reduced government regulation of business and opened up the free flow of capital across international boundaries. Clinton's trade agenda was unabashedly pro-capitalist. Economically, both parties are pro-capitalist and would lie on the right side of our continuum, as is roughly shown ("Dem" and "Rep") in Figure 2.3. Americans have been socialized to believe that there are enormous differences between the Democrats and the Republicans; but given their closeness on economic issues, many critical theorists argue that the United States has, essentially, a one-party system, a capitalist party (Noam Chomsky, renowned linguist and social commentator, refers to the Democrats and the Republicans as "the two factions of the business party"). Meanwhile, countries in Western Europe and elsewhere have multiple parties ranging across the continuum (e.g., Communist party, Socialist party, Green party, Labor party, Conservative party, etc.). When most Europeans go to the polls, they have far more choice (freedom) than Americans. Sometimes they elect leaders from the left, sometimes from the right, and sometimes candidates from multiple parties win enough votes that they have to form coalition governments—a freedom not possible in the American winner-take-all system.

The United States is famous, at least among Americans, as a bastion of freedom, yet has historically had very little tolerance for left-wing ideology and its proponents. In the past (some would argue even today), proponents of the left have been the targets of intense government scrutiny, discrimination, and smear campaigns. Eugene Debs, the last notable leader of the Socialist party, ran for president of the United States five times. The last time, in 1920, he received nearly a million votes, a sizeable number given that the electorate was much smaller back then. This was an exceptional campaign, not just because he was the last prominent Socialist in the United States, but because he ran his campaign as an *inmate* in a federal prison. Deprived of his freedom of speech, he had been imprisoned for speaking out against U.S. participation in World War I, claiming that it was a war fought in the interests of wealthy capitalists. Later, in the 1950s, left-wing writers and entertainers had their careers destroyed by inquests conducted by the U.S. Congress under the leadership of Senator Joseph McCarthy. And in the 1970s, the FBI was illegally investigating the activities of prominent leftists. Thus, political freedom has been rather limited in the United States in that it does not seem to encompass left-wing economic ideologies that are considered mainstream in much of the rest of the world. The fact that the image of the United States as being a bastion of political freedom does not correspond to the reality of a two- (or, according to some, a one-) party system, or with the reality of its history of political discrimination suggests that the image of American freedom is itself a social construction and not a fact.

In short, when the very idea of capitalism is seriously questioned, the government steps in to defend it. Further, the way our two-party system has evolved, Americans do not have the freedom to elect any presidential candidate other than one who is pro-capitalist. Moreover, we cannot expect the media to challenge this system.

While it seems that we may have digressed from the topic of inequality, the relatively extreme form of capitalism that is found in the United States explains a great deal of its inequality. Much of the wealth generated by the boom of the 1990s was indeed generated by capitalism, and the failure of that wealth to "trickle down" to the middle, working, and lower classes is also explained by the United States' position on the socialism/capitalism continuum.

THE GAP BETWEEN THE RICH AND THE REST

Despite the booming U.S. economy of the late 1990s, the gap between the rich and the poor was growing, while the incomes of working-class and middle-class families remained more or less stagnant. There is no doubt that there has been tremendous expansion in the U.S. economy over the last decade, but the vast majority of the profits from that expansion have been reaped by the upper class. "The United States," writes British economist John Gray, "is the only advanced society in which productivity has been steadily rising over the past two decades while the incomes of the majority—eight out of ten—have stagnated or fallen."[1] In the face of numerous recessions, median family income had been declining since the 1970s; the 1990s were remarkable in that the expanding economy had virtually no impact on the poor or on working-class and middle-class incomes.

The "Gini Index" is a measure of inequality reported annually by the U.S. Census Bureau. If everyone received the same income, there would be absolute equality and the Gini Index would equal "0"; on the other hand, a "1" on the Gini Index would indicate total inequality. The index has been rising since 1968. Ranging between .351 and .376 from 1947 to 1981, the index never reached .400 until 1989, and it has remained above that mark since 1992.[2] Further, the gap between rich and poor is larger in the United States than in any other industrialized country.[3] President Reagan's administration was guided by a policy known as "trickle-down economics." The reasoning behind this policy held that if the government made it easy for the rich to get richer (through fewer regulations and lower capital gains taxes), they would spend their money and it would trickle down to the poor. History demonstrates that this did not happen. Instead, the rich invested their new found gains and/or sent them overseas. During the 1980s, the income of the top 1 percent of U.S. families soared 78 percent,[4] median family income remained stagnant, and the income for the bottom 20 percent of workers fell 10 percent.[5] While Reagan was easily identified as a conservative— friend to the rich and nemesis of the poor—the same trends continued under the "liberal" Clinton administration. Overall, the Congressional Budget Office reports that between 1977 and 1994, after-tax income of the bottom 20 percent of families dropped by 16 percent, while the top 20 percent of families increased their incomes by 25 percent, and the top 1 percent of families saw their incomes shoot up 72 percent.[6]

"[T]he United States," writes sociologist William Julius Wilson, "has had the most rapid growth of wage inequality in the Western world."[7] In 1996, the richest fifth (quintile) of income earners earned 46.8 percent of all income in the United States; in 1970 it had been 40.9 percent. The poorest quintile earned 4.2 percent of all income in 1996, down from 5.4 percent in 1970. That is, the richest quintile earned more than eleven times the income share of the poorest quintile in 1996 compared to 7.6 times the share in 1970.[8] In Japan, the wealthiest quintile earns only four times more of the total income share than the poorest quintile.[9] The Luxembourg Income Studies, comparing the United States with many other industrialized nations, found that the rich in the U.S. had more disposable income (between one-quarter and one-half more) than any of the other nations studied and the poor in the U.S. had the least disposable income, suggesting that the rich in the U.S. are better off than the rich in most other industrialized nations and the "poor are among the poorest in the industrial world."[10] "Levels of inequality in the United States," writes John Gray, "resemble those of Latin American countries more than those of any European society."[11]

Income disparity is only one way of measuring inequality, as or more important are disparities in wealth. If one has wealth (or assets), then income becomes less important. Most Americans have little or no wealth because they cannot afford to invest much of their earnings.[12] While the majority of Americans are living in debt and are only a few paychecks away from financial catastrophe, wealthy individuals either do not have to work or can easily survive an interruption in income. Wealth also has a convenient way of generating more wealth through investments, interest, and dividends. Wealth, notes New York University economist Edward Wolff, is a "better indicator of long-run economic security. . . . Without wealth, a family lives from hand to mouth, no matter how high its income."[13]

Wealth inequality in the United States is greater than income inequality; just as the income gap between the rich and the rest has been expanding, so too has the wealth gap. In 1976, the top 1 percent of families in the U.S. held 19 percent of all wealth; by 2000, this figure had increased to roughly 40 percent.[14] Remarkably, during the "Reagan Revolution" of the 1980s, two-thirds of all gains in financial wealth were reaped by the top 1 percent of Americans.[15] The same trends continued under the Bush and Clinton administrations. According to Wolff's estimates, between 1983 and 1997, the top 1 percent of Americans reaped 86 percent of all stock market gains.[16]

High concentrations of wealth at the top are an indicator of how well entrenched the social classes are in a society, because these concentrations are almost always passed on from generation to generation. For most of the twentieth century, the wealth gap was generally greater in European societies than in the United States, leading to the assertion that the class system was more entrenched in Europe and that there was greater opportunity to advance in the United States. However, "By the late 1980s," writes Wolff, "the situation appears to have completely reversed, with much higher concentration of wealth in the United States than in Europe. Europe now appears to be the land of equality."[17] Wealth in the United States, notes Gary Wills, is "concentrated in fewer hands than at any time in our past—and in fewer hands than any other modern democracy tolerates."[18]

Many Americans, it seems, tolerate such concentrations of wealth because they would like to see themselves among those who possess such great wealth. Such dreams are part of one of the most powerful constructions in American society, frequently referred to as the "American Dream." The American Dream will be discussed in more detail later in this chapter, but for now we should note that one of its most important components is the belief in "America as the land of opportunity." This belief is easily identified as a social construction in that the power with which it is held does not correspond to the degree with which it can be supported by facts. Certainly, there is the opportunity to improve one's class position in the United States, but that opportunity does not distinguish the United States from many other countries in the world. Summarizing the research on class mobility, sociologist Harold Kerbo writes, "The United States has the reputation of being the land of opportunity among many people in the world. [The data], however, indicate that the United States is only about average with respect to its rate of circulation mobility, or the equality of opportunity in general."[19] While the media abound with rags-to-riches stories, "statistics on class mobility show these leaps to be extremely rare."[20] Research indicates that the majority of wealthy individuals featured in *Forbes 400*, writes Holly Sklar, "inherited their way to the roster, inherited already substantial and profitable companies, or received start-up capital from a family member."[21]

Just as the image of America as the land of freedom is socially constructed, so too is the image of America as the land of opportunity. The proof that there is not *equal* opportunity in the United States is simple and irrefutable: if one is born poor, it is far more difficult to become rich than it is for one who is born rich to stay rich. Most people remain in the social class into which they were born, and the United States is not exceptional in the proportion of individuals who move up or down the class hierarchy.

The Middle Class: Working Harder to Stay in Place

Economist Jeff Faux writes, "For the quarter of a century following World War II, Americans got richer faster and *together*, reinforcing the notion that our common citizenship contained claims on the American dream"[22] (emphasis in the original). As Figure 2.4 shows, from the mid-1940s until 1973, average household earnings rose continuously and considerably in the United States, increasing 104 percent from 1947 to 1973, in constant dollars.

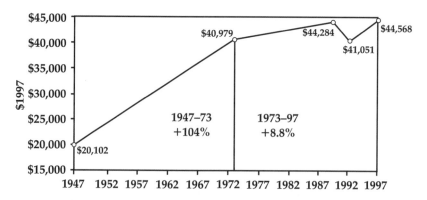

Median Family Income, 1947–1997

Source: *Economic Snapshots*, February 3, 1999, the Economic Policy Institute.

Figure 2.4

Thus it is quite possible that during the period in which your parents grew up, there was considerable economic optimism and that optimism had a basis in reality. Until recently, most middle-class parents took it for granted that their children would advance beyond them in their economic well-being. But since 1973, average earnings (especially for men) have either declined or stagnated, increasing only 8.8 percent from 1973 to 1997. It was not until 1997, well into the economic "boom," that median family income reached its 1989 level. In constant dollars, average weekly earnings dropped from $315 per week in the early 1970s to $256 per week in 1996. Average hourly earnings dropped from $8.55 in 1973 to $7.43 in 1996.[23] Those without a college education have been hardest hit. If economic trends had continued the way they had between 1947 and 1973, the average young, male high school graduate would have earned $33,000 by the mid-1990s, instead of the $13,000 he was actually earning.[24]

Women continue to earn less than men for comparable work, but there has been some improvement in women's earnings relative to men's earnings. Much of that improvement has been largely due to a decline in men's earnings. Consequently, even though at the beginning of this century more families are dual-income families than in the 1970s, there has been little change in the median *household* income since then, up a mere 4 percent since 1973.[25] In other words, six years into the most recent economic boom, it took two breadwinners to earn the standard of living that it used to take only one breadwinner to earn.

The remarkable thing about today's stagnating wages is that the average worker today is better educated than the average worker of 1973, and today's average worker is putting in more hours at work.[26] Employers are getting better educated workers, who work longer hours at approximately the same labor rates they were getting in the 1970s. Economists have long argued that a low unemployment rate would increase inflation because if there were "full employment," workers would command higher wages. Today's economy proves them wrong because the unemployment rate is low and, for most people in the workplace, there has been little or no improvement in their wages.

In 1985, average hourly compensation (wages plus benefits) in the United States was higher than elsewhere in the industrialized world. Today, the United States ranks thirteenth among industrialized nations in hourly compensation.[27] This is good news for American corporations, which are getting by with lower labor costs; it is bad news for the workers and their families. As we have seen, most of the economic expansion of the 1980s and '90s only improved the fortunes of the elite and little of it trickled down to the middle and lower classes. Much of this can be explained by the fact that corporations have been able to wring more work and productivity out of their workers without commensurate compensation. The resulting profits have inflated the price of stocks and been passed along to shareholders. While improved worker productivity has improved the fortunes of the rich, workers themselves have seen little in the way of improvement. In the recent past, we would expect workers to benefit more from the fruits of their labor and a booming economy. Indeed, higher productivity, lower unemployment, and stagnating wages are a historically unusual combination, baffling many economists. Richard Freeman writes, "Americans work considerably more hours and take less vacations than Europeans; according to the newest [data], we even work more than the Japanese. The experience of prolonged earnings declines and rising inequality in the context of job growth and economic expansion is unprecedented in U.S. economic history."[28]

THE PLIGHT OF THE AMERICAN WORKER

In the nineteenth century, Karl Marx was very concerned with the effects of capitalism and industrialization on the working class. Factory workers of that time had virtually no protections. Working long hours in often dangerous conditions for wages that kept them in poverty, they could be fired on a whim. Undoubtedly conditions have improved for Americans and workers in other First World countries. But many of the strides that have been made to establish a modicum of job security and to improve working conditions, wages, and benefits are steadily being eroded. While it is difficult to imagine we will ever see a return to nineteenth-century working conditions, work for most people in today's economy is far more precarious than it has been since the Great Depression.

Popular constructions hold that in order to compete in the global economy, U.S. businesses and industries must be able to change and adapt at a moment's notice and that the "boom" in the U.S. economy had been due to its "flexibility." The first and most precious casualty of such flexibility has been job security. The three decades following the end of World War II were marked by a period of enormous economic growth and by an unwritten "social contract" between corporations and their employees. It was implicitly assumed that if the employee dedicated his or her life's work to the corporation, the corporation was duty-bound to maintain the employment until their retirement. The economy would prosper and the middle and working classes, especially, would prosper as well. Writing in the *Wall Street Journal* in 1994, Hal Lancaster declared, "the social contract between employers and employees . . . is dead, dead, dead."[29] Today, job security is a thing of the past. The concept often seems foreign to college students and younger workers, and they likely have only a faint appreciation of its meaning and importance for their parents' and grandparents' generations. But for these generations, job security enabled workers to plan a family and then to plan for the future of their children. Job security lent predictability and stability to family life, and it had everything to do with peace of mind.

The greater the "flexibility" of a business or industry, the greater its ability to do whatever it takes to increase profits. Replacing assembly line workers with robots, replacing mid-level managers with computers, replacing full-time workers with part-time workers, replacing the labor of American workers with the labor of Third World workers, reducing health care insurance and other employee benefits—these are some examples of "flexibility" in business economics. Indeed, such flexible practices have made American businesses more competitive in the global economy; but, as we have seen above, the rewards of increased competitiveness have largely gone to the elite; and, as we will see below, the costs of increased competitiveness have largely been paid for by the middle and working classes in terms of their job security and their financial and psychological well-being.

Downsizing

Each year of the 1990s saw corporations lay off millions of American workers. According to U.S. Labor Department figures, from the beginning of 1995 to the end of 1997, eight million—one out of every fifteen—workers were laid off.[30] These layoffs occurred during the "boom" and signaled a new and unsettling trend. In the past, mass firings were associated with corporate failures, often accompanying a downswing in the economy; during the boom they were associated with corporate successes and an upswing in the economy. Ever focused on the "bottom line," anxious to cut labor costs, corporations are laying off employees, sometimes by the tens of thousands. Frequently, when they announce a massive layoff, the price of their stock shares rise, and their CEOs are awarded bonuses worth millions of dollars.

The beginning of the end of the "social contract" between employers and employees is frequently acknowledged to be the mid-1970s, when manufacturing jobs became very vulnerable to the export of labor to Third World countries. More and more companies were outsourcing labor, having their products assembled in Third World countries where labor is much cheaper, and importing parts assembled in these countries. With the money saved in labor, corporations could either lower their prices and compete more effectively, or they could pass the savings on to shareholders, or they could do both. During the 1970s and 1980s, blue-collar layoffs ran high. Corporations and their owners profited handsomely by the export of labor. Blue collar workers often suffered abysmally.

Corporations did not actually have to outsource their labor overseas to benefit from this trend; merely being able to threaten setting up shop overseas gave them considerable leverage over their employees and their unions. Much of the prosperity of the working classes during the postwar period came from the hard-won gains of the labor unions. Labor unions and corporate management have always had conflicting interests. Now, the unions are having to cut back on their demands and accept reductions in wages and benefits because management can always threaten to move their operations to another country.

In the 1970s and '80s, blue-collar workers suffered the most from downsizing. In addition to the outsourcing, or export, of labor, they were frequently displaced by new technologies and automation. New production techniques often required fewer workers. Robots replaced hundreds of thousands of assembly line workers. Corporate managers have been known to replace workers with new forms of automation, which are actually more costly than human labor, for the purpose of increasing their leverage over remaining workers, reminding them of their dispensability.[31] In the long run, such automation may save costs by undercutting the power of workers and their unions.

Today, new technologies are making white-collar workers increasingly vulnerable to downsizing as well. New computerized technologies are making business and industry all the more flexible, enabling the displacement "of telephone-answering secretaries by voice-mail interactive recordings; of letter-writing secretaries by word processing, faxboards, and e-mail; of filing secretaries by electronic memories; of clerical and administrative supervisors with nobody left to supervise; of junior administrators by automated processing; and of middle managers no longer needed to supervise dismissed clerical and administrative employees."[32] Jobs in corporate management were once among the most sought-after jobs, in part, because they were among the most secure jobs. Today, however, corporate managers are no less vulnerable to downsizing. A survey of large firms conducted by the American Management Association found that in 1997, 32 percent of layoffs were suffered by managers and supervisors.[33]

New satellite technologies have improved international communications to the point where it has become cost effective to export white-collar labor overseas, where such labor is cheaper. Katherine Newman notes, "Data-entry, airline reservations, and other clerical jobs are being exported to the English speaking Caribbean, to Ireland, and even to the People's Republic of China, where wages are one-fourth to one-fifteenth of those earned by American counterparts."[34] Even many of the more elite, "high-tech" workers in the United States are being displaced by technology and the export of labor. Computerized simulation programs, for example, have allowed Boeing to lay off many of its better paid aircraft design engineers. More and more of the code for computer software targeting First World markets is being written by Third World software designers who are being paid a fraction of what American software designers earn.

With the ever-increasing pace of technological change, few, if any, jobs are safe. Meanwhile, when a corporation announces plans for huge layoffs, it is not unusual to see the price of its stock increase. Unlike the past, in today's stock market, impending layoffs are seen as a good sign. Edward Luttwak notes, "Job cuts that will actually be implemented over a period of years—if they occur at all—are announced all at once to impress a stock market that equates them with guaranteed profits to come."[35] CEOs with reputations for implementing mass layoffs are frequently the best paid and most sought after of those in the corporate world. Katherine Newman writes,

Chainsaw Al is a legend in the annals of corporate downsizing. But he is hardly alone: Robert Allen pushed 40,000 AT&T workers out the door in 1996, mainly experienced managers; Louis Gertner ended the "life time" careers of 35,000 IBM employees between 1993–95; Stanley Gault chopped 12,000 from Goodyear Tire and Rubber over a five-year period. These contractions took place in the midst of a period of sustained economic growth, when unemployment fell to the lowest levels the U.S. has seen for nearly thirty years. The workers who lost their jobs were not the poorly educated, low-skilled labor force that poverty specialists worry about. Most were experienced, well-educated managers . . .[36]

The "Downsized."

At the time this book is being written, and as noted in the preceding passage, the unemployment rate in the United States is quite low relative to previous decades. Popular constructions hold that mass layoffs are frequently needed if corporations are to maintain their competitive edge and, further, that those who are "downsized" can easily find another job, especially given the low unemployment rate. While the mainstream news media frequently portray rags to riches stories and prefer to show how individual workers who have been displaced find better jobs or start their own successful businesses, research on the subject suggests that workers are not being done such a great favor by being laid off. Many of those who are laid off take weeks, months, or years to find another job (that is, if they do ever find another full-time job). Even for the fortunate few who take only a few weeks to find a job, the experience can have traumatic effects on the displaced worker's family, given the fact that most Americans have very little in the way of savings and given the uncertainty of future employment. Desperation leads many of those who find a job in just a matter of weeks to settle for one that pays considerably less than their former job. Many of those who job hunt for months or years still cannot find work that pays as much as their former job.

In a survey of workers who were laid off between 1981 and 1995, those who moved from full-time job to full-time job suffered an average 9.2 percent decline in income. If we also include those displaced workers who only managed to find part-time employment, the average income dropped 14.2 percent (and these figures do not include those who remained unemployed). The average displaced worker also suffered a decline in health care benefits with the new job.[37] Another study on the same subject finds that "over half of the country's displaced workers [lose] salary even when they find full-time jobs, with *more* than one-third losing more than 20 percent of their old income. Further, reemployed workers suffered lower wage losses in 1986 than those in 1996 when the economy was 'booming'".[38] Again, managerial workers are no less vulnerable to these trends. Of managers laid off in 1991–92, only 58 percent were able to find jobs in management afterward.[39] Managers laid off in their late 50s are likely to have even greater difficulties finding new employment, and when they do, they suffer an average 35 percent decline in salary.[40]

Many of those being laid off find themselves having to accept *contingency work*. Writes Beth Rubin,

> The contingent labor force includes both part-time and temporary workers—some voluntarily contingent, and some involuntarily so. Contingent workers receive lower pay, no fringe benefits, and little occupational protection. Their work is contingent on labor demand, and their security is up for grabs. Most would rather work full-time if they could. Research shows that since 1970 involuntary part-time work has grown 121%. . . . The involuntary, part-time workforce is growing more rapidly than the full-time work force and is becoming a permanent part of the modern workplace.[41]

While Rubin notes a 121 percent increase in contingency work since 1970, she notes an even more rapid increase of 250 percent since 1982. Contingency workers often work for "temp agencies" such as Manpower, Inc., now one of the largest employers in the United States. Temp workers average only 60 percent of the hourly wages of their full-time counterparts, and they get few if any benefits.[42] "[L]ess than half of the employees of temporary-help firms," states a *Boston Globe* article, "are covered by health insurance from any source."[43] The *New York Times* reports that more than a quarter of Microsoft's domestic employees are temporary workers, "who often call themselves permatemps because they work anywhere from six months to three years at the company. . . ."[44]

Contingency workers, of course, represent a cost savings to employers, and they greatly enhance the "flexibility" of the workforce in that they are employed on an as-needed basis. Until recently, most contingency workers were found in blue-collar and clerical work, but employers, anxious to cut labor costs, enhance their flexibility, and maintain their competitive edge, are hiring contingency workers throughout the occupational spectrum. Rubin notes, "Lawyers, doctors, college professors, and even top managers increasingly find themselves working on a part-time or temporary basis."[45] A striking indicator of the trend to replace full-time workers with part-time workers is the fact that many firms are laying off their full-time employees and then rehiring them as contingency workers. A survey of 720 recently downsized companies found that 30 percent had reemployed former full-time employees on a contingency basis without their former benefits.[46]

Missing from our discussion thus far is any mention of the psychosocial impact of job displacement, involuntary contingency work, and the downward mobility that so frequently accompanies them. Anthropologist Katherine Newman has studied the subject extensively for her book, *Falling from Grace: Downward Mobility in the Age of Affluence*.

> The experience of downward mobility is quite different. They once "had it made" in American society, filling slots from affluent blue-collar jobs to professional and managerial occupations. They have job skills, education, and decades of steady work experience. Many are, or were, homeowners. Their

marriages were (at least initially) intact. As a group, they savored the American dream. They found a place higher up the ladder in this society, and then, inexplicably, found their grip loosening and their status sliding.

Some downwardly mobile middle-class families end up in poverty, but many do not. Usually they come to rest at a standard of living above the poverty level, but far below the affluence they once enjoyed in the past. They must therefore contend not only with financial hardship but with the psychological, social, and practical consequences of "falling from grace," of losing their "proper place" in the world.[47]

Making the situation of the displaced and downwardly mobile all the more difficult is the fact that most Americans believe in the American economic system and blame the laid off worker for his or her fall from grace. Those who are downsized also frequently believe in the system and, therefore, blame themselves. "We are far more likely to 'blame the victim,'" Newman writes, "than to assume that systemic economic conditions beyond the influence of any individual are responsible. This tendency is so pervasive that at times even the victims blame the victims. . . ."[48] The American emphasis on financial success, the media's predilection for rags to riches stories, the constant refrain about the economic "boom" extending from the mid-90s into the new millennium—these provide little framework for the displaced worker to understand what has happened to him or her.

Those who are laid off are not the only ones traumatized by downsizing; those who made the cut and managed to keep their jobs are also psychologically impacted. Having seen their co-workers "axed," and suspecting future cuts, they find themselves in a very stressful work environment. Working units are expected to be as productive after downsizing as they were before; consequently, workers remaining on the job frequently have to work harder and put in longer hours, with the proverbial axe hanging over their heads. The respected British medical journal, *The Lancet*, reports a study examining the health effects of downsizing on remaining employees. The study found that

> . . . the biggest 'losers' were professional workers; they went from being the most secure group of workers in 1986 to the most insecure in 1997. Unsurprisingly, poor general health and tense family relationships are the result for many, with "the sheer quantity of work" being perceived as the main contributor.

Interestingly, the article further reports, ". . . but the study coordinators also discovered that lack of colleagues is pushing many professionals to the brink: half of the interviewees described their current staffing levels as either inadequate or very inadequate"[49]

The ease with which companies downsize gives rise to fear among employees and this fear translates into increased power for the corporate executives. Though they may be working harder and longer, pulling the weight of their missing (i.e., laid off) co-workers, the remaining employees are not likely to be asking for raises or complaining when their benefits are cut, as they fear they could lose out in the next round of job cuts. "Despite high levels of employment and labor shortages in some areas," notes William Julius Wilson, "workers have been surprisingly hesitant to demand higher wages."[50]

Workers in the manufacturing industries are rapidly coming to realize that their jobs are *passé*, that they cannot compete with the price of Third World labor, and that the new job openings in the United States are primarily in the service sector. "Not to worry." write Donald Barlett and James Steele,

> As Washington and Wall Street were quick to point out, new jobs were created throughout the economy to replace the old. Why, employment at Wal-Mart alone has increased by 2,890 percent in less than two decades. . . . Wal-Mart has roared ahead of GM, Ford and Chrysler as a major American employer.
>
> There are to be sure, several significant differences. First, 30 percent of Wal-Mart's workers are part-time; the Big Three autoworkers are full-time. As for pay, a GM assembler earns $18.81 an hour; a tool and die maker $21.99 an hour. Most Wal-mart employees earn a dollar or two above minimum wage. . . .
>
> Then there's the matter of benefits. The autoworkers have a guaranteed annual pension. The Wal-Mart employees do not. The autoworkers receive fully paid health care. Wal-Mart part-time workers receive no company benefits and full-time workers must pay part of the cost of health insurance.[51]

With marketplace and technological changes taking place so rapidly, and with millions of workers facing impending "restructuring," layoffs, and/or Wal-Mart-type employment, economists and social commentators frequently console and advise workers that they need to keep abreast of changes and learn new skills that are more appropriate in the modern labor market. They simply need to "retool" themselves. This is often more easily said than done. And accelerating marketplace and technological changes suggest that if the future worker is to remain steadily employed, he or she will have to spend ever-increasing amounts of time learning new skills. Today's workers are already spending increasing amounts of time at work and decreasing amounts of time with family; from where will they find the additional time to learn new job skills?

Despite the alleged "boom" of the past several years, though the official unemployment rates are considerably lower than we have seen in decades, unemployment has never loomed on the horizon of so many workers, over such a large spectrum of occupations, as it does today—not since the Great Depression. Earlier in this chapter, we mentioned working conditions in the early days of the Industrial Revolution, stating that these conditions have certainly improved. But with regard to job security, the clock has been turned back decades, if not centuries. British economist John Gray writes, "[I]n their ever-greater dependency on increasingly uncertain jobs, the American middle classes resemble the classic proletariat of nineteenth-century Europe. They are experiencing economic difficulties similar to those which confronted workers who have lost protective support of welfare provisions and labor unions."[52]

In short, true to critical constructionism, popular constructions of the health of the American economy are skewed toward the interests of corporate executives and corporation shareholders. The years 1994 to 2000 were indeed boom times for these elites; but far less so for the working and middle classes, who saw their wages remain relatively stagnant. Further, some have argued that the boom was brought in on the backs of the working and middle classes, that it was made possible by exacting more productivity from these workers—partly through newer technologies, but mostly through more work hours—without compensating them with higher wages.[53] Meanwhile, corporate executives and conservative politicians have used the banner of global competition to hold back wage increases and to turn back advances made by American workers in the decades following World War II. The balance of power between employers and employees—once mediated by labor unions and progressive government policies—is now shifting rapidly in favor of the employers, where it had been from the Industrial Revolution through the Great Depression.

Holly Sklar tells her reader to "imagine a country":

Imagine a country where the top 1 percent of families have about the same amount of wealth as the bottom 95 percent. . . . It's not Mexico. . . . Imagine a country where wages have fallen for average workers, adjusting for inflation, despite significant growth in the economy. Real per capita GDP (gross domestic product) rose 33 percent from 1973 to 1994, yet real weekly wages fell 19 percent for nonsupervisory workers, the vast majority of the workforce. It's not Chile. Imagine a country where the stock market provides "payoffs for layoffs." Imagine a country where workers are downsized while corporate profits and executive pay are upsized. The average CEO (chief executive officer) of a major corporation was paid as much as 40 factory workers in 1965, 60 factory workers in 1978, 122 factory workers in 1989, and 173 factory workers in 1995. . . . It's not England. Imagine a country where living standards are falling for younger generations despite the fact that many households have two wage earners, have fewer children, and are better educated than their parents. . . . It's not Russia.[54]

Sklar, is, of course, describing the United States.

The United States vs. Other Industrialized Countries

Defenders of the American economic system often point to the fact that unemployment rates in European countries today are considerably higher than in the United States. But cross-cultural comparisons of unemployment rates can be deceptive. Different countries calculate unemployment rates differently. For example, many European countries include "underemployed" contingent workers in their unemployment figures, whereas "Americans working a mere hour a week do not get counted as unemployed."[55] Further, most countries require a person to be actively seeking employment to be included in the unemployment rate. In some European countries, a recent look through the job ads in a newspaper counts as an "active search," whereas in the United States, a person actually has to contact potential employers to be counted as actively searching for employment.[56] The extraordinarily high incarceration rates in the U.S. (discussed in more detail in Chapter 4) also confound comparisons of unemployment figures. Most of the people in prison today were poor and unemployed before they got there. Prison inmates are not counted in the unemployment rates, but if they were, U.S. rates would rise far more substantially than European rates. If prisoners were included in U.S. unemployment rates, the national rate for unemployed males would have risen by about 25 percent in 1996 and considerably more than that in some states.[57]

More important than these confounding factors, we cannot compare U.S. and European unemployment rates to draw inferences about levels of suffering. While the rates of unemployment may or may not be lower in the United States than in Europe, depending on the definition of "unemployed," the unemployed in the U.S. likely suffer more than those in most European countries. Most of the countries in Europe are much more generous with their unemployment compensation benefits. "The United States," writes Newman, "is conservative—some would say mean—in this regard. We provide 35 to 40 percent of an individual's prior wages for a period of twenty-six to thirty-nine weeks. Most European countries (and Japan) offer support equivalent to 60 to 80 percent of previous earnings for nearly one year."[58] Most European countries are also less stringent in determining eligibility requirements for unemployment compensation. In the United States, one must have been at his or her previous job for a certain period of time to qualify for benefits, and part-time workers are unqualified. Thus only about one-third of workers who are out of work are qualified to receive unemployment benefits, compared with 89 percent of unemployed workers in Germany and 98 percent in France who are qualified for benefits.[59]

Defenders of the stringent and relatively stingy unemployment compensation policies in the United States argue that they encourage laid off workers to find new employment quickly. This may be true, but these policies also explain why displaced workers so often end up with jobs that pay less than their former employment. They do not have the comfort zone that their European counterparts have to take their time to look for more suitable employment; instead, financial exigencies frequently force them to settle for lower paying jobs.

Aside from unemployment compensation, many European countries do far more to protect their workers. In most Western European countries, it is much more difficult to fire employees than it is in the United States. For example, "In Germany," economist John Gray writes, "the slash-and-burn, hire-and-fire culture which permitted the American downsizings . . . is unheard of—or rejected."[60] In a bold move to reduce its unemployment rate, France is phasing in a 35-hour workweek. Larger companies are being required to reduce their employees' workweek without cutting their pay; smaller companies will eventually be required to comply. The rationale: "if people work less, it will take more people to do the work. That means more jobs."[61] Other European countries are considering similar plans. In Japan, during times of economic recession, and with the help of special government subsidies, corporations "do everything possible to keep valuable workers by making cuts elsewhere when profits are down."[62]

Capitalism

European restrictions on downsizing, France's government mandated 35-hour workweek, and Japan's government subsidies to reduce the need for layoffs—all of these are anathema to American corporate capitalism. The reason the United States is considered the most capitalist society in the world is because the government does so little to intervene in the economy. Consequently, the U.S. government does far less than most European countries and many other countries throughout the world to protect workers from the vagaries of global competition. Such government policies, it is said, limit the flexibility of business and industry and, thereby, inhibit their competitiveness and, consequently, their profits. Few economists—American or European—dispute this claim. But the United States is distinguished from its industrialized counterparts in the emphasis that its citizens, politicians, and economists place on the market. As we shall see throughout this text, American social and economic policies are guided by the preeminence of the market. Other countries have different priorities, and they frequently hold to the opinion that unbridled capitalism can have destructive effects on societies and communities. These governments—more than the United States—have policies intended to moderate, or harness, the effects of the market on the common good. "Why," asks former conservative British economist John Gray, "should a civilized and successful social institution [a government-moderated economy] be traded off for the endemic insecurity, social divisions, and multiplying ghettos of the American free market?"[63] Or, as a spokesman for the French employment minister states, "We say OK to the market *economy*. . . . But what we don't want is the market *society*"[64]

A government-moderated market smacks of "socialism" to most Americans and, indeed, government intervention in the economy is the critical variable distinguishing left from right on the socialism/capitalism continuum (see Fig. 2.1). But we need to remember that "socialism" and "totalitarianism" are not equivalent and that the European and Japanese governments, referred to above, are democratically elected. Their people have freely gone to the polls and chosen government leaders who would step in to moderate the harmful effects of their markets. Though these countries have fewer individuals who go from rags to riches, they do not have the radical inequalities in income and wealth that exist in the United States. Their workers are less threatened by the possibility of massive layoffs and, if they are laid off, workers and their families do not face the same degree of financial upheaval as their American counterparts. As we shall see later in this chapter, these nations also do not have as much poverty as the United States.

The key to capitalism's success, some say, is a process known as "creative destruction." According to this principle, policies, practices, businesses, or industries that are not competitive will ultimately be destroyed by, or give way to, ones that are more competitive. The modern-day version of capitalism is in many ways a new form of capitalism made possible by new technologies and increasingly permeable international boundaries. Improved telecommunications have made it possible to shift vast sums of money around the globe with a mere keystroke. Telecommunications have also made it far easier for executives in the United States, for example, to manage and direct operations in Third World countries (i.e., to "export labor"). Further, shipping costs have been steadily declining (especially for new technologies such as computer chips, which are often light and take up little space). At the same time, it has been fashionable in the U.S. Congress to deregulate business and industry and to lower trade barriers. All of these factors add up to what Edward Luttwak calls "turbo-charged capitalism," which has contributed to the ever-increasing pace of creative destruction.

Businesses and industries that compete successfully in this environment have reaped enormous profits for their shareholders, but, faced with the threat of creative destruction, they frequently have left significant casualties in their wake in the form of massive layoffs, unemployment, financially disrupted families, and communities disrupted by uncertainty and crime. Creative destruction is not new; it is the speed at which creative destruction occurs in today's economy that is new and that makes the majority of Americans vulnerable. "[A]ny production anywhere and the related employment can be displaced at any time by cheaper production from somewhere else in the world. Life in the global economy," writes Luttwak, "is full of exciting surprises and catastrophic downfalls."[65] It is the rapid pace of change, according to many commentators, that makes the U.S. government's policy of nonintervention so dated.[66] An interesting and destabilizing cycle is in effect: while the accelerated pace of change has increased the need for the government to moderate its destructive effects, the U.S. government is becoming increasingly noninterventionist in its economic policies, which, in turn, further increases the pace of change and the need for government moderation of its destructive effects.

Unfortunately, in many ways, the European democratic socialist model is competing with the American corporate capitalist model and may itself be in danger of creative destruction. The American model, with all of the flexibility described in previous pages, is a very strong competitor. In response to this challenge, many European countries are combining their economies with a phased-in common currency. Beyond this, most European countries are demonstrating a great deal of ambivalence about how they are going to compete effectively in the global economy. There is talk in the European press about how, if they are to compete, there will have to be downsizing and governments will have to cut back on some of their welfare provisions and worker protections. Indeed, on the one hand, various European countries have cut back on their welfare provisions. On the other hand, some countries, like France, as described above, are beginning new worker protection initiatives. Countries like Germany have managed to maintain very strong worker protection policies, while simultaneously exporting a good deal of their labor. Ambivalence is further reflected in that people in many European countries seem to alternate between electing conservative pro-capitalist candidates and liberal pro-socialist candidates. As the American corporate capitalist model spreads across the globe, countries around the world are facing the same question as these European countries: Can they effectively compete in the global economy without abandoning their government-moderated economic models that have, thus far, helped them to maintain a civil society? The answer to this question remains open.

POVERTY

The Numbers

Despite the fact that the unemployment rate in the United States was dropping significantly by 1997, emergency food requests were rising.[67] The United States, recognized as the wealthiest and most powerful country in the world also has higher rates of poverty than other industrialized nations. The data in Table 2.1 reveal what sociologists refer to as *relative poverty:* the condition of not being able to afford what is considered normal in a given society. In Table 2.1, people are considered poor if their income is less than half of their country's median income. Another, more serious, type of poverty is *absolute poverty*, which is defined as the inability to afford the basic necessities of living. Using this definition, the United States ranks even worse than it does for relative poverty. In the early 1990s, other industrialized countries had an average of between 2 and 5 percent of their populations living in absolute poverty, while the U.S. had between 13 and 14 percent.[68] A study by the U.S. Department of Agriculture (USDA) reports that almost 10 million people in the United States experienced hunger as a result of financial constraints in 1998. As we shall see in the next chapter, the United States ranks worst of all when considering the rates of children living in poverty. The USDA report reveals that more than three million of those experiencing hunger in 1998 were children.[69]

Beyond these figures, we are more used to hearing about the numbers and percentages of Americans living below the official "poverty line" or the "poverty threshold." The poverty line was first calculated by the U.S. gov-

Table 2.1   Percentage of People Living in
Poverty in Major Industrial Nations

	All People	Children
United States	19.1%	24.9%
United Kingdom	14.6	18.5
Australia	12.9	15.4
Japan	11.8	12.2
Canada	11.7	15.3
(Western) Germany	7.6	8.6
France	7.5	7.4
Netherlands	6.7	8.3
Norway	6.6	4.9
Italy	6.5	10.5
Finland	6.2	2.7
Belgium	5.5	4.4

Adapted from Kerbo (2000), Smeeding (1999), and The Luxembourg
Income Study

ernment in the 1960s, using data from 1955, by estimating the cost of a bare
minimum diet (known as the "thrifty food plan") and then trebling that figure to take into account other necessities such as clothing and shelter. Today, the poverty threshold stands at just over $17,000 for a family of four.
In 1997, 13.3 percent of the population lived below this threshold, down
slightly from 1990 when it stood at 13.5 percent, but up from what it was in
1970, when it was 12.6 percent. The 13.3 percent figure in 1997 represented
more than 35 million people living in poverty in the United States in boom
times.[70]

Many social scientists, however, are critical of the official poverty threshold, arguing that it underestimates the true number of people living in
poverty. One problem is that its estimated cost of a minimal diet is quite
meager, amounting to less than 75 cents per meal. Another problem is that
the official poverty threshold—other than deriving separate figures for
Alaska and Hawaii—makes no allowances for the fact that the cost of living (food, rent, utilities, etc.) is higher in some areas than in others. In fact,
frequently lacking transportation, the poor often have to purchase their gro-
ceries from the only grocery store in their neighborhood, which quite likely
charges exorbitant prices because there is no competition in the area and its
customers are "captive."

A more fundamental problem is that, though the poverty threshold has
been adjusted for inflation in food prices since it was first calculated using
1955 data, it has not been adjusted for other types of inflation, or for changes
in living standards. The poverty threshold is calculated by multiplying the
cost of a minimal diet by a factor of three because the typical family in 1955
spent about one-third of its budget on food; today it spends about one-sixth

of its budget on food.[71] Today, the costs of housing, transportation, and utilities take up a far larger proportion of the family budget than they did in 1955.[72] Depending on where they live, if parents are to go to work to earn their living, they quite likely need a car and must pay all the expenses necessary to keep it running—another cost not included in the formula. They often must incur child care costs as well. In 1955, the calculation assumed a two-parent family with working father and stay-at-home mother and, therefore, it made no provisions for the costs of child care.

According to journalist John Schwarz, if we made these adjustments to the government's estimates of the minimal diet in 1994, the poverty threshold should have been around $26,000 for a family of four, instead of the official figure of $15,100. Interestingly, $26,000 is very close to the $25,000 that respondents to a Roper survey estimated was the "lowest income required for a family of four just to get by" in 1994.[73] Schwarz writes,

> In 1955 the official poverty-line income for a family of four would have stood at 59 percent of the median income for all married-couple families; by 1994 it had dropped to 33 percent. In other words, whereas the poverty line originally measured the poor, it has come to measure the very poor. Imagine a family of four living on $15,100 . . . trying to find decent housing with no more than about $300 a month for rent and utilities combined, having no more than $52 a week to spend on food for four people—sixty-three cents a meal per family member.[74]

Government officials have long resisted any efforts to reform the calculation of the poverty threshold because to do so would dramatically increase the number of people considered to be living in poverty. No presidential administration wants to be associated with the year in which the number of people living in poverty jumped more than 100 percent.

Even so, such reforms in the calculation of the poverty threshold take into account only needs associated with absolute poverty. Conceivably, they could also take into account needs associated with relative poverty, such as the costs of entertainment, a vacation, and perhaps an occasional ice cream sundae for the kids. Sociologist Kathryn Edin notes that the poor often feel compelled to make purchases that, at first glance, others might regard as frivolous, "such as the occasional trip to the Dairy Queen, or a pair of stylish sneakers for the son who might otherwise sell drugs to get them, or the cable subscription for the kids home alone and you are afraid they will be out on the street if they are not watching TV."[75]

Whether one accepts the official poverty thresholds or not, one of the most disturbing economic trends in the United States has been the rise in the number of people who live "deeply in poverty." Since 1975, the percentage of the poor with incomes *below* 50 percent of the poverty line has been increasing, from 30 percent in 1975 to 41 percent in 1997. The actual number of people living below 50 percent of the poverty threshold has nearly doubled during this period, rising from 7.7 million to 14.6 million people.[76]

The Homeless

Among the hardest to count when calculating the extent of poverty in the United States are the homeless. It is very difficult to estimate the extent of homelessness because those in this situation have no address and are frequently on the move. Until the 1980s, public discussions of homelessness almost always focused on homeless men, who were often stereotyped as tramps, hobos, or skid-row alcoholics. During the 1980s, the Reagan administration had begun cutting back on welfare programs and federal housing programs. When the issue of homelessness came up, the focus was still on individuals, and administration officials typically characterized the homeless as either mentally ill or drug addicted. "This view, of course," writes Joseph Dillon Davey, "exonerate[d] the Reagan administration for housing cuts and makes no distinction between the 'new homeless' and the 'old homeless' and the skid-row alcoholics who made up the old homeless."[77] The "new homeless," to which Davey refers, is increasingly made up of families with children. According to the U.S. Conference of Mayors, each year since 1973 has seen an increase in the proportion of the homeless that is made up of families. In 1999, an article in *Political Science Quarterly* reported that there were 400,000 families living in shelters, representing 1.1 million children. "Many Americans," the authors state, "refuse to believe, however, that entire families are homeless in the richest country of the world." This, they argue, explains why there has been no effective policy response to the problem of homelessness in the United States.[78]

Health Care and the Poor

As mentioned earlier in this chapter, though the United States is more capitalist than any other country on the socialist/capitalist continuum, it is not purely capitalist. Among other things, its police departments, fire departments, and public schools are socialized. Almost all Americans would agree that everyone has a right to police protection, fire protection, and an education paid for at public expense. But the United States is the only industrialized country that does not feel the same way about health care; it is the only one without a nationalized ("socialized") health care system. On any given day in 1996, an estimated 41 million Americans were uninsured.[79] Eligibility for Medicaid benefits varies from state to state. While many of the poor do qualify for Medicaid benefits, many others do not. It is often the working poor and their families who do not qualify, earning wages that keep them below the poverty line, yet above the eligibility threshold in their state. When the poor do receive health care, it is typically substandard, frequently in underfunded, understaffed, overcrowded "charity hospitals" or state or county hospitals.[80] The poor typically do not have a regular family physician who is familiar with their medical histories. Poor children frequently go without immunizations, poor women frequently go without regular gynecological check-ups, and poor pregnant women frequently go without prenatal or postnatal care. This lack of care would be unconscionable to our counterparts in most other industrialized countries.

Not surprisingly, research has shown a correlation between social class and life expectancy in the United States. Those of lower social classes have lower life expectancies.[81] The rich live an average of seven years longer than the poor.[82] In large part, as a result of its lack of a nationalized health care system, the United States ranks poorly in some of the more critical international standards, though it ranks toward the top in many others. A recent report from the World Health Organization ranked the United States health care system 37th out of the 191 countries that they studied, even though the United States spent more per capita on health care than any other country.[83] The United States ranks 17th in the industrialized world in terms of life expectancy.[84] And as far as how long people live in "good health," the average Japanese citizen lives four more healthy years than the average American, and the average French citizen lives three more healthy years than the average American.[85]

Perhaps the most embarrassing ranking for the United States is for its infant mortality rate. This statistic measures the chances that a baby will die in its first year of life. In 1994, with a rate of 8.1 deaths per 1,000 live births, the United States ranked 18th in the world for infant mortality (Japan, for example, had a rate of 4.3; some Third World countries frequently have rates over 100).[86] By 1996, the U.S. rate had dropped to 7.3 deaths per 1,000 live births, but this was still more than twice as high as Sweden's at 3.5, and at least six other countries had rates lower than 5.[87] Researchers at the Centers for Disease Control have found that much of the variation in infant mortality rates within the United States is indeed due to social class. They found that the rate for children born to low income women was 60 percent higher than the rate for children born to women of higher incomes.[88] The maternal mortality rate is another statistic for which the United States does not fare too well compared with its industrialized counterparts. This rate refers to the chances of a mother dying from complications due to childbirth. It is very strongly related to poverty and the quality of medical care provided and, consequently, 99 percent of maternal mortality occurs in the Third World. The United States, however, ranks 13th in the world, with a rate of 12 maternal deaths per 100,000 births, compared with rates of 6 per 100,000 in Canada, Switzerland, and Norway.[89]

As with many of the problems associated with the U.S. government's failure to control private industry, it is not only the poor who suffer. "The United States," reports USA Today, "is the only industrialized nation in the world that doesn't control the prices of prescription drugs."[90] As a result, Americans typically pay much higher prices for most of their prescription drugs. The elderly are hit with a double whammy: very often living on fixed incomes, Medicare pays little or nothing of the costs of their prescription medicines (whereas the health care systems throughout the rest of industrialized world pay all or most of the costs), *plus* their medicines are priced much higher. Poor, elderly Americans who are not poor enough to qualify for Medicaid (remember eligibility varies from state to state) face difficult choices between food, medicine, and other necessities. In the meantime, the prescription drug industry, states Senator Orrin Hatch, "is the most profitable sector of [the U.S.] economy."[91]

In 1993, the Clinton administration was considering health care reform. The most often talked about reform would have been a move in the direction of Canada's "single payer" plan. (All citizens of Canada are covered by its national health insurance which is paid for by public taxes.) Of the interest groups that were most threatened by health care reform in the United States, the multibillion dollar health insurance industry, of course, figured most prominently, as people would no longer need private health insurance. The health insurance industry mounted a multimillion dollar advertising campaign designed to discredit any move toward a national health care plan. Among the misinformation propagated by the health insurance industry, and the media in general, were the following messages: (1) under a national health care plan, people would lose their choice of physicians; (2) a national heath care plan would require an enormous increase in taxes; and (3) national health care plans like Canada's can only function by "rationing" medical treatments. These can all be characterized as exaggerations or distortions because (1) most Americans who are insured are covered by health maintenance organizations that limit their policyholders' choice of physicians; consequently, most Canadians have more choice than their American counterparts;[92] (2) in between Americans and their medical treatment are the multibillion dollar insurance companies; money that is spent to keep them in business and their shareholders happy could instead be paid in taxes to support national health insurance; and (3) *all* health care systems ration their services; in Canada, rationing is based on need; in the United States, rationing is based on social class (i.e., the patient's ability to pay). Almost all of the criticisms of a national health care plan that appeared in various media could have been systematically refuted, but they were not, and the reform initiative lost its support. With more resources at their disposal, the health insurance industry and its allies successfully reconstructed the problem at hand, and the poor lost out.

Why?

The widespread poverty in the United States, relative to other industrialized countries, begs for an explanation. Basically, most of the characteristics of the U.S. economy already discussed above go a long way toward an explanation. The extreme form of capitalism that exists in the United States means that there is little in the way of government assistance to the poor. Yet popular constructions of poverty and welfare in the United States suggest that the U.S. is far too generous in its welfare provisions to the poor. But relative to other industrialized countries, welfare provisions for the poor are quite meager in the United States. Sociologist Harold Kerbo writes, "From the political rhetoric of the 1990s one gets the idea that the United States has had the most extensive and costly welfare system in the world. . . . Nothing could be farther from the truth. To begin with, of the sixty-three most industrialized nations in the world, *only one nation* does not have some form of guaranteed income program for all families in need. That one exception is the United States."[93]

Another popular construction related to poverty in the United States is that there is plenty of opportunity for the poor to improve their economic standing. This is, in fact, the basis of what is so often referred to as the "American Dream," the belief in "America as the land of opportunity." But like other patriotic rallying cries throughout history, it is, at best, an exaggeration. Perhaps the American Dream had its greatest element of truth in the early decades of the 1900s. It was during this period that the United States became the biggest industrial giant in the world. Factory jobs became plentiful and the "American Dream" became accessible to millions of Americans, even the poor. Factory jobs were good jobs because they paid relatively well and they required little in the way of skilled experience. One did not even have to speak English to perform well at most of these jobs. Poor, uneducated, illiterate, non-English-speaking people from all over the world flocked to American cities for these factory jobs. In the 1920s, for example, an assembly line worker at Ford Motor Company could earn $5 per day. That was a considerable sum of money for a poor person in those days, enough to support a family and to set some aside as savings. In this way, millions of people were able to move from poverty into the middle class. In the 1970s, however, a process known as *deindustrialization* got underway. For reasons discussed above (namely, automation and the export of labor), manufacturing jobs grew scarce, leaving mostly low-paying service-sector jobs available for the poor. Today, it is far more difficult for someone making close to minimum wage flipping burgers to make enough money to support a family *and* to set some aside as savings. Deindustrialization made the route from poverty to the middle class a far more difficult prospect, and the American Dream became far less viable for millions of Americans.

The American Dream, however, is such a powerful construction and is so much a part of the American ethos that it is virtually sacrosanct. To many Americans, questioning it, as critical constructionism is apt to do, is almost a form of heresy. To challenge the validity of the American Dream is to challenge both our collective and our individual identities. The very presence of the poor in the United States represents such a challenge, and the response to the poor in the United States—more so than in almost all other countries—is often one of contempt. Contempt for the poor could be considered a form of American patriotism in that it is a reaffirmation of the belief in America as the land of opportunity.

Contempt for the poor explains why Americans are so frequently attuned to alleged character flaws in poor people. As a professor who talks about poverty in my classes, I frequently hear students complaining about the "welfare system," citing cases of poor people driving luxury automobiles, or the time they were behind a poor person in the grocery checkout who was paying for luxury items with food stamps. These cases are likely to have been selected out of contempt, because these students seem to have failed to notice the hundreds of other times when they have seen poor people driving old, beat-up automobiles, or taking the bus, or walking because they cannot afford an automobile. They've also failed to notice the scores of other times they have been behind someone in the grocery checkout purchasing cheap, subsistence foodstuffs with their food stamps. That they instead notice the "abuses" committed by poor people suggests that they *want* to see such abuses because these reaffirm their belief in the American Dream. Such contempt for the poor makes it all the more difficult to be poor in the United States. In terms of absolute physical necessities, it is more difficult to be poor in most Third World countries, but emotionally, it is more difficult to be poor in the United States because of all of the blame and self-blame that accompany the conditions of poverty here.

Conservative politicians can gain a good deal of political capital by tapping into and nurturing this contempt. Ronald Reagan, for example, on a number of occasions, held up the "help wanted" sections of major newspapers while indicating that the problem of poverty had nothing to do with the lack of job opportunities in the United States. "[I]n the Washington daily paper on Sunday," he once said at a Republican campaign rally, "you pick it up and see 70 full pages of those tiny help-wanted ads, employers looking for people to come work. . . ."[94] The message he was imparting was simple: poor people prefer poverty and welfare to work, and the problem of poverty is a problem of motivation on the part of the poor. But when holding up these want-ads, what Reagan failed to note was that (1) most of those job ads required experience, education, or skill levels that disqualified most poor applicants; (2) of the jobs for which poor people were qualified, there were frequently several to dozens of applicants; and (3) most of the jobs for which there were ads were eventually filled, and filling them did nothing to lower the poverty rates. Sociologists John Pease and Lee Martin systematically examined the want-ads in one edition of the *Washington Post*. Of the 696 ads in that edition, most required experience, education, or skill levels that disqualified most poor applicants. "Only 13% of all vacancies," they write, "and only 8% of all full-time vacancies offered work for the unemployed poor. Although these menial jobs," they continue, "paid low wages and rarely offered fringe benefits, they received an average of 21 applications and were quickly filled."[95]

Indeed, the fastest growing category of those living in poverty is the "working poor." More of the jobs being created in the "new economy" are in the lower paying areas of the service sector, such as fast food and retail. These jobs are often part-time and frequently pay little more than minimum wage, with few or no benefits. Even a full-time job or several part-time jobs amounting to 40 hours per week at minimum wage would put a single-parent and his or her—most likely *her*—two children well below the poverty line. This, in part, explains why a 1997 survey of 11,000 charitable agencies found that 40 percent of those requesting emergency food had at least one member of the household with full-time employment.[96]

In the United States, the poor receive relatively meager financial assistance, plus a great deal of blame. In other industrialized countries, the poor receive generous financial assistance and relatively little blame. The latter combination seems to be more effective in moving people out of poverty. Perhaps most confounding to the notion of the American Dream is the relative ease with which the poor in other industrialized countries are able to "escape" poverty. In the Netherlands and Sweden about 40 percent of those living in poverty are able to escape in a year or less. In France, Germany, and Ireland, the escape rate is about 30 percent. In the United States, only about 14 percent of those living in poverty are able to escape in a year or less. Even poor immigrants in Germany fare better, with an escape rate of about 20 percent.[97]

Welfare vs. Wealthfare

Given the contempt that so many Americans have for the poor, it is not surprising that welfare programs for the poor are popularly held in disdain. It is interesting to note, however, the contrast between opposition to financial assistance available to the poor and the toleration of financial assistance available to corporations and the non-poor in the United States. Both money given out by the government and money not collected by the government in the form of taxes represent "tax expenditures." They both negatively affect the amount of money in the treasury. Welfare given to the poor and tax breaks available to corporations and the non-poor—all represent tax expenditures. Tax deductions could then be regarded as a form of "welfare" given to corporations and to the non-poor. They are sometimes referred to as "corporate welfare" and/or "wealthfare." The amount of money "given out" in welfare to the poor pales in comparison to the amount given out in wealthfare; but wealthfare is not as controversial. While many Americans complain bitterly about the size of their tax bill, sometimes blaming welfare going to the poor, cutbacks in welfare to the rich could have a far more substantial impact in reducing their tax bills. Journalists Donald Barlett and James Steele, who have written extensively about the subject, write

> It is possible to structure a tax system that imposes taxes in such a way that people at the top are left with sufficient money to buy several houses, and everyone in the middle can buy one house. Or it is possible to structure it in such a way that people at the top are left with sufficient income to buy many houses, and a large number of people in the middle cannot buy one. In the 1950s, the United States had the former tax system. In the 1990s, it has the latter. Why? Because Congress effectively jettisoned the progressive income tax—which held that tax rates should rise along with income [as it does in most Eu-

ropean countries]—and replaced it with comparatively low rates plus a generous mix of preferences, and exceptions, and deductions that are designed to benefit the more affluent individuals and families. . . .[98]

Over the last three decades, Congress has cut the tax rate for the wealthiest taxpayers by more than half.[99] With the deductions and exceptions available to them, it is not the least bit uncommon for rich people to pay similar or even lower rates of tax than people in the lower and middle income range.

Corporations have enjoyed similar tax privileges. "The Federal Government alone," write Barlett and Steele "shells out $125 billion a year in corporate welfare."[100] The alleged justification: corporate welfare helps create jobs. However, some corporate tax breaks make it easier for corporations to set up shop overseas. Indeed, many of the corporations subsidized by corporate welfare have been downsizing. "Fortune 500 companies . . . have erased more jobs than they have created [in the 1990s] . . . and yet they are the biggest beneficiaries of corporate welfare."[101] AT&T, Bechtel, Boeing, General Electric, and McDonnell Douglas, all beneficiaries of corporate welfare, reduced their workforce, *in toto*, by 38 percent.[102] State and local governments have provided billions of dollars in services and tax breaks to attract jobs to their areas. The value of these services and tax breaks often seems excessive. For example, economic incentives provided to Sears Roebuck and Co. in Illinois amounted to $44,000 per job "saved," and such incentives provided to United Airlines in Indiana amounted to $72,000 for each job.[103]

These are monies that, essentially, are being paid for out of public taxes; and yet public outcry is more likely to be vented against the poor. The incongruity is often rationalized by the belief that society as a whole benefits from corporate welfare, but only the undeserving poor benefit from the other kind of welfare. Mark Zepezauer and Arthur Neiman write,

> It's sometimes argued that corporate welfare benefits society as a whole, by recirculating money back into the economy. Of course, that's also true of welfare to the poor, which benefits landlords, supermarkets, variety stores, etc.
>
> What's more, a lot of welfare programs pay for themselves many times over in future savings on health care, prisons, and welfare payments. (Head Start is a perfect example—according to conservative estimates, $1 invested in Head Start saves $3 in future costs to society.)[104]

RACE AND INEQUALITY

To begin a discussion on race, we should note that "race" is itself a social construction. We are all descended from the same first human ancestors and have almost all of the same genetic material in common. To select one feature, such as skin color, as distinguishing one race from another is an arbitrary selection. And since there is a continuum of human skin colors, it is another arbitrary decision to judge where one race ends and another begins. "The development of the "race" doctrine," writes Prince Brown, Jr., "is a social and political process that tells more about the history of relations between people who thought/think of—and define—themselves as different than it tells about what can be known using and practicing science."[105] In other words, genetic or physical features do not establish one's race; society does. Thus, "race" has little or no scientific meaning; but in the United States and many other societies, it has tremendous social and economic meaning.

Though the majority of people living in poverty are white, poverty rates are higher among minorities. According to U.S. Census data, rates of poverty among African Americans and Hispanics, year after year, are consistently two to three times higher than the poverty rate among whites. Over half of African American children under the age of six are living in poverty.[106] A recent study conducted by Cornell and Washington University researchers reports that "nine out of every 10 black Americans, or 91 percent, who reach the age of 75 spend at least one of their adult years in poverty."[107] "African Americans," writes sociologist Martin Marger, "exhibit much higher rates of poverty, unemployment, and low income. They are also underrepresented in jobs at the top of the occupational hierarchy and overrepresented at the bottom."[108] While many Americans are under the impression that blacks have made considerable strides since the civil rights movement of the 1960s, by at least one critical measure, they have not: the median family income for black families in 1950 was 54 percent of that of the median white (non-Hispanic) family income. By 1997, it had inched up only to 58 percent.[109]

Prejudice and discrimination, despite improvements, remain a stumbling block for millions of African Americans. If we accept what people say in surveys as accurate reflections of their beliefs and attitudes, very few Americans still believe that African Americans are biologically inferior. However, the belief that African Americans are somehow "culturally inferior" is still pervasive among white Americans. Such surveys frequently show that blacks are believed to have a weaker work ethic than their white counterparts. Further, recent surveys indicate, in the words of sociologists Lawrence Bobo and James Kluegel, "blacks are rated as less intelligent, more violence prone, and more likely to prefer living off of welfare than whites."[110] These qualities are seen not so much as being derived from the biological make-up of blacks, but from their environments and upbringing. These attitudes are routinely reinforced by the media, in that African Americans are so frequently depicted in stories covering welfare issues and crime.

Whether or not African Americans are disproportionately represented among welfare recipients or violent criminals, these prejudices also afflict the vast majority of African Americans who are law abiding and motivated to work. Holding such prejudicial attitudes, employers often avoid hiring black applicants, suspecting they will be poor workers. As is always the case with prejudice, a self-fulfilling cycle emerges. Acknowledging the economic gap between blacks and whites, whites are inclined to blame blacks for their lack of motivation; then, perceiving them to be poorly motivated, employers are less likely to hire blacks. Thus, as a consequence of existing prejudices, African Americans are given only limited opportunity to close the economic gap between blacks and whites—and then they are blamed for the gap.

The poor, as we have noted, are often blamed for their poverty, and they are told that they should go out and get a job—any job. Anthropologist Katherine Newman found job acquisition is not quite so simple for poor blacks, even in the black community. Examining minimum-wage job openings in fast-food restaurants in Harlem, she found, first, that there were far more applicants than there were job openings; and, second, that employers frequently opted to hire immigrants from outside the community than blacks who resided in the neighborhood. "Employers are exercising a preference for applicants who are not African American," Newman writes, "even in central Harlem, which is overwhelmingly African American in its residential population. . . . It is harder for African Americans to get these jobs than for equivalently educated individuals from other racial and ethnic groups."[111] If resident blacks encounter such adversity finding jobs in their own community, we can imagine that finding employment elsewhere could be a monumental task.

There is good news, however. In the face of adversity, increasing numbers of African Americans are making their way into the middle class. The civil rights movement, laws protecting minorities, affirmative action policies, and the immigration of blacks from the South to the North have all helped to facilitate the expansion of the black middle class. But there is one critical difference between the black middle class and the white middle class, and that is wealth. Actually, throughout the class structure, if we compare black and white families that are similar in income, the white family is likely to possess more in the way of financial assets.[112] As discussed earlier in this chapter, wealth has much more to do with financial security and peace of mind than does income. Isabel Wilkerson writes,

> [U]nlike the white middle and upper classes, which include 70 percent of all white households and have been a fixture for three generations, the vast majority of the black middle class is starting from scratch. . . .
>
> Perhaps equally important, economists say, black people often enter the middle class with a slight fraction of the financial assets of middle class whites whose parents and grandparents were middle class. So blacks lack the reserve of money and property needed to buy a house, to finance a college education, to weather a personal catastrophe or a national recession.[113]

Wealth brings with it more far-reaching benefits than income, and it accumulates over generations.

Dalton Conley has examined the issue of race and wealth in his recent book, *Being Black, Living in the Red*. In the first chapter, Conley asks his reader to imagine two families: one white, the other black. (For the sake of simplicity, I will modify some of the conditions presented by Conley.) The husbands in both families were the main breadwinners. Both were just recently laid off from their manufacturing jobs, which provided the same incomes. Twenty-five years earlier, the white couple was able to borrow $3,000 from their parents so they could make a down payment on a $30,000 home. The black couple was unable to borrow money from their parents, so they had to rent an apartment. The white couple was able to deduct the majority of their house payments from their annual tax bill. They could put the money they saved through these deductions in the bank. The black couple could not deduct their rent payment. When it was time for their son to go to college, the white couple had enough equity in their house (which is now worth three times what they originally paid) that they could get a second mortgage and help him with his tuition. The black couple, of course, had no equity in their apartment and could not afford to help their daughter through college. At the time the two breadwinners were dismissed from their jobs, the white man had enough money in savings (money saved in mortgage interest deductions, plus interest) to serve as a buffer while he looked for a new job. The black man had no money in savings and quickly had to take a job far below his skill level that paid less than his former job and had fewer benefits.

Conley, of course, simplified these cases and I have simplified them even more, but the message is an important one. The grandparents of the black couple described above experienced a great deal of discrimination. The black couple's parents faced a great deal of discrimination a generation later—probably less—but were lucky to earn a living, even though they accumulated no wealth. But because they had no wealth, the parents of the black couple could not afford to lend their children the $3,000 that so improved the fate of their white counterparts. Because of that $3,000 given to them 25 years earlier, the child of the white couple could go to college, and the husband could afford to wait for a better job. The child of the white couple will eventually be able to help his own kids out financially because he has a college education and because he will likely inherit more from his parents than the child of the black couple will inherit. And the cycle goes on. Thus, wealth, says Conley is a far better indicator of one's life chances (i.e., "class") than is income, and blacks, in whatever social class they are according to their income, are likely at a disadvantage. "Since wealth accumulation depends heavily on intergenerational support issues such as gifts, informal loans, and inheritances," writes Conley, "net worth has the ability to pick up both the current dynamics of race and the legacy of past inequalities that may be obscured in simple measures of income, occupation, or education."[114]

Affirmative Action

If the disadvantages of being black have been cumulative over generations, then it follows that the advantages of being white have also accumulated over generations. White people in American society today have benefited and continue to benefit from the fact that their ancestors were given preference over black people in generations past. "[Recognizing] that racism and sexism are systemic inequalities, requiring sustained, long-term, ongoing policy initiatives if they are to be alleviated,"[115] affirmative action policies were developed to counteract cumulative injustice and to give the victims of generations of discrimination a "step up" in the competition for jobs, college admissions, public works contracts, etc.

Not surprisingly, such policies have always had their opponents, but today their opponents are winning considerable victories, and affirmative action programs are rapidly being dismantled. The fate of affirmative action is, in part, intertwined with many of the processes discussed earlier in this chapter; namely, the declining prospects of the working and middle classes help to explain the frequently bitter reactions to affirmative action policies. When affirmative action policies emerged from the civil rights movement in the 1960s and early '70s, the United States was prospering and the fortunes of the great majority of Americans were improving. They could afford "sacrifices" in the name of justice and improved race relations. Writes William Julius Wilson, "When affirmative action programs were first discussed in the 1960s, the economy was expanding and incomes were rising. It was a time of optimism, a time when most Americans believed that their children would have better lives than they had. During such times, a generosity of spirit permits consideration of sharing an expanding pie."[116] Since then, with their economic prospects on the decline or stagnating, many Americans are feeling far less generous.

Critics of affirmative action claim that it amounts to reverse discrimination, that if two equally qualified candidates apply for a job, preference is given to the minority candidate. Further, they claim that when quotas are involved, preference may be given to a *less* qualified minority applicant. There is validity to these claims, but before discussing them, it might be useful to recount briefly a short documentary segment broadcast on one of the major television network's "newsmagazines" a few years ago. In this film, a middle-class black man and a middle-class white man with equivalent educational levels were followed around a midwestern city with a hidden camera for several weeks. Time after time, we witnessed acts of discrimination directed toward the black man. In the shoe store, a salesperson goes right up to the white man, offering assistance. No one offers to help the black man. In the music store, the white man is assisted; the black man is "tailed" to see if he is shoplifting. At the car dealership, the white man is offered a car at a certain price with a certain down payment; the black man is offered the *same* car at a higher price with a higher down payment. Responding to job ads, the white man is welcomed and told all about the job; shortly afterward, the black man is told the (still unfilled) job is no longer available. Looking at apartment rentals, again the white man is welcomed and cordially shown around; the black man is told the (unrented) apartment is no longer available.

Certainly for dramatic effect, the segment's producers were selectively editing the film clips to show acts of discrimination; we were not shown the times when the two men were treated equally. Furthermore, the city in which the segment was filmed may not be representative of the rest of the country with regard to its race relations. However, there is little doubt that on any given day hundreds of thousands of African Americans encounter similar acts of discrimination. There are millions of white Americans who, if given the chance, will actively discriminate against blacks. When it comes to jobs and housing, such discrimination is illegal. But *how do we enforce these laws?* Such discrimination is often subtle and could never have been detected without the hidden cameras and microphones. Given that everybody cannot be expected to carry around hidden surveillance devices, "quotas" emerged; not legal quotas, but unofficial quotas were adopted by government agencies as a means of directing the enforcement of antidiscrimination statutes. If an employer had 100 employees and only two were minority group members, this became grounds for suspicion and further scrutiny. Employers, therefore, felt compelled to hire a given percentage (quota) of minorities to avoid government scrutiny or antidiscrimination lawsuits. Indeed, quotas *do* mean reverse discrimination. But, given that illegal acts of racial discrimination occur thousands of times a day, how, other than hidden surveillance devices or quotas, can antidiscrimination statutes be enforced? (This is not meant to be a rhetorical question.)

Critics of affirmative action argue that discrimination on the basis of race (or gender) is wrong, whether the victim is black or white (or male or female). But we should remember that these critics are frequently the beneficiaries of generations of discrimination. For the white critics, odds are that their median income is higher than the median black income, and part of the reason they are faring better than their black counterparts is because for generations their ancestors have been given preference over the ancestors of their black counterparts. White critics of affirmative action may also benefit from other preferences that they find less objectionable. Colleges and universities, for example, frequently give admission preference to their "legacies," that is, to children of their alumni. In the past, generations of African Americans and other minorities were less likely than whites to have gone to college, so it is mostly whites who benefit from such admission policies. "A recent study of the nations' ten most selective educational institutions," recounts Deborah Rhode, "found that they have admitted far more whites through alumni preferences than blacks and Hispanics through affirmative action."[117] Interestingly, there has been very little outcry, even from the "victims," concerning legacy preference and the *de facto* racial discrimination that it engenders.

Another claim of affirmative action's critics is that it does minorities more harm than good. When some minority group members are given preference through affirmative action programs, they argue, the abilities of all minority group members become suspect. Resentful co-workers come to suspect that their minority colleagues are only there because of affirmative action and not because of their abilities. Further, minority group members come to question their own ability, wondering if they got the job only because of affirmative action. These are interesting claims that, again, do not seem to come into play with regard to other preferential selection policies. Over the generations, when whites had been given preferential treatment over blacks, this did not cause them to be held in low regard, nor did it seem to have a negative effect on their self-esteem. College and university legacy entrants do not seem to be held in lower regard by their fellow students, nor do they seem to suffer lower self-esteem. Stanford law professor Deborah Rhode writes, "Affirmative action is not responsible for adverse stereotypes. Racism and sexism are. White males who have long benefited from preferences by schools, jobs, and clubs have suffered no discernable loss of self-esteem. Nor have the children of alumni who get special treatment in school admissions; they certainly aren't clamoring for policy changes that would spare their children such injuries."[118] (When Barbara Babcock, an assistant attorney general during the Carter administration, was asked how she felt about getting her job because she was a woman, she replied "It's better than not getting your job because you're a woman."[119])

Given the current economic situation, it is not surprising that critics of affirmative action maintain their opposition, despite many of the contradictions to their arguments, because minority hiring preferences are perceived to have an impact on their ability to earn a living. Like so many of the criticisms of affirmative action, this perception is partially valid, but easily exaggerated. Affirmative action often can become the scapegoat of individual failure and of the economy's failure to provide enough job opportunities. For example, if 100 people apply for a job and a minority group member gets hired, all 99 of those rejected can blame affirmative action. If the hiring was indeed based on affirmative action, then it may have, in fact, had an impact on *one* of the white applicant's livelihood, but 98 other white applicants also have affirmative action to blame instead of themselves or an economy that pits 100 applicants against each other for one job.

While the negative impact of affirmative action on majority group members is exaggerated, its successes have been quite significant. Much of the minority representation in management positions in private sectors of the workforce has been achieved largely through affirmative action. Racial and ethnic diversity in public sectors of the workforce, such as police and fire departments, welfare agencies, and public education have been brought about through affirmative action policies. The expansion of the black middle class over the past few decades has, in large part, been made possible by affirmative action. And the presence of millions of African Americans, Hispanics, and other minorities on college campuses and faculties, thanks, in part, to affirmative action, have added a richness and diversity to the college experience that enhances the education of all students, not just minority students. Without affirmative action policies, minorities would not have progressed as far as they have, and the statistics on racial inequality would be even worse than they are today.

Whether or not affirmative action has outlived its usefulness depends on the answers to three questions: (1) have the accumulated injustices that have been heaped on minorities over generations been sufficiently overcome; (2) are there still significant numbers of employers, managers, realtors, etc. who will discriminate against minorities if left to their own devices; and (3) is there another way to address these concerns other than affirmative action? The answers to these questions can be found in the previous discussion and can be summarized as follows: (1) at the very least, the wealth inequality between blacks and whites *at all class levels* indicates that accumulated injustices have not been sufficiently overcome; (2) although beliefs about the biological inferiority of blacks have declined significantly over the past few decades, beliefs about their cultural inferiority (e.g., their lack of work ethic) still abound and, therefore, if left to their own devices, we can expect significant numbers of employers, managers, realtors, etc., to discriminate against African Americans if left to their own devices; and (3) affirmative action's critics have proposed no alternative that would adequately address these issues and "level the playing field."

GLOBAL INEQUALITIES

Much of the affluence found in the First World and much of the dire poverty associated with the Third World have been due to the wholesale exploitation of Third World countries over the last several hundred years. Possessing superior military technology, especially in the way of navies and armaments, European countries established colonies all over what is today known as the "Third World." The purpose of these colonies was quite simply to enrich the colonizers and their home countries. Wealth was extracted in the form of natural resources and in the form of labor performed by indigenous peoples. Labor was frequently extracted through enslavement, or by capturing or destroying alternative means of earning a livelihood. Political scientist Michael Parenti writes,

> The process of extracting the natural resources of the Third World began centuries ago and continues to this day. First, the colonizers extracted gold, silver, furs, silks, and spices, then flax, hemp, timber, molasses, sugar, rum, rubber, tobacco, calico, cocoa, coffee, cotton, copper, coal, palm oil, tin, iron, ebony, and later on oil, zinc, manganese, mercury, platinum, cobalt, bauxite, aluminum, and uranium. Not to be overlooked is the most hellish of all appropriations: the abduction of millions of human beings into slave labor.[120]

The extraction of wealth from these countries hundreds of years ago continues to have effects on the Third World today. Parenti continues,

> What is called "underdevelopment" is a set of social relations that has been forcefully imposed on countries. With the advent of Western colonizers, the peoples of the Third World were actually set back in their development, sometimes for centuries. . . . The enormous wealth extracted should remind us that

there originally were very few poor nations. Countries like Brazil, Indonesia, Chile, Bolivia, Zaire, Mexico, Malaysia, and the Philippines were and in some cases still are rich in resources. Some lands have been so thoroughly plundered as to be desolate in all respects. However, most of the Third World is not "underdeveloped" but overexploited. Western colonization and investments have created a lower rather than a higher living standard.[121]

Similar kinds of wealth extraction by First World countries are still going on today in the Third World. At least three-fourths of the known mineral resources in the Third World are controlled by First World corporate interests.[122]

Besides natural resources, as in the past, Third World labor continues to be extracted. The export of labor from First World to Third World countries, as we have seen, has had serious negative effects on workers in the First World. But according to popular constructions, it is supposed to play a key role in improving the living standards of the billions of people living in the Third World. Instead, the evidence indicates that poverty has only been on the rise in the Third World since the arrival of the manufacturing jobs that left the First World. Jobs started leaving the First World for the Third World *en masse* in the 1970s. Between 1985 and 1990, U.S. corporate investments in the Third World rose 84 percent, "with the most dramatic increase in cheap-labor countries."[123] In the meantime, standards of living in the Third World were on the decline.

"Most people in the [Third World]" writes Bello, "remember the 1980s not as the decade of triumphant capitalism but as the decade of reversal. By 1990, per capita income in Africa was down to its lowest level at the time many African countries achieved their independence in the 1960s. And in Latin America, per capita income in 1990 had not exceeded its 1980 level."[124] Between 1980 and 1993, according to World Bank data, low-income countries (except India and China) experienced no growth in their GNP.[125] A more recent World Bank report indicates that the number of people living on less than $1 per day is on the increase.[126] Author Hazel Henderson writes, "[T]here are 1.6 billion people in the world who are worse off now than they were 15 years ago. Furthermore, 3.3 billion people—60% of humanity—make less than $2 a day. Thirty years ago there was a 30-to-1 difference between the richest 20% and the poorest 20% of humanity. Now, it's 60-to-1. The incomes of the poorest 20% have actually declined."[127]

One of the biggest impediments to economic progress in the Third World is foreign debt. "The political economy of debt," write sociologists Buttell and Taylor, "has become the principal parameter affecting Third World development prospects."[128] Many Third World countries are indebted billions of dollars to First World creditors. To the benefit of First World corporate interests, Third World countries are frequently forced to sell off more of their natural resources to generate the income to service their debts. Robert Weissman writes, "As long as foreign countries are forced to organize their economies toward earning foreign exchange to meet outrageous debt-repayment schedules, they will have almost no choice but to pillage their resource bases."[129] Moreover, Third World countries are competing with each other for foreign "dollars." They compete with one another on the basis of their labor costs, workers' rights, and environmental regulations. Thus, the countries with the lowest wages, fewest worker protections, weakest labor unions, and laxest environmental regulations often win out in the competition to attract First World corporate investments. The effects on working conditions and the environment in the Third World have been devastating.

Most Third World countries are so poor and their debts so large that they are often, at best, only able to pay the interest on their loans, not making a dent in the principal. Sometimes they have to borrow more money to keep up with old debts. For such loans, they frequently go to the World Bank or the International Monetary Fund (IMF). These agencies often make loans conditioned upon the country's acceptance of a "structural adjustment program" (SAP). SAP conditions usually require the country to adopt austerity measures such as cutbacks in welfare, educational, or health care spending so that the country will be better able to pay off its debts. These are harsh conditions, given the deprivation and suffering that already afflicts these poor countries. Often criticized for serving First World corporate interests, SAPs may also require a country to open its markets to First World imports and, thereby, undercut its local economy and the livelihood of its indigenous farmers, craftspeople, and manufacturers. Weissman writes, "[I]n the 1980s and into the 1990s, military power has receded as the key to ensure multinational corporate access to Third World resources. The new favorite club of industrialized power brokers is the massive foreign debt of Third World countries."[130]

There is growing recognition of the Third World's need for debt relief. "Nearly everyone agrees," writes Richard Stevenson in *The New York Times*, "that it would be a good thing if the world's rich nations could do more to ease the huge burden of debt that is weighing down the poorest countries. Far better, after all, to allow governments of impoverished nations to put what money they have into improving health care and education than to force them to sink as much as a third of their paltry budgets into futile efforts to keep up with loans from governments and international agencies—loans that their creditors have all but written off anyway."[131] In 1999, leaders from the United States, Britain, France, Germany, Italy, Canada, and Japan agreed on the need to relieve the poorest countries of their foreign debt. They agreed, at least, in principle. There has been little indication of any substantial effort to appropriate the funds necessary to accomplish this task. Given that foreign debt has provided First World corporations with leverage over Third World markets and labor conditions, it remains to be seen whether the First World can muster the will to alleviate the problem.

APPLICATION: THE GROSS DOMESTIC PRODUCT

A recurring theme in this chapter is the paradox of declining and/or stagnating prospects for so many sectors of the American population in the midst of the economic boom that took us into the new millennium. It is time now to look critically at one of the principal measures that goes into popular constructions of the health of the economy, the Gross Domestic Product (GDP). Basically, the GDP is a measure of all the money that changes hands in a country. Whenever money is spent, the GDP goes up.

While a rising GDP is taken to be a good sign, the GDP makes no distinction between "good spending" and "bad spending." In other words, if a hurricane devastates an area, money is spent to bring in emergency equipment, for rising medical expenses, and for funerals, so the GDP goes up. When divorce rates rise, former couples spend more money on lawyers, may sell their old home or buy two homes, and get counseling for the kids, so the GDP goes up. When street crime surges, more police are hired, police equipment is updated, more defense attorneys are hired, the prosecutor needs more assistants, more jails are built, more security devices are installed, money is spent on more emergency medical treatment and more funerals—and the GDP goes up. When white collar crime inflates the price of commodities and utilities, the GDP goes up. When billions of dollars are spent to clean up toxic waste dumps, the GDP goes up.

When people spend more time sitting in front of a television, advertisers spend more money to capture their audience, and the GDP goes up. When obesity rates rise (as they have been in the United States) because people are buying more and more food that they see advertised on television (as they have been in the United States), the GDP goes up.[132] When people require more prescription medicines to lower their cholesterol levels, the GDP goes up. When teen magazines glorifying the sleek physique increase their sales, the GDP goes up. When the girls who read those magazines develop anorexia or bulimia and require counseling, medical treatment, or funeral services, the GDP goes up. When cigarette sales increase, the GDP goes up, as it does when rates of lung cancer are on the rise. Not surprisingly, health care costs make up a significant contribution to the overall GDP.

Subsistence farming, which is certainly a type of productivity, does not involve the exchange of money and, therefore, is not figured into the GDP. Social behaviors that may improve the health of the family, community, environment, or society, but that do not involve the exchange of money, are not figured into the GDP. Hence the amount of money spent manufacturing bombs and building prisons becomes a measure of a country's success; unpaid household work, child care, the preservation of family ties, or of forests and water supplies are irrelevant when measuring success. (It is not unlike measuring your value as a person according to the amount of money you exchange in a given year instead of by all of your other attributes.)

Jonathan Rowe and Judith Silverstein write, "A human economy is supposed to advance well-being. That is elementary. Yet politicians and pundits rarely talk about it in those terms. Instead they revert to the language of 'expansion,' 'growth' and the like, which mean something very different. Cut through the boosterism and hysterics, and growth means simply 'spending more money.' It makes no difference where the money goes and why. As long as people spend more of it, the economy is said to 'grow.'"[133]

As a measure of the amount of money changing hands, a rising GDP does indeed suggest that business is good in the United States. However, as we have seen in the examples above, economists' principal measure of the "health" of our economy makes a poor measure of the "health" of our society—although celebratory declarations about the booming economy implicitly connected the two. It is, of course, an enormous benefit to the corporate world for us to equate the health of corporate interests with that of society's interests. This equation is very powerful in American economic constructions and has a powerful influence on American economic policy. But if the purpose of the economy is to serve the society (and not simply corporate interests), then this equation can be misleading and perhaps dangerous when it serves to direct the nation's social and economic policies.

A statement from the New Economics Foundation reads, "For all our sophistication, modern society still persists in making one huge leap of faith. We blithely assume that if, at the end of the day, one key indicator of economic output—[GDP]—goes up, the quality of life of the citizenry will improve.[134] In a similar vein, I've written elsewhere,

> Despite the class, gender, racial and ethnic inequalities, despite the decline in wages, and the disappearance of job security, despite the need for Americans to work harder to stay where they are, despite serious problems in health care, despite the fact that the United States suffers more violent crime than any other Western industrialized country—the GDP says we are a success. Well, perhaps the GDP is a better measure of the success of the corporate world than of the average citizen. When corporations are doing well the GDP is up; but that does not mean the average citizen's lot has improved. Perhaps we need a new measure of success.[135]

Indeed, progressive organizations (such as Redefining Progress in the United States and the New Economics Foundation—NEF—in Britain) are working to develop new social and economic indicators that count negative outputs as negatives (to be subtracted) and positive outputs as positives. An NEF publication reads, "New indicators such as these go to the heart of democratic debate, by looking at how we measure the success of politicians, economists, and society. If we continue to ask the wrong questions, we will continue to get the wrong answers."[136] It remains to be seen whether such indicators will ever become a popular alternative or supplement to our current measure of corporate success, the GDP. But true to critical constructionism, as long as the GDP is taken to be the principal measure of the health of our society, and as long as it drives social and economic policy, elite interests are served, often to the detriment of the middle, working, and lower classes.

SUMMARY

The U.S. economy is considered to be among the most capitalist economies in the world. As such, it gives its businesses and corporations more free rein than most or all other countries. A critical examination of the United States indicates that its political system is organized around its economic system, much like the former Soviet Union, but unlike most Western European countries. Unlike the European electoral systems, the two-party system in the United States allows little other choice but the election of pro-capitalist candidates. Non-capitalist economic ideas that are considered mainstream in Europe and in many countries throughout the world come under formidable attack in the United States. Historically, these attacks have come from the media, the U.S. Congress, the U.S. courts, and the FBI, calling into question whether the United States is indeed the "land of freedom."

From 1994 until the writing of this book, politicians, economists, and the media triumphantly proclaimed that the United States was in the midst of an economic boom. But this was an unusual "boom" in that productivity rates went up, unemployment rates went down, and the lower, working, and middle classes saw almost no improvement in their standard of living. Instead, most of the wealth generated by the boom went to the upper class—corporations, their CEOs, and their shareholders. With the threat of "global competition" dangling over their heads, workers have been forced to accept stagnating wages even when they are working longer and harder. Consequently, the income and wealth gaps between the rich and the rest expanded throughout most of the economic "boom."

The most striking loss for workers over the last few decades has been job security. Once taken for granted throughout most of the workforce, it has become a thing of the past, first for blue-collar workers, and then for white-collar workers. The export of work to the Third World, where labor is cheap, has led to massive downsizing in the United States. Workers who are "downsized," if they eventually find new jobs, usually get jobs that pay lower wages and offer fewer benefits. Those who are not downsized often work harder in more stressful work environments, fearing the time when the "axe" will fall on them. Another ominous trend for the American worker is the expansion of the contingency workforce. Across the occupational spectrum, more and more work is being performed by part-time workers who usually work for lower wages, have little or no job security, and have few if any benefits. The big winners from these trends are the corporations which are increasing their profits by decreasing their labor costs. The losers are the vast majority of the workforce.

Most European countries, Japan, and many other industrialized countries do far more to "moderate" the effects of global competition. Some restrict corporations in their ability to lay off workers; France has reduced the work-week to 35 hours in order to "spread" the work around. Most industrialized countries have far more generous unemployment compensation with fewer eligibility restrictions than the United States. U.S. corporations complain that such policies and programs would limit their flexibility, and they would not be able to compete as well in the global market. However, with the pace of technological and market changes, the harmful effects of globalization will only be exacerbated, and the need for some form of government moderation/intervention will increase.

In the meantime, the wealthiest country in the world, the United States, has one of the highest rates of poverty among industrialized countries. The percentage of people living below the official poverty line has dropped slightly in the last decade, but many critics charge that the method used to calculate the poverty line is obsolete and that a more realistic calculation would produce a much higher poverty rate. In any case, there are over 35 million people living below the poverty line, and the U.S. government does far less to help them than most other industrialized countries. This can be explained partly by the fact that Americans typically hold the poor in contempt. Believing that the United States is the land of opportunity, they blame the poor for their circumstances. Cross-cultural data, however, suggest that the United States is not exceptional in providing opportunities for upward mobility. Research shows that jobs available to the unskilled poor are not as numerous as many believe. Furthermore, one of the fastest growing segments of the poor are the working poor. Moreover, the United States compares unfavorably to many other industrialized countries in regards to the rates at which the poor are able to "escape" from poverty.

Just as the U.S. government does far less than most industrialized nations to help displaced workers and to help the poor, it also does far less to ensure that everyone has access to health care. It is the only industrialized nation that does not have a nationalized health care system. Consequently, the poor in the United States typically receive substandard medical treatment and very little in the way of preventative care. In the United States, popular constructions of nationalized health care systems in other countries have been distorted by very biased negative publicity. Much of that publicity is orchestrated by vested interests in the United States that profit from the present system.

Disproportionately represented among the poor are African Americans and other minorities, especially African American children. While beliefs about the biological inferiority of blacks have declined substantially, beliefs about their "cultural inferiority" are still pervasive and are likely to be translated into acts of discrimination. Even blacks who make it into the middle and upper classes are still not on a par with their white counterparts in terms of wealth. Wealth is accumulated over generations and, therefore, African

Americans are usually at a disadvantage. This compromises their children's prospects and makes them far more vulnerable to economic downturns; therefore, their class position is far less secure.

Affirmative action policies have been very beneficial to millions of African Americans and other minorities and have helped to counteract the effects of prejudice and discrimination. They have, however, become very unpopular with millions of people, especially among the white population. Part of the backlash against affirmative action can be explained by the declining economic prospects of the working and middle classes. They feel they cannot afford the "sacrifices" implied by affirmative action. However, many of them have advanced as far as they have financially because of generations of preferential treatment accorded their ancestors. Further, the "sacrifices" implied by affirmative action are usually exaggerated in the public imagination. The disproportionate representation of African Americans and other minorities among the poor, as well as the wealth gap that exists between blacks and whites in all classes, suggests the need for remedy. Affirmative action is one such remedy and its critics, if they want to dismantle affirmative action, should suggest an alternative remedy.

The discussion of inequality concluded with an examination of global inequalities. Well over a billion people in the Third World live on less than $1 a day. Many Third World countries are as poor as they are today because of hundreds of years of exploitation by Western imperialist nations. Such exploitation still goes on today, subsidizing First World lifestyles and corporate profits. Many Third World nations face a foreign debt crisis, forcing them to serve First World interests instead of using their money, labor, and resources to develop their own infrastructure and improve the prospects of their majority poor. If First World countries were to forgive these debts, a major obstacle to Third World development would be overcome.

Finally, critical constructionism was applied to an analysis of the GDP. In that the GDP fails to make distinctions among the ways money is spent, it is a better indicator of the health of businesses and corporations than it is of the health of society. Inasmuch as the two are confused by popular constructions, the use of the GDP as the primary economic indicator well serves the interests of the upper class, often to the detriment of the other classes. Nothing, in fact, better suits the interests of the upper class than the frequently held belief that what is good for the upper class is good for the other classes. Holding to this belief, the people willingly approve of economic policies and legislation that enhance the interests of the elite, even when such policies and legislation—as we have seen so often in this chapter—do them more harm than good. Interpreting the GDP as a measure of the health of a society contributes to this phenomenon.

Problems of the Family

THE FAMILY IN HISTORICAL PERSPECTIVE

The family is such a basic institution—and so near and dear to us all—
that a great variety of problems in society are often believed to em-
anate from problems in the family. Social problems as varied as
poverty, drug abuse, crime, and deficiencies in educational achievement are
often blamed on the "breakdown" of the family. While there are many who
think the family is on the verge of extinction, it has been and continues to
be one of the most enduring institutions throughout the world and throughout history. Many people think the family is undergoing dramatic changes
today. They are right. But many think that these changes have only begun
relatively recently and that these changes spell the doom of the family and
of civil society. They are wrong. The family in America has been undergoing change since the first settlers arrived, and the colonists—much like their
modern-day descendants—prophesied the downfall of the institution.[1] "The
'crisis of the family,'" writes Arlene Skolnick, ". . . is a national tradition,
and not just in America: historians of the family in other countries have
made much the same discovery."[2]

Thus, significant numbers of people have always felt the family to be on
the verge of collapse when, in fact, history has demonstrated that it was not.
Problems of the family, then, are a prime subject for a critical constructionist analysis because there is a considerable discrepancy between perceptions
of reality and objective conditions. Popular constructions of problems of the
family are based on some dubious assumptions.

Notions about the breakdown of the family, almost by definition, make
assumptions about the history of the family. The words "breakdown," "extinction," and "collapse" suggest a process going from some reasonably
healthy state in the past to a relatively unhealthy state in the present and/or
future. Those who argue that the family is breaking down assume a knowledge of the state of the family in the past, and they assume that that former
state was better than that of today's family. These are questionable assumptions. To put these assumptions in critical perspective, we need to
know something about the history of the family. Writes John Demos, "To
study the history of the American family is to conduct a rescue mission into
the dreamland of our national self-concept. No subject is more closely bound
up with our sense of a difficult present—and our nostalgia for a happier

past. How often, in reference to contemporary problems, does the diagnostic finger point in the direction of family life."[3]

Not until recently have a good many historians begun systematically studying the history of the family. More has been learned about the history of the family in the past three decades than in the previous two centuries.[4] A review of the history of the family reveals, "First and definitely foremost," writes Demos, "there is no Golden Age of the Family gleaming at us from far back in the historical past. And there is no good reason to construe recent trends in terms of decline and decay."[5] Every family pattern that has developed and then faded has had its own advantages and disadvantages. Many of problems associated with the family today are either exaggerated or falsely dissociated from the family of the past. For example, while divorce rates are inordinately higher today than they have been in the past, we cannot then assume that marriages were more successful in the past. Demos notes that, "In earlier times, countless marriages were ended by simple, and legally unrecognized, desertion."[6] Besides those opting for desertion ("the poor man's divorce"), there were many more people trapped in loveless marriages, who were spiritually and emotionally separated, with little hope of moving on to a better marriage in a world where divorce was severely stigmatized. The proportion of marriages "invisibly" separated in the late nineteenth century may not have been much different from the proportion visibly separated today.[7]

Many of those who fear the breakdown of the family identify the changing role of women as the principal source of the family's decline. They long nostalgically for the "breadwinner/housewife" form of family that, writes historian Stephanie Coontz, "produced a sentimental, almost sacred, domestic sphere whose long-term commitments and nurturing balanced the pursuit of self-interest in the public arena. Recent social problems, they argue, stem from a self-defeating superegalitarianism that denies men's and women's differing needs and abilities and desanctifies family relations."[8] Many believe this traditional division of gender roles to be part of the "natural order" of things and that departures from the breadwinner/housewife model are unnatural. However, the breadwinner/housewife form of family did not emerge as a dominant family form until the nineteenth century. Before that, in an agrarian society, the family—mother, father, and older children—made up an economic unit, with each member contributing to production (harvesting, making clothes, milking cows, churning butter, etc.). Not until the Industrial Revolution did father go off to work and become the "breadwinner," leaving mother at home to become the "housewife" and perform unpaid housework. It is questionable, then, just how natural and traditional the breadwinner/housewife form of family is. In cross-cultural and historical perspectives, it seems to be an unusual and transient form of family. The breadwinner/housewife model is, according to sociologist Kingsley Davis an "aberration that arose in a particular stage of development and tends to recur in countries now undergoing development."[9]

It should also be noted that the breadwinner/housewife model that emerged in the nineteenth century appeared as the dominant form of family only in the middle and upper classes, only among those who could afford it.[10] Popular constructions blame the problems of the poor on their departure from the breadwinner/housewife model, yet the poor have never been able to afford such a lifestyle in significant numbers.

While many believe the family that is based on "traditional" gender roles to be the natural order of things, it produced some unnatural and disaffecting results. In the nineteenth century, men were perceived to have uncontrollable sexual desires, while women were supposed to have none. This could hardly have been conducive to satisfying sexual relations. Studies in the history of gynecology have uncovered an "astonishing number of cases" in which women sought clitorectomies in order to control their sexual desires.[11] Prostitution was rampant in the nineteenth century. Many married men sought prostitutes as a sexual outlet, in part, because (a) they had been socialized to believe their sexual appetites were uncontrollable, and (b) their wives had been socialized not to enjoy sex. "But," writes Demos, "sex was merely an extreme case of a pattern that affected every sort of contact between men and women. When their appropriate spheres were so rigorously separated, when character itself appeared to be so gender-specific, what was the likelihood of meaningful communication? . . . [It] was a new mode of partnership—formal, self-conscious and contrived."[12] Divorce rates began to rise in the middle of the nineteenth century, and the "tramp phenomenon" had begun to emerge with, eventually, hundreds of thousands of disaffected men who had run away from their wives, wandering the cities and countryside.[13] The nineteenth century also saw the rapid proliferation of "voluntary," often single-sex, organizations, such as the Elks, the Mother's Association, and the Women's Christian Temperance Union. These, according to Demos, signaled a "deficit in family life" and a search for companionship "preferable to what could be found at home."[14]

Though the conditions described above may be grim, there certainly were happy families in the nineteenth century, but this could hardly be thought of as the Golden Age of the Family. Following World War II came a brief, but unusual, period in the history of the American family that still plays a pronounced role in the American psyche and continues to affect popular constructions of problems relating the family. This new and historically odd family was the post-war family, or the "'50s family."

THE FAMILY OF THE 1950s

Today, those who glorify the breadwinner/housewife form of family do not harken back to idealized images from the nineteenth century, but to idealized images from the 1950s. If they had a television in the 1950s, they likely had a steady dose of idealized images of the family broadcast into their house through such programs as *Ozzie and Harriet, The Donna Reed Show, Father Knows Best,* and *Leave It to Beaver.* Some of these shows, *Leave It to Beaver,* for example, continue to be broadcast in syndication. But if you are too young to have caught these on television, you can be sure that a great many of the baby-boomers—a large proportion of today's parents, teachers, professors, and legislators—grew up watching the '50s construction of the ideal family on TV. There were usually two or three kids; the division of labor among father and mother was quite specific, and gender roles were mutually exclusive. Father worked 9 to 5, mother was the homemaker/nurturer; and when father came home from work, he took charge of the family. Other family patterns were rarely, if ever, seen.

Today, many social problems are seen as the result of deviations from this family form, the so-called "traditional family." Mary Ann Mason and her colleagues write,

> ... The current debate starts from the idealized American family of the 1950s—middle class, two biological parents, a breadwinner husband and homemaker wife, and two or three biological children—and assumes that any departure from that pattern is negative. Since most contemporary families do depart in one way or another from this pattern, most commonly because the wife and mother is in the paid work force, the fifties norm implies by definition that the family is in decline or in trouble.[15]

The family of the '50s—both on and off television—however, was far from traditional. It was, in fact, most unusual and, historically, almost freakish. Men returned home from the war, and a great many of the women who had been in the workforce during the war left their jobs (either willingly or not so willingly). New families were being formed at an astonishing rate, and the baby boom was under way. "In fact," writes sociologist Arlene Skolnick, "the decade stands out as an unusual one for twentieth-century family life, whose historical trends have been falling birth rates, rising divorce rates, and later ages of marriage."[16] And, according to Coontz,

> [T]he "traditional" family of the 1950s was a qualitatively new phenomenon. At the end of the 1940s, all the trends characteristic of the rest of the twentieth century suddenly reversed themselves: for the first time in more than one hundred years, the age for marriage and motherhood fell, fertility increased, divorce rates declined, and women's degree of educational parity with men dropped sharply. In a period of less than ten years, the proportion of never-married persons declined by as much as it had during the entire previous century.[17]

"Domestic bliss" was supposed to be the principal goal of everyone—especially of women. The home became a sanctuary and was to be the primary source of self-fulfillment—especially for women. "The legendary family of the 1950s . . . ," writes Elaine Tyler May, "was not as common wisdom tells us, the last gasp of 'traditional' family life with deep roots in the past. Rather, it was the first whole-hearted effort to create a home that would fulfill virtually all its members' personal needs through an energized and expressive personal life."[18]

From the turn of the century until the 1950s, women had been steadily gaining new freedoms, more independence, and increasing parity with men. Such progressive steps came to a screeching halt with the family of the fifties. In the first half of the century, more women were going to college and planning to establish a professional career. By the 1930s, women represented half of all professionals. "But in the 1950s," notes Skolnick, "most women who attended college had no career plans and dropped out in large numbers to marry."[19] Women had always been at a disadvantage, but in 1950s America, with "a birthrate that approached that of India, the insistence that marriage and motherhood take up the whole of a woman's identity, and the increased emphasis on gender difference," women's social and economic status began moving backward rather than forward.[20]

Perhaps most women would have testified that, like their television counterparts, they found all of the fulfillment they needed as housewives and mothers. But there were signs of widespread despair that were never depicted on television and rarely brought to the public's attention through any other medium in the 1950s. According to Coontz, "The hybrid idea that a woman can be fully absorbed with her youngsters while simultaneously maintaining passionate sexual excitement with her husband was a 1950s invention that drove thousands of women to therapists, tranquilizers, or alcohol when they actually tried to live up to it."[21] Women who had difficulty accepting their domestic roles were sometimes diagnosed as schizophrenic, then institutionalized, and sometimes administered shock treatments to force them into submission.[22] Psychiatrists introduced a new term to their diagnostic regimen, "housewife's blight," and doctors began prescribing record numbers of antianxiety drugs. A favorite prescription drug was called Miltown. By 1957, with the drug out for just three years, 1.2 million pounds of these pills had been consumed in the United States.[23] When magazines did recognize the plight of the '50s housewife, by printing articles such as "The Plight of the Young Mother" and "The Mother Who Ran Away," their sales often increased dramatically. When *Redbook* asked its readership to submit examples of "Why Young Mothers Feel Trapped," 24,000 people replied.[24] And in the 1960s, commentators, nostalgic for the '50s, noted the resurgence of increasing divorce rates, but they failed to note that a great many of those getting divorced in the '60s had gotten married in the '50s.

In the '50s, nobody heard much about marital strife, or about wife abuse, child abuse, or incest. The fact that nobody heard about these phenomena did not mean that they did not occur at rates comparable to those of today; it only means that these phenomena had not surfaced in the public consciousness. They had not been constructed into social problems. Yet it is quite likely that these incidents occurred as or more often then as they do today because the family was much more shielded from public scrutiny in the 1950s than it is today. Wife abuse was dismissed as "nobody else's business;"[25] incest involving a daughter, if it did come to anybody's attention, was quite likely to be defined as female "sex delinquency;"[26] and evidence of child abuse was more likely to be shrugged off by emergency room physicians as being the result of an "accident" than it is today.[27] Family violence has received a good deal of public attention in recent years from both professionals and the media; law enforcement officers have been alerted, and neighbors have been sensitized. Consequently, there is less opportunity to perpetrate such acts with impunity than there was in the 1950s.

Fifties TV showed us only the middle-class families who could afford a particular standard of living. In the '50s, 25 percent of the U.S. population was poor.[28] Yet television never showed poor families that could not afford the kitchen appliances and vacuum cleaner that made June Cleaver's life so much more tolerable. Fifties TV did not show us the families that could not afford the breadwinner/housewife model because both parents had to work to eke out a living.

Fifties TV also showed nothing about social inequality, nor did it show anything about the diversity of American society. Television families, writes Coontz, "were so completely white and Anglo-Saxon that even the Hispanic gardener in *Father Knows Best* went by the name of Frank Smith."[29] Yet during the '50s, the United States was undergoing major changes in regard to its racial and ethnic composition. Prior to that decade, most blacks and Mexican-Americans lived in rural areas and most blacks lived in the South. But by the end of the decade, most blacks and Mexican-Americans lived in the cities, and the majority of blacks had moved to the North. Puerto Ricans were immigrating in such large numbers that by 1960, there were more Puerto Ricans living in New York than in San Juan.[30] Such demographic changes must have been unsettling to many in the white majority, who likely found comfort in the virtually all-white world depicted on television.

Finally, for those who believe many of society's problems would disappear if only we could return to the fifties-style family, when people were independent, self-sufficient, and able to manage without government subsidies—we should be mindful of the fact that the middle-class family of the fifties was one of the most well-subsidized in U.S. history and would not have existed without generous government subsidies. Through the "GI Bill," World War II veterans were eligible for generous benefits, including educational subsidies and extremely low-interest housing loans subsidized by the government. With the help of these benefits, people were able to marry earlier in life than in times past; they bought their houses in the suburbs, and millions improved their lot in life. Sylvia Ann Hewlett and Cornel West note,

> More than any other government program before or since, the GI Bill helped a broad spectrum of Americans—blue-collar as well as white-collar workers, black as well as white workers—attain the American Dream. . . . In the 1990s, an age of disillusionment with government, it is hard to comprehend that the

conservative 1950s, that golden age of the American family, was largely a creation of public policy. . . . Contemporary conservatives who espouse family values but attack social spending seem unaware of the degree to which the families of the 1950s were subsidized by public programs. . . . [31]

Furthermore, the federal government pumped billions of dollars into highways, sewage systems, and other projects that made middle-class suburban life all the more attractive. Enormous amounts of government monies went into the subsidizing of middle-class suburban family life. Meanwhile, the conditions of the cities were being ignored. Cities became increasingly dilapidated and dangerous, spurring a further exodus from the cities; those who could afford it moved out to the suburbs, leaving the poor behind to face a host of social problems for decades to come.

In summary, popular constructions that hold to the view that the family is breaking down and that the decline of the family is the cause of numerous other social problems are based on the belief that the family was once a healthier institution and, consequently, engendered fewer social problems. An examination of the history of the family provides little basis for such a belief. Throughout American history, there have been significant numbers of people or numbers of significant people who have believed the family was on the brink of disaster, blamed then-current social problems on the woeful condition of the family, and have waxed nostalgically for the golden age of the family. Today, substantial numbers of people wax nostagically for the family of the fifties which (1) was a very unusual family pattern brought about by a unique set of historical conditions, (2) had its own problems as well as many of the problems experienced by today's families, (3) was inaccessible to millions of poor families, and (4) to the extent that it was a healthy institution, it derived much of its strength from government subsidies, often at the expense of the poor.

THE CURRENT STATE OF THE FAMILY

Historically, there have always been people alarmed about the state of the family because the family has always been undergoing changes. One of the most significant changes taking place in the past few decades, the one that has had a pronounced effect on millions of families, causing considerable concern, has been the movement of women into the workplace. Since the Industrial Revolution, lower-class women have always worked in as well as outside the home. Until recently, most middle-class women did unpaid work within the house, but did not do paid work outside of the house. Today, they do both. This change has had momentous effects on women, on children, on men, on marital relations—on families.

After World War II, most jobs in the labor force were in manufacturing; since the 1970s , the economy has depended increasingly on service sector jobs (i.e., providing services, such as word-processing, teaching, computer repair, social work, etc.). The demand for high-paying blue-collar work in automobile and steel manufacturing, for example, began to shrivel, and the demand for low-paying "pink-collar" workers, sales clerks and secretaries, for examples, began to expand. With several economic recessions in the 1970s, men faced unemployment and stagnating wages. Women moved into those pink-collar jobs, and into other jobs as well, and though their wages were lower, they were able to offset the declining financial situation of their families.

In that women demanded less in terms of salary, they began competing with men for jobs, driving down wages for men and making it even more difficult for a man to support his family without the help of a working wife. In fact, many company owners and managers came to prefer hiring women because they were "better adapted, cheaper, more reliable and more easily controlled" than men.[32] In 1960, 32 percent of married women were in the labor force. By 1985, this figure had climbed to 54 percent and, in 1996, it stood at 61 percent. Even more striking is that the proportion of working married women with children under the age of six rose from 19 percent in 1960 to 63 percent by 1996.[33]

In the meantime, the cost of living has been rising, while the buying power of young families, in particular, had been declining since the 1970s. In 1978, the median price of a new home was 3.2 times the median income; by 1994, the median price of a new home had risen to 4.2 times the median income.[34] Put another way, between 1970 and 1994, the median family income rose by 9.5 percent in real dollars (keep in mind, this is a very small increase, considering that the 1994 family was much more likely to be a dual-income family); during this same period the cost of a single family home rose by 44 percent.[35]

The problem is especially acute for young families and families with young children. While the median inflation-adjusted income of families, in general, barely changed between 1976 and 1996, the income of families headed by parents under the age of 30 declined by 33 percent between 1973 and 1994, from roughly $30,000 to less than $20,000 (in 1994 dollars).[36] These figures include both parents' income, which is declining despite the fact the numbers of young mothers entering the work force had been steadily increasing during those years, thus, underscoring the need for mothers to work outside of the home.

Today, millions of middle-class wives have to work outside of the household if their family is to maintain a middle-class lifestyle. Of course, securing middle-class status for their families is not the only reason for women to work outside of the home. "Economic necessity, the traditional reason for women working," write Grubb and Lazerson, "has increasingly come to co-exist with positive assertions of choice: work allows women to become independent, to develop a career, and to terminate unsatisfactory marriages, and it gives them greater power both outside the family and within it."[37]

Housework

Despite the fact that most married women who are working outside of the home may be working full-time, and even though they may be making more money than their husbands, most women today perform most of the housework and child care duties. Though there are exceptions, even among better-educated couples with "liberated" husbands, wives tend to do a disproportionate amount of housework. True, today's fathers are more involved in housework than their fathers, but, write Cowan and Cowan, "studies in every industrialized country reveal that women continue to carry the major share of the burden of family work and care of the children, even when both parents are employed full time."[38] When a woman gets off from work, she still has to look forward to working what Arlie Hochschild refers to as "the second shift" when she gets home.[39] Studies show that men tend to devote only about one-third as much time to housework as do their wives.[40] Thus, while there has been a substantial departure from the breadwinner/housewife family, marital relations remain far from egalitarian. Based on their study of middle-class couples, Cowan and Cowan write, ". . . we find the attack on family egalitarianism puzzling when the fact is that, despite the increase in egalitarian ideology, modern couples move toward more traditional family role arrangements as they become parents—despite their intention to do otherwise."[41]

Does a woman working outside of the family increase a couple's likelihood of divorce? The research data is inconclusive, but does suggest that dual-earner families are indeed more likely to divorce.[42] There are a number of possible explanations for this correlation. For one thing, most women working outside of the home basically have two jobs because they also do most of the housework. This undoubtedly causes stress and resentment, and decreases marital satisfaction among many women. Another part of the correlation between dual-earner families and divorce is explained by the fact that a woman earning an income has greater independence and is better able to exit a failed marriage and live on her own.

Stress in the Modern-Day Family

We should keep in mind that divorce rates today are also quite high among breadwinner/housewife couples. Both dual-earner and breadwinner/housewife marriages face considerable challenges in today's society. Cowan and Cowan write,

> The challenge to juggle the demands of work, family, and friendship presents different kinds of stressors for men and women, which propels the spouses even farther into separate worlds. When wives stay at home, they wait eagerly for their husbands to return, hoping the men will go "on duty" with the child, especially on difficult days. This leaves tired husbands who need to unwind facing tired wives who long to talk to an adult who will respond intelligibly

to them. When both parents work outside the family, they must coordinate schedules, arrange child care, and decide how to manage when their child is ill. Parents' stress from these dilemmas about child care and lack of rest often spill over into the workday—and their work stress, in turn, gets carried back into the family atmosphere.[43]

Cowan and Cowan refer to the modern couple as "pioneers," because they are crossing uncharted territory. "[A] brief survey of the changing context of family life in North America suggests the transition to parenthood presents different and more confusing challenges for modern couples creating families than it did for parents of earlier times."[44] Today's family, they argue, must get along with less support than families of the past. Parents today are more isolated from their parents and siblings who, in the past, were more available to help out in child-rearing. People today are less likely to know their neighbors who, otherwise, might be able to help out. Or, even if they do know their neighbors, their neighbors—both male and female—are more likely to be off working during the day. "Many women who stay at home to care for their babies find themselves virtually alone in the neighborhood during this major transition, a time when we know that inadequate social support poses a risk to their own and their babies' well-being."[45]

Further, they argue that today's family must deal with more ambiguity than families of previous generations. In the past, the family's life was more tightly scripted. The purpose of the family was to produce and raise kids. The father had his specified role, and the mother hers; there were few acceptable choices available to them with regard to how they played their roles. Consequently, there was less ambiguity. Today's parents have "more choice about whether and when to bring children into their lives . . . will the mother return to work, which most were involved in before giving birth, and, if so, how soon and for how many hours?"[46] Such ambiguity leads to anxiety and this is one of the many sources of stress families face in today's society.

In addition to these stressors, which are relatively new to today's parents, real wages have stagnated, home ownership is becoming more difficult to attain, men and women are working longer hours on the job, and their jobs have become less secure. The restructuring of the global economy and corporate downsizing have placed untold pressures on families, depriving them of both their job security and the time they had to spend together. Writes David Elkind, "The postmodern global economy makes unceasing demands on adults to constantly update their skills or to change occupations, and has robbed postmodern parents of their sense of vocational security."[47] Not only are jobs less secure, but people are putting in longer work hours than they did twenty years ago. According to Juliet Schor's research, the average worker puts in an additional 163 hours of work on the job per year, or the equivalent of about an extra month's work.[48] This work increase cuts across the occupational spectrum to include assembly-line work, hospital orderlies, and Wall Street attorneys. Parents, consequently, have less time to spend with their children. This is a primary source of concern both for those who would like to see the return of the fifties family and for those couples who feel they cannot afford to have the wife stay home to care for the children. A *National Journal* article comments, "Whether or not the 1950s represented heaven, the twin hells for those trying to raise children in the 1990s are less money and less family time. . . ."[49]

CHILDREN, OUR MOST PRECIOUS RESOURCE?

We often hear politicians, religious leaders, and pundits refer to children with such phrases as "tomorrow's leaders," "our nation's future," and "our most precious resource." One would think that such phrases would indicate the importance of our country's investment in children. And yet, in the United States, the wealthiest country in the world, our government invests very little in the welfare of its children relative to other Western industrialized countries and many other countries around the world. The message from today's legislators to American parents is fairly clear: "you do the investing because we won't." Consequently, the United States has higher rates of child poverty and lags behind other Western industrialized nations in terms of day care and parental support programs.

Child Care

Most middle-class mothers must remain in the workplace if their family is to maintain their standing in the middle class. It is the goal of recent welfare reform to move more and more lower-class mothers into the workplace also. The Personal Responsibility and Work Opportunity Act of 1996 that "ended 61 years of guaranteed aid to poor children"[50] was designed to force poor "welfare mothers" out of the home and into the workplace. Oddly enough, many of the interest groups that would like to see middle-class mothers leave the workplace and return home to their children also want to see lower-class mothers leave their children at home while they go to work. This might not be such a glaring contradiction if these interest groups also supported adequate government funding for child care services and facilities.

Consistent with its insubstantial antipoverty programs, the United States ranks miserably in the world in terms of providing for the care of young children with working parents. Part of this is explained by the belief that mothers should be at home caring for the kids. (A Baptist church in Berryville, Arkansas, for example, recently closed its day-care center in the belief "that working mothers too often neglect their children and set bad examples."[51]) But adding to our list of contradictions, despite the desire of many to see mothers do more "mothering," the United States provides very little in the way of legislation that allows working mothers to spend time at home caring for their children. Every Western European nation, for example, guarantees *paid* maternity leave. The U.S. guarantees only leave *without* pay, and only to women working in organizations with more than fifty employees. In Sweden, even fathers are allowed up to ten "daddy days" to stay at home and help care for their newborn, and they are compensated at 90 percent of the regular income. Swedish law also allows parents with children under the age of eight to opt for a six-hour workday instead of the usual eight-hour day, with a proportional reduction in pay.[52]

Recognizing that mothers often have to work outside the home, most Western European countries offer state-subsidized day-care. Danish public policy, for example, ensures that parents have to pay no more than 30 percent of operating costs of day-care facilities; low-income families pay no fees at all. The vast majority of Western European countries provide child care for children from the age of two-and-one-half or three until primary school. In most of these countries, such care is part of an educational system that allows parents to start their kids in the system at such early ages, but only if they choose to do so. Many countries are cutting back on the provision of child care services. Sheila Kamerman and Alfred Kahn estimate that "these countries meet about 67 to 75 percent of the 'need,' not enough, but far more than in the United States."[53] Though the United States does allow child care tax credits and subsidizes child care for some low-income families, child care remains a tremendous financial burden for most families with young children.

The U.S. government does little to nothing to regulate the quality of child care provided by day-care centers, while our European counterparts set strict standards for the training of staff members and for limiting staff-to-child ratios. Of course, one of the best means of maintaining quality is by offering providers a decent salary. Yet in the United States, day-care providers are often paid at minimum wage, and their jobs often do not include benefits. A *U.S. News and World Report* article sums up the problem, asserting "the warped dynamic of the child-care market is all too plain: There are too many parents chasing too few day-care openings in settings where there is too much turnover of providers who receive too little training and pay. The average salary for a year-round, full-time child-care provider in 1997 was a hair over $12,000—less than a family of three needs to stay above the poverty line"[54]

A study of child care centers conducted by a team of researchers from a number of prominent universities throughout the country found, among other things, that (1) "child care at most centers in the United States is poor to mediocre," (2) "children's cognitive and social development are positively related to the quality of their child care experience," and (3) "states with more stringent licensing standards have fewer poor-quality centers." They also found that the centers that offered higher quality care depended less on parent fees for their operating costs, paid higher wages and provided more benefits to their staff members, had higher staff-child ratios, and had staff members who were better educated, better trained, and had longer tenure at the center.[55] These happen to be many of the features that distinguish child care in European and many other countries from that in the United States. While many argue that the U.S. cannot afford to ensure that high-quality care is available at reasonable costs to all those in need, Kamerman and Kahn write, "most of what we have urged also is done in many countries and is popular with citizens and a range of political parties. Their economies have not collapsed, and their families thrive."[56]

Again, the critical constructionist is concerned with the disjuncture between perceptions of reality and objective conditions. If Americans think that children are "our most precious resource" and "our nation's future," then there is a considerable discrepancy between these beliefs and the priority given to children on our national agenda.

Children in Poverty

What is not on the table, and perhaps most significant, is a set of social arrangements that allows children to be the most poverty-stricken group in America. There is no concept of justice or virtue that justifies our willingness to allow millions of children to suffer in poverty (Paul Wellstone).[57]

As mentioned earlier, critical constructionists are concerned with alternative ways various problems can be explained. And as mentioned in Chapter 2, popular American constructions place the blame for poverty on those individuals suffering the condition rather than on current economic arrangements. This construction of the problem suggests that the solution lies in changing the behavior of those individuals rather than changing the economy. This construction, therefore, works to the advantage of those who have an interest in keeping the economy just the way it is, namely, of those benefiting the most by current economic arrangements: the elite. But what about the children of the poor? If we are to believe that poor adults have only themselves to blame and, therefore, deserve to suffer from poverty, do their children deserve the same? Are the children of the poor counted among "our most precious resource?"

Twenty-three percent—almost one in four—of American children live in poverty.[58] In 1996, a family of four had to make less than $16,036 to fall below the Census Bureau's official poverty line. Those who fall below that line often fall far below. In 1996, the average poor family with children earned only $8,632, barely over half the official poverty threshold for a family of four.[59]

Of children, adults, and the elderly, children represent the largest group living in poverty. In his study of poverty in the United States, Smeeding, compared the U.S. to seven other countries that were similar in terms of their "economic profiles" (these included, Australia, Canada, France, Germany, The Netherlands, Sweden, and the United Kingdom). Based on his data covering the years 1979 to 1987, he concluded that American children "have by far the highest poverty rate of any group, in any nation at any time."[60] Columbia University's National Center for Children in Poverty similarly concludes "the United States continues to have the highest rate of young child poverty of any Western industrialized nation."[61] Especially at risk are children under the age of three, who experience the highest poverty rate of any age group.[62] Dr. David Hamburg, director of the Carnegie Corporation, a foundation dedicated to the study of children's well-being, states,

> Early childhood is clearly one of the most crucial periods of development. It is characterized by rapid growth, specific environmental needs, maximal dependence on caretakers, great vulnerability, and long-term consequences of failure in development. It is a dramatic period, with great changes and striking contrasts. First, the nine months of pregnancy—from a single cell to a very complex organism. Next, the critical transition from living inside the mother's body to living in the world outside. Then the period of forming the initial human attachments that shape so powerfully the possibilities for human relationship and social skills. So this initial phase has a strong bearing on a child's entire life. Especially in poor communities, the risks of permanent—and largely preventable—damage are formidable.[63]

Contrary to popular constructions about poverty, three in five poor children are white, one in three lives in suburban America, one in three lives in a family with married parents, and two in three lives in a family with a parent(s) who works.[64] However, minorities do, indeed, account for a disproportionate number of the poor. In 1996, 40 percent of Hispanic children, 40 percent of black children, and 16 percent of white children were living in poverty.[65] Black and Hispanic children are more likely to be living in families without fathers, and their mothers are more likely to be unemployed; but they are also more likely than white children to be living in poverty *whether or not* their mothers are working. About 20 percent of white children under the age of three are living in poverty; most of them are living with single unemployed mothers.[66]

Thus, there is reason for some of the traditionalist alarm about the breakdown of the breadwinner/housewife family. High rates of out-of-wedlock births, as well as of divorce, do indeed have a negative impact on the economic status of millions of families, especially minority families. With regard to the welfare of children, however, it makes no difference whether out-of-wedlock births and divorce rates are the result of individual decisions or grander structural and economic factors; *the children of the poor still suffer for reasons beyond their control.* Furthermore, it must be noted that even having a working father living at home is certainly no guarantee that a family will rise out of poverty. In fact, "traditional" families have been among the hardest hit. The poverty rates of young children living in breadwinner/housewife families more than doubled between 1975 and 1996.[67] Despite the economic expansion of the 1990s, wages have not increased commensurately, especially the minimum wage. "Thirty-two percent of all men between twenty-five and thirty-four when working full-time now earn less than the amount necessary to keep a family of four above the poverty line."[68] According to Judith Chafel, 45 percent of all two-parent families living in poverty had a full-time worker employed year-round.[69] And according to Rebecca Blank, "The emphasis in this country on encouraging the poor to work harder ignores evidence that the vast majority of the poor either cannot participate in the labor market, are already looking for more work and not finding it, or are already working full-time."[70]

The Consequences and Costs of Child Poverty

Poverty can affect virtually every aspect of a child's life. Poverty increases the likelihood of marital instability, alcoholism among parents, and child abuse.[71] Compared to non-poor children, poor children are one-third as likely to have had adequate prenatal care, almost twice as likely to be born prematurely, almost twice as likely to be of low birth weight, twice as likely to repeat a grade in school, and about three and a half times more likely to be expelled from school.[72] State health officials in Kansas report that low-income children are three times more likely to die before reaching age 18 than higher income children. According to the same report, before reaching age 18, low-income children are four times more likely to die from fires and five times more likely to die from infectious diseases and parasites.[73]

Poor children also tend to score lower on IQ tests and on tests of their cognitive abilities. Such correlations help to explain their lower school achievement and suggest that poverty is, to an extent, self-perpetuating. If it is more difficult for poor children to succeed in school, then there is an increased likelihood that they will fail to generate higher incomes than their parents. Some would argue that correlations between test achievement and poverty can be explained by inadequate parents, inadequate parenting, or a number of other variables. Research cited by Arloc Sherman for the Children's Defense Fund indicates "that poverty's ill effects *cannot be explained away* as mere side effects of single parenthood, teen parenthood, race, or parents' low IQs or lack of education"[74] (emphasis in the original), and that poverty is correlated with IQ irrespective of growing up in a single-parent family or of the mother's education.[75] Therefore, it seems that poverty itself generates an environment that produces these effects. Poor families are less able to afford an adequate diet necessary for a child's proper mental development; a poor child's environment is less likely to be filled with books and educational toys that might better facilitate the child's intellectual development; and a poor child's home life is characterized by a variety of deprivations, distractions, and "setbacks" that make achievement extremely problematic.

BOX 1. PROBLEMS THAT ADD UP AND INTERACT

Picture a seventh grader struggling to do well in school. Perhaps child poverty means she cannot concentrate properly on her homework one night because the power company has shut off the lights. The next night she cannot concentrate because she's hungry. The night after that she cannot concentrate because people are shouting and arguing in her crowded apartment building. The next night she cannot concentrate because her brother's asthma has flared up and the family must make a long nighttime trip to the emergency room by bus. By the end of the week, she is tired and has fallen further behind in her studies.

The number and breadth of problems assailing poor children wears down their resilience by forcing them to fight battles on many fronts at once. A child with a wealth of resources can absorb a minor illness or other setback and then compensate or catch up. But for poor children who are faced with more setbacks than other children, the cumulative weight of assaults can be overwhelming. . . . Some experts believe that the number of setbacks a child suffers often matters as much or more than what the setbacks are.

Source: Arloc Sherman, (1997) *Poverty Matters: The Cost of Child Poverty in America.* Children's Defense Fund, Washington, D.C., p. 27 and p. 29.

Poverty does not have costs and consequences just for poor children and their families, but, of course, for society as well. With the help of University of Michigan researchers, Mary Corcoran and Terry Adams, the Children's Defense Fund estimates that each year of childhood lived in poverty reduces future earnings for young men by 2.5 percent and 1.65 percent for young women. They argue that reduced earnings results in reduced consumption and, therefore, reduced production. They conclude that "for every year 14.5 million American children continue to live in poverty . . . society will lose a total of $130 billion in future economic output."[76] Poverty also costs citizens and taxpayers. Poor children are more likely to repeat a grade in school and/or be in need of special education. Poor children are more likely to grow up and become violent, costing citizens in terms of their potential for victimization and in terms of taxes spent controlling the poor through the criminal justice system. As Arloc Sherman states, "A nation that does not invest to end child poverty now will inevitably pay for its consequences later."[77]

As we begin to think of children in terms of their potential contributions and/or costs to society, we begin to approach a *human capital* perspective. From this perspective, children are seen as future assets or future liabilities to society, depending upon how society invests in them. Children are, in the words of Kamerman and Kahn, "an investment good, not merely a consumption frill. They are society's future."[78] The phrases "our nation's future" and "our most precious resource" imply a human capital perspective, and they imply an appreciation for the importance of investing in children. Yet, the United States invests very little in its poor children.

Responding to the Problem

The way the causes of a social problem are constructed will affect the way the solutions to the problem are constructed. In the United States, the causes of poverty are often believed to be laziness and a lack of moral fortitude among the poor. While such constructions undoubtedly apply to some poor persons, they do not apply to most. The media, however, on those rare occasions when they do attend to the problem of poverty, rarely portray anything other than the stereotypes.

William Scarborough sums up typical constructions of poverty and the problem with such constructions.

> There are many commonly held stereotypes about poor families with children in the United States. For example, many believe that all poor families are alike— that they are lazy (in that their parents do not work), that they are persons of color, that they are uneducated, that they have many unrelated members, and that they have been poor all of their lives. The facts are that many of these families are white, are composed of relatively small numbers of related individuals, and the adults in the families generally work and have high school educations. . . . The problem is that these and other important facts rarely receive adequate media attention, thus perpetuating the stereotypes.[79]

By their effect on public policy, *constructions of the poor as lazy and undisciplined have severe effects on poor children—even though no one actually believes that poor children are themselves to blame for their poverty.* As mentioned earlier, many of the negative consequences poverty has on poor children occur irrespective of the parents' marital status, educational attainment, or parenting abilities. In other words, the principal cause of these negative consequences is a lack of family income. This suggests that the best remedies would be policies targeting the enhancement of family income, such as income subsidies, minimum wage increases, and programs boosting the number and availability of employment opportunities. If family values and the welfare of children are indeed primary policy concerns, then these should be the focus of our efforts. This is not a new argument, but it seems to have been lost in much of the debate about the family.

Unfortunately, rather than increasing its efforts to deal with child poverty, the federal government has in essence divested itself of much of the responsibility by turning welfare over to the states and abandoning AFDC (Aid for Families with Dependent Children). With the passage of the 1996 welfare reform bill, the number of individuals receiving food stamp assistance dropped an astounding 3.9 million between September 1996 and September 1997. Some attribute the decline to an improved economy, yet at the same time, the U.S. Council of Mayors reported sharp increases in requests for emergency food assistance.[80] True, the federal government still invests in Head Start programs for poor children and in job development programs for parents of poor children; but these investments are small relative to what could be done and what other countries are doing. As of 1997, federal tax law also provides for a $500 per child tax credit. But this pales in comparison to the $600 per dependent deduction in the 1940s—an amount equivalent to $6,500 in 1996 dollars.[81] Further, this tax credit is of little use to the millions of families who are too poor to owe taxes.

Responding to child poverty is largely a matter of priorities. Priorities are such that, for example, every 66 year old in the United States is entitled to health care at public expense, but not every 6 year old, because many of the poor do not qualify for Medicaid. Few take issue with providing Medicare to the elderly, who have a hard time taking care of themselves. But what rationale could legitimize depriving children of the medical care they need? The answer is that it is not so much a matter of rationale as it is the fact that the health care needs of poor children have not been successfully constructed into a social problem. They have not been made a priority. Meanwhile, "every six days we spend more on the military than we do annually on Head Start, which still serves only one in three eligible children."[82] The U.S. military budget is greater than the total military budget of the next twelve largest spenders. In 1996, the year Congress passed the welfare reform bill ending AFDC, it also voted to give the Pentagon $12 billion more than it requested.[83] President Eisenhower himself (a Republican and former five-star general) recognized the woeful priorities that placed child welfare below military expansion when he stated "Every gun that is made, every warship launched, every rocket fired signifies . . . a theft from those who hunger and are not fed, those who are cold and not clothed. This world in arms is not spending money alone. It is spending the sweat of its laborers, the genius of its scientists, and the hopes of its children."[84]

Despite the U.S. view of itself as being "child-centered," as this book is being written, the United States is one of only two countries in the world that has not ratified the U.N. Convention on the Rights of Children. (The other country is Somalia, which does not have an internationally recognized government.) Having been ratified by 198 countries, it is the most widely accepted of all U.N. Conventions. Among other rights, the document includes access to food, shelter, and health care. The Convention best represents an ideal to which its signatories pledge they will aspire. Many of these countries, of course, have a worse record on child welfare issues than the United States. But most of these are themselves poor countries that might argue that they cannot afford to assure every child access to food, shelter, and health care. The United States, though, is the wealthiest country in the world and cannot make such an argument.

Other Western industrialized nations are much more sensitive to the welfare of their children—all of their children. A great many European countries, for example, provide family allowances to *all* families with children. These countries' family welfare policies are based on the human capital perspective discussed above, viewing children as "a societal good, a societal investment, rather than only a private 'consumption' pleasure for the individual family. The family's economic situation is a major factor in how children fare and develop. Therefore," write Kamerman and Kahn, "society should share some of the costs of child-rearing as a matter of justice, solidarity, and societal self-interest."[85] In Sweden, as in the United States, absent parents are expected to contribute financially to the child's welfare; however, if the parent fails to do so in Sweden, the government provides a "maintenance advance" to the child. "The parent responsible for paying child support," writes Sidel, "is required to repay the amount advanced, but in the meantime, the child will not have to suffer because of nonpayment"[86] Such progressive policies reflect very different priorities than those seen in U.S. policy. Consequently, it is not surprising to find that in European countries, Kamerman and Kahn report, "Infant mortality rates are consistently lower than those in the United States, fewer babies have low birth weights, childhood immunization rates are higher, and therefore certain disease rates are lower than in the United States."[87]

Using data from the Luxembourg Income Study (LIS), Timothy Smeeding (1992) examined the impact of the U.S. "antipoverty" system relative to those of seven other countries with economic profiles similar to the United States.[88] Smeeding standardized the poverty level across nations by setting the threshold at 40 percent of the median income level. (The official poverty line in the U.S. is indeed about 40 percent of the median income level.) Then he compared poverty rates among children in these countries before and after taxes and transfers. ("Transfers" refer to government payments to the poor in the form of welfare, tax credits, food stamps, etc.) Data pertain to various countries in various years during the mid-1980s, depending upon the "availability of the other nation's datasets." As seen in Table 3.1, before taxes and transfers, poverty rates among the countries is closer than might be expected. The United States, with a rate of 22.3 percent living below the poverty threshold, was exceeded only by the United Kingdom with a figure of 27.9 percent. However, after taxes and transfers, the United Kingdom reduced its rate of child poverty to 7.4 percent, a proportionate reduction of 73.5 percent, while the United States only reduced its rate to 20.4 percent, a proportionate reduction of only 8.5 percent. The U.S. after tax and transfer rate of 20.4 percent is more than double any of the other nations' rates. And the proportionate reduction of 8.5 percent is less than one-sixth of the average reduction achieved among the other nations.

If we look at the poverty rate of children in single-parent families (Table 3.2), we see equally striking differences between the United States and the other countries that were compared. Before tax and transfer, poverty rates

Table 3.1 The Impact of Taxes and Transfers on Percentage of Children Living in Poverty in Major Industrial Nations

	PERCENTAGE OF CHILDREN UNDER AGE 18 LIVING IN POVERTY		
	Before Taxes and Transfers	After Taxes and Transfers	Proportional Reduction
Sweden	7.9	1.6	79.7
France	21.1	4.6	78.2
United Kingdom	27.9	7.4	73.5
Netherlands	14.1	3.8	73.0
Germany	8.4	2.8	66.7
Australia	16.4	9.0	45.1
Canada	15.7	9.3	40.8
United States	22.3	**20.4**	**8.5**
Average	*16.7*	*7.4*	*58.1*

Adapted from Smeeding (1999) and the Luxembourg Income Study

tend to be considerably higher than those rates seen in Table 3.1. The after tax and transfer rates tend to be higher as well. But U.S. assistance brings very few children out of poverty compared with assistance offered in the other countries. U.S. assistance brings about a proportional reduction in child poverty of only 6.7 percent, far below the 62.6 percent average, and light years behind several countries that managed to reduce their numbers of children from single-parent families living in poverty by more than 90 percent!

Table 3.2 The Impact of Taxes and Transfers on Percentage of Children *in Single Parent Families* Living in Poverty in Major Industrial Nations

	PERCENTAGE OF CHILDREN IN SINGLE PARENT FAMILIES LIVING IN POVERTY		
	Before Taxes and Transfers	After Taxes and Transfers	Proportional Reduction
Sweden	23.2	2.0	91.4
France	43.1	13.1	69.6
United Kingdom	71.2	8.5	88.1
Netherlands	70.3	3.8	94.6
Germany	46.0	15.9	65.4
Australia	70.2	34.6	50.1
Canada	56.6	37.1	34.5
United States	58.1	**54.2**	**6.7**
Average	*54.8*	*21.2*	*62.6*

Adapted from Smeeding (1999) and the Luxembourg Income Study

From these data, it appears that, unlike its peers, the United States simply does not have an antipoverty system.

Child welfare and antipoverty programs are expensive, but not as expensive as many of the programs to which the United States has given priority, such as the military. Many European countries are cutting back on their child welfare and antipoverty programs, but these programs still remain a much higher priority than they do in the United States. The constructions of children as "our most precious resource" and "our nation's future" do not correspond with where children rank in our nation's list of investment priorities. A critical constructionist analysis calls for a reexamination of these priorities, keeping in mind that countries not as wealthy as the United States have done much more to improve the lot of their children and, therefore, the prospects for their nations' futures.

CAPITALISM VERSUS THE FAMILY

It is generally agreed that the two principal ingredients in a capitalist economy are (1) the pursuit of individual self-interests and (2) a free market. Under these conditions, according to Adam Smith, the best possible products will be made available at the lowest possible prices. According to Smith, there's no better way to ensure the efficient production and distribution of goods and services in society. A free market is one in which the government does not intervene. The less government intervention, the freer the market, the more capitalist the economy. As was mentioned in Chapter 2, the United States is, by most accounts, the most capitalist society in the world. But it does not represent a pure form of capitalism because the U.S. government does intervene in the production of goods and services in a number of ways. Some of these interventions include minimum wage, Social Security, unemployment compensation, and state-funded educational, police, and firefighting services. Note that in one way or another, each of these "interventions" serves to ensure the well-being of millions of families. So while most Americans have been socialized to take a negative view of the phrase "government intervention," virtually all of us benefit from one or another interventionist policies.

A great many countries provide far more in terms of government policies ("interventions," in capitalist terminology) that ease economic strain on family life than does the United States. While some may argue that the United States is the financial powerhouse that it is today because of its relatively anti-interventionist/capitalist policies, we should note—as noted above—that the most pro-family program in U.S. history was the GI Bill, which made the American Dream a reality for millions of families, which was implemented during American economic ascendancy throughout the world, and which helped to prolong that ascendancy for almost three decades.

Whether or not one subscribes to the belief that poor adults are to blame for their own poverty, few people believe that poor children are to blame, yet capitalist anti-interventionism means that higher proportions of our children suffer from poverty than those in other Western industrialized nation. While providing children with substandard nutrition, substandard housing, and substandard education would be unthinkable in many of the less capitalistic Western nations, such provisions are tolerated in the United States.

As we have seen, economics plays a crucial role in the well being of the family. While it may be preferable to have a stay-at-home parent (mother or father), especially in the early years of a child's life, most families can ill afford the loss of wages involved. Efforts to enable more parents to spend more time at home with their children—such as family leave legislation—are often opposed by powerful constituencies as unwelcome government intervention. Often these are the same constituencies that are heard bemoaning the decline of the breadwinner/housewife couple and calling for the return to "traditional family values."

In short, "family values" and capitalist values are often antithetical. Capitalists, write Hewlett and West "undermine family life because they fail to see the ways in which market values destroy family values. Committed as they are to free and unfettered markets, they forget that values are the 'black hole of capitalism,' to use Lester Thurow's memorable phrase. Indeed, market capitalism leans on some of the least attractive human traits—avarice, aggression, self-centeredness."[89]

Americans who identify themselves as "conservatives" are typically against both government regulation of the economy and government assistance to families. But it is the scarcely regulated economy that so frequently disrupts families. As we saw in Chapter 2, the lack of government regulation does indeed make business more flexible and competitive; at the same time, it allows for social change to take place at such a rapid pace that millions of families have been, are, and will be devastated. For example, Edward Luttwak writes of the deleterious effects of deregulation in the airline industry in the 1980s,

> From a strictly economic point of view, the greater efficiency brought about by unregulated competition justifies all. But from a social point of view there is no such compensation. With its stable well-paid jobs, the regulated airline industry of the past enhanced the stability of employees' families and their communities as well as those of the aircraft industry that supplied the airlines.
>
> Today's chaotically unstable airlines are by contrast very disruptive, as they rapidly expand or drastically shrink over a matter of months or even weeks, as they abruptly shift "hubs" and maintenance bases from one place to another, each time hiring and firing employees in their constant maneuvering. It would be a nice bit of sociological research to calculate the number of divorces (and therefore problem children) caused by deregulation-induced economic stress on the families of airline employees.[90]

Of course, the airline industry is just one among thousands of industries, and its employees among tens of millions workers (and parents) who have and/or will undergo the effects of "creative destruction" as the United States drags the world's economy toward an even more extreme mode of capitalism.

In the meantime, other democratic, but less capitalist societies, are mindful of the effect free markets can have on families, and they have enacted policies to prevent or reduce the kinds of family devastation that have been seen in the United States. While their economies might be less competitive, their families are arguably much healthier. If unemployed, parents have generous unemployment compensation available to them. If employed, parents are more secure in their jobs and can rest assured their children are being well cared for in government-subsidized child care centers. Further, government policies ensure that they have more time to spend with their children—especially when they are newborn or very young—without serious reductions in their incomes. These policies, far more than the policies found in the United States, do indeed seem to reflect "family values."

APPLICATION: "CHILDREN HAVING CHILDREN"

In his 1995 State of the Union address, President Bill Clinton called teenage parenthood the nation's "most serious social problem." Indeed, teen parenthood is often assumed, without question, to be a negative social condition. Reactions to the concept of teen pregnancy and/or parenthood are so universally negative (in the United States) that its mention elicits an almost knee-jerk response, and its detractors rarely have to state what is wrong with it. Some think it is a principal cause of poverty, some are concerned that the mother (as it is usually the mother who is implicated) is not mature enough to raise a child, others argue that she is not physiologically ready, and still others are concerned because teen pregnancy is indicative of trends in teen sexual behavior that they find alarming. But those who express alarm are rarely called upon to specify their concerns. British researchers Sally MacIntyre and Sarah Cunningham-Burley note similar concerns with the construction of the problem in the United Kingdom,

> This failure to specify why we should be worried often proves particularly irritating because it leads to a lack of precision about the nature of the perceived problem of adolescent pregnancy. It is often simply taken for granted that conceptions (or births or abortions) occurring in the teenage years are problematic. For whom they are problematic, and in what ways, are topics that are too infrequently discussed. But unless we are clear in our definition of the problem, how can we analyze its features or proper solutions to it?[91]

Teen pregnancy/parenthood did not become part of popular discussions of social problems until the early 1970s.[92] The issue did not suddenly become a matter of public concern because of increases in adolescent fertility at that time or just before that. In fact, rates of childbirth among teenagers were declining between 1957 and 1983.[93] The construction of the phenomenon as a problem persisted; in 1993, Annette Lawson and Deborah Rhode commented "Contrary to much alarmist rhetoric, neither the United States nor the United Kingdom is experiencing an epidemic of 'children having children'. The frequency of teenage childbirth has varied considerably over time and culture, and current levels are by no means unprecedented."[94] Yet, popular concern has been unprecedented. Thus, because of the lack of correspondence between public perceptions and objective realities, the problem is particularly amenable to a critical constructionist analysis. Such an analysis starts with the fact that teen parenthood has not always been held in such disregard and goes on to examine the reasons, other than the ostensible ones, that account for its present status as a social problem.

Many people's concerns about teen pregnancy have to do with their moral objections to premarital sex. Though proscriptions against premarital sex have always been prevalent in American culture, the historical evidence from the seventeenth and eighteenth centuries indicates a certain tolerance for premarital sex *and* teenage pregnancy as long as the couple was willing and financially able to marry. In the latter half of the eighteenth century, it is estimated that almost 30 percent of first births were premaritally conceived.[95] At the end of the nineteenth century, 23 percent of the babies born in the United States were conceived out of wedlock, mostly to young, urban, working-class women who were less subject to the oversight of their family or community. (To the extent that there was opprobrium, most of the wrath of family and community was focused on *women* who engaged in premarital sex, not their male partners.) Rates of out-of-wedlock births were also high among lower class black families, especially among tenant farming families for whom child labor was an economic asset. These children were cared for by extensive kinship networks—a system that still survives in parts of the black community today.[96]

In addition to the concern about premarital sex, many people object to the notion of teenagers bearing children, whether married or not. But, this too, is a relatively new concern. Teenage childbearing has been common throughout American history and was far more common in the 1940s and 1950s, for example, than it is today. Of course, most of the teenage mothers were married; yet they experienced far less stigma than the married teenage mothers of today. Popular constructions of teen pregnancy/parenthood, then, include prevailing notions of childhood ("children having children"), youth, adolescence, and the appropriate age at which people can engage in sexual relations and begin families. It is important to note that the vast majority of teenage mothers are in their late teens. Two-thirds of them are 18 or 19 and only a small fraction are below 16.[97] It should also be noted that such notions of age-appropriate behavior are themselves social constructions. "The appropriate age for sexual relations and parenthood has always been a matter of cultural definition, and in the United States it has varied considerably across time, region, class, race, ethnicity, and gender."[98] Diana Pearce writes, "In the strictly physiological sense, 'children having children' is an oxymoron. In fact, in our national history and in much of the world today, marriage and childbirth for teenage women are the norm. Thus the definition of teenagers who become pregnant as children reflects a cultural construction of the ending of childhood that is considerably later than the actual physical transition."[99]

If not in terms of physiological maturity, then in what ways do popular constructions suggest teenage mothers are different from older mothers? Many associate teenage pregnancy with unplanned pregnancy. Yet about three-fourths of all unplanned pregnancies are to women beyond their teens.[100] Another common perception associates teen parenthood with out-of-wedlock births. Yet 69 percent of births out of wedlock are to women over twenty.[101] As McIntyre and Cunningham-Burley point out, popular constructions do not recognize that "many women over 20 have unplanned or unwanted pregnancies and may be unmarried or unsupported. It is also worth pointing out that no one expresses much concern about older mothers—for example those having children when they are 35 or 40—even though they may face obstetric and social hazards and may often be unsupported, and even though the rates of pregnancy among these age groups are increasing."[102]

Popular constructions also question the motives of a teenager who decides to have her baby, while they do not question the motives of her older counterpart—even though they might be the same motives. Sally MacIntyre and Sarah Cunningham-Burley write, "Of the first it is often said that her motives . . . are suspect because she seeks an object to love and to return her love, that she desires to achieve adult status, or that she wants to gain independence from her parents. But a 26-year-old might have identical motives, which in her case are taken to be normal and possibly admirable"[103]

It is also believed that the teenager will have fewer supports available to help her with her child than her older counterpart. Yet she is more likely to be living at home with her parents than, for example, her older counterpart, and more government-assistance programs are available to her than to her older counterpart. The implication of most constructions about teen motherhood is that the teenager will live to regret her choice of having a baby, but there is little empirical evidence to suggest that this is the case any more for the teen mother than for her older counterpart.[104]

Race and Class

Much of the attention focused on teen parenthood emphasizes its occurrence within the black community. The media portray teen motherhood as largely a problem of the black community. Ann Phoenix writes, "The issue of teen motherhood provides an excellent example of the intersection of the negative constructions of teenage mothers with those of people of color. Although teenage motherhood is stigmatized generally . . . concern about black teenage mothers is expressed more frequently and is often more heightened than that about their white peers."[105] Indeed teen motherhood does occur disproportionately in the black community. But there are far more white teen mothers than black teen mothers in the United States, and the rate of teen motherhood is increasing much faster among whites.[106] The rates among white women in the United States are also far higher than they are among white women in most other industrialized countries.[107]

Singling out black single mothers became a popular exercise in the 1960s, with the release of Senator Daniel Patrick Moynihan's report blaming much of the plight of the black poor on the increased incidence of female-headed families in the black community. Poverty is indeed one of the more frequently cited objections to teen motherhood. The problem, as it is popularly constructed, is that if a teenager decides to have a baby, she is foregoing education and training that would otherwise allow her to achieve financial success. Teen motherhood, especially black teen motherhood, usually comes to the attention of the public when calls for welfare reform heat up. Welfare critics charge that teenagers are having babies just so that they can live on the dole, thus attacking the motives of teen mothers and accusing the welfare system of encouraging teen motherhood. There is little evidence substantiating these claims, however. In fact, teen motherhood rates are frequently higher in the states that provide the least amount of public assistance.[108]

The relationship between poverty, teen motherhood, and race is far from obvious. But to the extent that it can be delineated, a good deal of research indicates that being black in the United States increases one's likelihood of being poor, and being poor increases the likelihood of teen motherhood. "Teens from low-income or poor families," writes Jane Mauldon, ". . . are nine times more likely than teens from higher-income families to have a child."[109] As for teen mothers foregoing their education in favor of having a child, studies indicate that a great many of them dropped out of school *before* becoming pregnant.[110] In other words, teen motherhood was not the *cause* but often the *result* of foregoing an education, *and* the young woman's inability to succeed in school may explain both her decision to have a child while in her teens as well as her remaining poor into her later adulthood. Among poor teenagers who have a child while still in school, their odds of finishing high school or obtaining a GED are comparable to poor teenage women who do not have children.[111]

Further, if a young woman from a low-income family does indeed drop out of school—"forego" her education—to have a baby, research indicates that she will likely be in no worse shape in her adulthood than her peer who delayed maternity. Hotz, McElroy, and Sanders compared poor women who had babies in their teens to an interesting control group—poor women who had miscarriages in their teens and had their first child at the age of twenty or twenty-one—and they found that the former group worked more, earned more, and received less public assistance in their later adulthood than the women who delayed maternity.[112] This seemingly paradoxical finding is explained fairly easily. The poor women who had children in their teens were likely still living at home and still linked to a social support network that could help them raise their children. On the other hand, the poor women who delayed maternity were less likely to be living at home, were more distant from such a support network, and therefore, less able to leave their children to go to work and more in need of public assistance. In other words, having their children in their teen years may actually be adaptive for low-income women, especially poor black women. Mauldon writes,

> While by most people's standards few of the teenagers who become parents are well equipped to raise a child, these women might not be in a much better position if they waited. These young women probably have greater claim on familial resources (however limited) if they are teenage parents than if they give birth in their twenties. They may also have greater claim on social resources, in the form of specialized education programs for teenage parents, health care, or counseling. The employment picture for them could also favor childbearing: they probably cannot find good jobs as teenagers, but by the time they are in their mid-twenties, when employers might be more inclined to hire them, they will have completed their childbearing and their children will be in school full time.[113]

Frank Furstenburg, who has studied teen pregnancy extensively, writes, ". . . the advantages of delaying parenthood are not so great for black [women] . . . The cruel fact is that for blacks delaying childbearing has relatively low payoff. They are damned if they do and damned if they don't."[114]

The "obvious" drawbacks of teen motherhood become less than obvious from the viewpoint of critical constructionism. As we can see, a critical constructionist analysis illustrates the fact that many of the assumed disadvantages of teen pregnancy are often exaggerated or unsubstantiated. Nevertheless, the way the problem of teen motherhood is popularly constructed serves to reaffirm the ideology of abundant opportunity in the United States and, in doing so, it remains an effective scapegoat for the problems of the poor, especially the black poor, blaming them rather than the social structure for their impoverishment. This is not to suggest that there are no drawbacks to teen motherhood nor that teens should be encouraged to have children, but such an analysis does challenge us to reconsider where this problem is placed on our list of priorities. If poverty is more often the cause than the effect of teen motherhood, then perhaps poverty and its structural causes should be placed higher on that list.

SUMMARY

Popular constructions of the breakdown of the modern day family are based upon idealized impressions of the family of the past. Yet there has never been a "Golden Age" of the American family. Even in colonial times, people were bemoaning the decline of the family. While divorce rates are quite high today, in the past when divorces were rare, it was not uncommon for people to be trapped in loveless marriages, or to be unofficially separated, or to opt for the "poor man's divorce," separation. Today, those who are the most alarmed about the state of the family often identify the "working mother" as the source of the problem. Yet the "breadwinner/housewife" form of family is a relatively new pattern that did not emerge until the Industrial Revolution, and when it did emerge, it was common only in the middle and upper classes and made possible only through the labor of the lower classes.

The breadwinner/housewife form of family reached its apotheosis in the 1950s, following World War II. The baby boomers—that is, many of today's parents, writers, politicians, and political pundits—grew up on a steady diet of idealized images of the '50s family, which made up a substantial proportion of television broadcasting. Those images inform a good deal of the rhetoric in current debates about the family. References to the "traditional family" often allude to this form of family. The family of the fifties, however, was far from traditional. It in fact represented a setback in a longstanding and continuous progression in the status of women. Women were marrying younger, having more babies, and giving up career ambitions, and the educational gap between men and women began to widen. Women were suddenly supposed to find all of their happiness within the confines of the family. Many did not. Of those who did not, their frustration was indicated by the new psychiatric diagnosis of "housewive's blight" and by the thousands upon thousands of women being prescribed antianxiety drugs. When the divorce rates did increase in the 1960s, "traditionalists" often fail to recognize a substantial proportion of those couples getting divorced were the ones who had gotten married in the 1950s.

The family of the fifties was also far from traditional in that it was very heavily subsidized by government monies. Traditionalists—who proclaim the values of independence and self-sufficiency and who are often the fiercest opponents of welfare—also fail to recognize that the family of the fifties was made possible by some of the most generous government subsidies in U.S. history. The GI Bill enabled World War II veterans to establish themselves, marry early, support their wives and children, and achieve the American Dream with relative ease.

Since the fifties, married women have taken jobs outside the home in substantial and increasing numbers. A series of recessions, wage stagnation, and a rising cost of living have made it necessary for families to have both husband and wife working in order to maintain a middle-class lifestyle. So while the traditionalists argue that mothers should be at home with their kids and not out working, the lost income would represent far more sacrifice today than it would have in the 1950s. Not only are more middle-class women working outside the home, contributing substantially to the family income, but most are still performing a disproportionate amount of the work inside the home, namely, most of the housework and child care. While there are plenty of exceptions, this pattern exists even among better educated couples with more "liberated" husbands.

While "family values" are often proclaimed to be the country's first priority when election time rolls around, the United States has fewer policies and programs to support the family than a great many countries around the world. Many other countries have far more generous laws providing for maternity leave (usually paid), and some even provide for paternity leave (often paid). Relative to other industrialized countries, the United States also ranks poorly in the provision of child care services. As a result, many poor single mothers feel the need to stay at home with their children, and many middle-class children receive inferior child care.

When the family is identified as a serious social problem, children are usually considered the most important casualties. Of those problems facing children, the critical constructionist is most concerned with those associated with poverty. While Americans often speak of children as "our most precious resource," the United States, though the wealthiest country in the world, is willing to tolerate child poverty rates that would be unconscionable in Western Europe and other parts of the globe. The belief that individuals are to be blamed for their poverty and not the social system accounts for the American tolerance of high poverty levels. Yet few, if any, actually believe that children are to be blamed for their poverty. Minimal efforts to resolve this contradiction are to be found in U.S. social and economic policies.

One popular method of blaming poverty on individuals lies in the identification of teenage pregnancy as one of the more serious problems in society, especially within the black community. Teen pregnancy has only recently been constructed as a social problem. Today it has such negative connotations that its detractors rarely feel compelled to say what is wrong with it. But it is generally regarded as irresponsible behavior that leads to the diminution of the mother's life chances and to the perpetuation of poverty, especially within the black community. Research, however, reveals that poverty is more the cause of teen pregnancy than the effect. Further, there is evidence indicating that teen pregnancy may well be an adaptive behavior for poor women. That is, a poor woman who has children earlier in life often still lives with her parents, and thus has a support network and child care immediately available. This allows her to finish school and/or get a job. There are also government programs tailored to the needs of teen single mothers. The poor woman who delays maternity, on the other hand, often finds herself quite isolated, with no one to help her with her parenting responsibilities and fewer government programs available to her.

In summary, throughout this chapter, a critical constructionist analysis reveals numerous inconsistencies in the way problems of the family are popularly conceived. Popular constructions about the current state of the family often work from false assumptions about the history of the family. Popular constructions usually place blame on individuals, whereas there are grander social and economic forces accounting for many of the problems facing the family. And in placing blame on individuals, popular constructions reinforce the status quo and offer inadequate remedies relative to the remedies found in countries that implement policy based on a human capital philosophy.

4

Crime and Deviance

Of all the social problems considered in this and other texts, crime and deviance consistently rank among the more serious in the minds of most Americans. Because we are constantly being bombarded with images and accounts of murder, random violence, drug abuse, and various other signs of "moral decay," millions of Americans alternate between feelings of concern, fear, disgust, and outrage. As we shall see in this chapter, however, those feelings stand in the way of a sociological understanding of crime and deviance.

UNIVERSALITY AND RELATIVITY

Crime is certainly not new to the United States, nor is it unique to the United States. Crime is universal. All societies have had, do have, and will always have crime. Therefore, according to Emile Durkheim, crime is not a sign of social pathology. That is, crime is normal, and it is not an indication that there is something wrong with a society. Furthermore, since crime occurs in all societies, Durkheim postulated, it must be functional; it must serve some purpose.[1] Besides providing society with millions of jobs—law enforcement officers, defense attorneys, prosecuting attorneys and their assistants, judges, bailiffs, court recorders, prison guards, counselors, the people of who build the prisons and the courts, probation and parole officers, people who sell insurance, those who make and sell security devices, criminologists, crime writers and their publishers, and the list goes on—crime also provides members of society with a common purpose. Crime, though disruptive, also has a unifying effect, uniting society against a common enemy. Crime and deviance provide the opportunity for *mutual* moral outrage. Rarely do social problems produce such a unifying effect. (However, while Durkheim felt that crime was functional, he did not feel the more crime the better; he most likely would have been quite distressed by the levels of crime we experience in the United States today.)

Not only are crime and deviance universal, but they are also relative. Conceptions of crime and deviance vary from time to time and culture to culture. Behavior that is normative in one culture may well be deviant in another. For example, it is often stated that the incest taboo is universal. Though there is truth to this statement, it is also misleading. It is true that all societies have an incest taboo. However, different societies define incest differently. Hence, some societies may permit sexual relations between certain family members that are prohibited in other societies, and vice-versa. Likewise, behavior that is normative at one time may be deviant at another time in the same culture. For example, before the turn of the century in the United States, large segments of the population regularly consumed opiates (derivatives of the opium poppy). Shortly after the turn of the century, these drugs became strictly regulated and such consumption came to be considered deviant.

The relativity of crime and deviance suggests that there is not something inherent in an act that makes it "wrong," "criminal," or "deviant." Instead, sociologists emphasize that the "wrongfulness" of an act is extrinsic to that act. That is, whether or not an act is considered "wrongful," "criminal," or "deviant" depends upon the norms of the society and the perceptions of the audience, *not* upon the evil that resides in the act, *nor* upon the harm caused by the act.[2]

EXAMPLES OF THE RELATIVITY OF CRIME AND DEVIANCE

Homosexual Behavior

Not long ago, homosexual behavior was thoroughly condemned in the United States. Until the 1960s the subject was rarely mentioned in polite conversation or in the media. To the extent that homosexuality was recognized, it was generally seen as a sign of moral depravity or mental illness. So deviant was homosexuality that it was extremely rare that an individual would openly admit to his or her own homosexual orientation. Today, while there are still those who would like to return to previous times, most people would agree that homosexuality is far less deviant than it was in the not-so-distant past. Most of us are aware of friends, relatives, or public figures who have openly acknowledged their homosexuality. This marked change in public attitudes towards homosexuality—the fact that homosexuality is far less stigmatized today than it was, for example, in the 1950s—illustrates the temporal relativity of deviance.

Homosexuality also provides a very good example of the cross-cultural relativity of deviance. While the deviant status of homosexuality has lessened considerably over the last few decades in the United States, there are other societies in which homosexual behavior is quite normal. In their classic study of sexual behavior in preindustrial societies, Clellan Ford and Frank Beach write, "Our own society [the United States] disapproves of any form of homosexual behavior for males and females of all ages. In this it differs from the majority of human societies. Some peoples resemble us in this respect, but a larger number condone or even encourage homosexuality for at least some members of the population."[3] In some societies—among the Siberian Chukchee, for example—the homosexual may assume the role of *shaman*, a religious figure who enjoys considerable power and prestige. Amongst the Siwans of Africa and the Keraki of New Guinea, boys routinely engage in anal intercourse. Likewise, in some Latin American countries, such as Brazil and Nicaragua, where *machismo* is highly valued, it does not compromise a male's manhood to play the insertor role in same-sex anal intercourse.[4]

Thus, the cross-cultural and historical relativity of the deviant status of homosexuality suggest that there is something external to the behavior—something in the culture—that makes it deviant, rather than something in the behavior itself.

Drug Consumption

Another example of the relativity of crime and deviance can be seen in the variable attitudes and laws regarding the consumption of different mind-altering drugs across time and across cultures. Today, most Americans take the regulation of various drugs for granted. Few people question that such drugs are inherently harmful and, therefore, few question the right of the government to restrict them. However, such attitudes have only come to represent the majority of Americans during this century.

Before the turn of the century, the consumption of mind-altering substances in the United States and in Europe was widespread and generally accepted. Opiates were especially popular, advertised in newspapers and available over the counter at the general store. There were likely hundreds of thousands of addicts.[5] Morphine was used in the treatment of pain. In Britain, it had been rubbed on the gums of babies to ease teething pain. In the United States, thousands of Civil War veterans were addicted to it, having had their war injuries treated with morphine. Various patent medicines were laced with opium. One in particular, laudanum, was especially popular among upper-class women. Also during the latter part of the nineteenth century, preparations from the coca leaf (from which cocaine is derived) began achieving some popularity in the United States and Europe. At first, it was mixed in wine, and its developer received a medal of appreciation from Pope Leo the XIII; later, another coca preparation was developed, and it was named *Coca-Cola*.[6] (Eventually, of course, the coca had to be removed from the cola, and it was replaced by a more socially and legally acceptable drug, caffeine.)

All of this drug consumption went on with very little negative attention from the press or the public. Writes Troy Duster, "From 1865 to 1900, then, addiction to narcotics was relatively widespread. . . . In proportion to the population, addiction was probably eight times more prevalent then than now. . . . It is remarkable, therefore, that addiction is regarded today as a problem of far greater moral, legal, and social significance than it was then."[7]

With regard to the cultural relativity of attitudes and laws affecting drug consumption, there's surely no shortage of data. The consumption of mind-altering drugs is normative behavior in many if not most societies through-out the world. Such drugs often play an integral role in the performance of important rituals in these societies. For example, in the United States, wine is consumed during the Catholic mass; and almost all weddings involve the provision and consumption of alcohol. Peyote, a hallucinogenic drug, plays a critical role in religious rituals among Native American Indians in the west-ern U.S. and in Mexico. Another hallucinogen, *ebene* is used in the rituals of the Yanomamo Indians of northern Brazil. The Rastafarians of Jamaica con-sider marijuana to be an important part of their religious experience. While alcohol is strictly forbidden in Yemen, the consumption of the stimulant *qat* is quite popular. And coca leaves are appreciated for their stimulating qual-ities amongst numerous peoples in the Andes.[8]

Since drug consumption patterns vary so tremendously across cultures, it is not surprising to find considerable variations in the way societies reg-ulate drug consumption. In some countries, Malaysia and China, for exam-ple, drug traffickers are executed. In the Netherlands, while they are tech-nically illegal, coffee shops are allowed to sell small quantities of marijuana and hashish. In Liverpool, England, a clinic has been established where drug addicts can receive prescriptions for the drug of their choice—e.g. heroin or crack cocaine—and redeem them at the local pharmacy. In the United States, the official stance on illegal drugs is quite punitive relative to other West-ern industrialized countries. In the 1980s, the American incarceration rate doubled—becoming one of the highest rates in the world—largely due to the "War on Drugs."

The Significance of Relativity

The fact that crime and deviance are relative to time and culture is extremely significant to the sociologist because it demonstrates the importance of his-tory and social structure to the understanding of these social problems. His-torical changes in attitudes toward homosexuality and drug consumption suggest important changes in institutions, values, beliefs, and norms—all of which make up a social structure and its culture.

Changes in the deviant status of homosexuality, for example, were the result of changes in social structure and culture. During the civil rights move-ment of the 1950s and '60s, momentous changes were taking place in soci-ety's institutions and in its values, beliefs, and norms. Disenfranchised mi-norities were demonstrating, writing, marching, boycotting, and rioting, demanding equal rights. Institutions were forced to become more inclusive of women and racial and ethnic minorities. Attitudes, values, and stereo-types began to change. People's beliefs about the differences and abilities of minority groups began to change. And one such minority that demanded justice was homosexuals.

In addition to the civil rights movement, values, beliefs, and norms with regard to sexual behavior and sexuality began to change. People, especially younger people, became more free and open with the expression of their sexuality. Together, the civil rights movement and the "sexual revolution" led to increasing tolerance and increasing demands for tolerance. The most probable turning point in the struggle for the acceptance of gay lifestyles in the United States was the Stonewall Riot on June 28th, 1969 in New York City. A few days later, the Gay Liberation Front was founded, and ever since, more and more gays have come out of the closet to fight for inclusion.

The conflict theorist would emphasize that another lesson to be learned from the relativity—especially the historical relativity—of crime and deviance is that these phenomena, as well as all other social problems, are very political in nature. Politics is the arena in which different groups fight to uphold their own interests. Gays entered this arena to fight against discrimination and for their acceptance into mainstream society. As late as 1972, homosexuality was classified by the American Psychiatric Association (APA) as a psychiatric disorder. Gay groups, including the Gay Psychiatric Association, organized and entered the arena to fight this classification. They lobbied the APA's leadership, and they picketed and caused general mayhem at the annual meetings of the APA. Eventually, under pressure, the APA took a vote among its members as to whether or not the classification of homosexuality should be dropped from the official classification manual. With a vote of 58 percent to 37 percent, the classification was deleted.[9] This series of events provides a prime example of the political nature of deviance. Thanks to the political maneuverings of gay activists, strides were made in making homosexuality less deviant.

Likewise, the laws that eventually criminalized various types of drug consumption were the result of political processes. Among the first antidrug laws passed in the United States was the law prohibiting opium *smoking* passed in California in 1873. While there were various forms of opiates used throughout the state, *smoking* opium was done almost exclusively by the Chinese immigrants of the time. It has been argued that this legislation was aimed primarily at the Chinese (as were many other legislative efforts in California in the 1870s). Chinese immigrants competed with the white majority for jobs working on the railroads. The white majority was able to use the new law to persecute their Chinese competitors. In other words, the white majority entered the political arena and fought for the exclusion of the Chinese from the labor market, and they won.[10]

This series of events set a precedent for much of the drug legislation that was to follow. That is, much of the legislation was preceded by public images and debate that associated the target drug with a given minority that, at the time, was the object of public scorn. Addressing this historical trend, Musto writes,

> The most passionate support for legal prohibition of narcotics has been associated with fear of a given drug's effect on a specific minority. Certain drugs were dreaded because they seemed to undermine essential social restrictions

which kept these groups under control: cocaine was supposed to enable blacks to withstand bullets which would kill normal persons and to stimulate sexual assault. Fear that smoking opium facilitated sexual contact between Chinese and white Americans was also a factor in its total prohibition. Chicanos in the Southwest were believed to be incited to violence by smoking marijuana. Heroin was linked in the 1920s with a turbulent age group: adolescents in reckless and promiscuous urban gangs. Alcohol was associated with immigrants crowding into large and corrupt cities. In each instance, use of a particular drug was attributed to an identifiable and threatening minority group.[11]

In other words, according to the conflict theorist, antidrug legislation resulted when representatives of the white majority entered the political arena and fought for and won control over the offending minority group.

Today, crack cocaine is of particular concern to the criminal justice system and the public imagination. It is associated with poor, young, urban black males who are associated with much of the street violence in our urban centers. Consequently, whites have stepped into the political arena to fight for what they believe to be their safety. Meanwhile, the possession of powder cocaine—which is largely associated with upper- and upper-middle-class whites—receives far less attention from the public and the criminal justice system. Most prosecutions are for crack cocaine, and the sentences for crack cocaine are far more severe than they are for powder cocaine. An understanding of history and social structure help to account for these differences.

Thus, the critical constructionist asks why is it that alcohol and tobacco are viewed benignly relative to heroin and crack when, in fact, they are relatively more harmful, both physiologically and societally? Alcohol use is implicated in thousands of murders and more than ten thousand drunken driving deaths each year. Tobacco use is implicated in hundreds of thousands of lung disease deaths every year. There are tens of millions of alcohol and tobacco addicts. All of these figures arguably add up to more harm than the combined effects of heroin and crack.[12] Yet heroin and crack are illegal while alcohol and tobacco are not. The reason, states the critical constructionist, is that the advocates of alcohol and tobacco have more political power than the advocates of heroin and crack. Alcohol and tobacco are the drugs of choice among those in power, and the alcohol and tobacco industries have more political sway than the heroin and crack industries.

THE CULTURAL PRODUCTION OF KNOWLEDGE ABOUT CRIME

The social problems perspective emphasizes that crime constitutes a social problem primarily because the public defines it as such, while most people are inclined to think that crime is a social problem because it is harmful and there is so much of it. Citizens are mostly concerned with street crime or stranger-to-stranger violence. Indeed, despite recent declines in crime rates, relative to most other societies in the world, the United States has very high rates of crime. However, it should be noted first, that crime rates are very difficult to measure and second, that public concern about crime and the crime rate are not directly related.

Measurements of Crime and Deviance

Crime and deviance are difficult to measure because their perpetrators want to keep their activities secret. The "official" criminal statistics are generally considered to be the *Uniform Crime Reports* that are published every year by the FBI. These are a compilation of reports from thousands of local law enforcement agencies across the country. Generally speaking, the crime rates are comprised of those crimes that are *reported* to the police. They do not include the so-called "dark figure" of crime: those crimes that do not come to the attention of the authorities. Some types of crimes are more likely to be reported to the police than others. For example, murder rates are highly reliable because when a homicide occurs, it is almost always reported to the police (that is, the dark figure is minuscule). However, drug offenses are less likely to be reported because they usually involve willing participants (hence, the dark figure would be quite large). Likewise, certain crimes may be more likely to be reported at certain times or in certain places than in others. For example, a date rape that occurred in the 1950s was probably less likely to be reported than one that occurs today, because in the '50s the victim was more likely to be blamed for her own victimization than she is today. By the same token, a rape occurring in a rural area may be less likely to be reported than one occurring in an urban area, because in the rural area the victim and the rapist are more likely to be known by everyone in the community and each one's guilt or innocence may become a source of contention throughout the community for years to come.

All such factors that affect the "reportability" of crime affect the dark figure of crime. Consequently, it is very difficult to interpret official crime rates—so difficult that rising crime rates may actually be a good sign with regard to the crime problem. Rather than indicating that more crimes are being committed, rising crime rates may indicate that the crimes that are being committed are more likely to be reported than they were in the past.

Problems with the official statistics should not be taken to mean that they are useless, nor should rising crime rates usually be seen as a good sign. The most reliable measure in the *Uniform Crime Reports* is, as explained above, its murder rate. These are higher in the United States than in most countries in the world; however, as seen in Figure 4.1, contrary to the beliefs of many people, homicide rates are not "skyrocketing." If there have been any trends, it has been one of recent decline. It has not been until recently that the media began reporting a decline in violent crime and homicide rates. But well

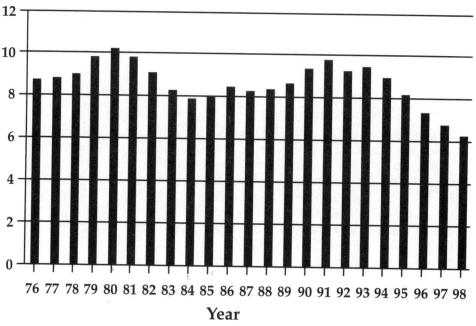

U.S. Homicide Rates 1976–1998

Data obtained from *Sourcebook of Criminal Justice Statistics*.

Figure 4.1

into 1995, the public was being bombarded with a steady barrage of crime reporting. In 1993, for example, the three major television networks broadcast 1,632 crime segments on their evening news shows, up from 785 the previous year—more than 100 percent increase. There had been no corresponding increase in crime during those years. In fact, the crime rate actually decreased between 1992 and 1993. In 1992, 104 segments focused on homicide; this figure rose to 329 the next year—a more than three-fold increase.[13] Meanwhile, the homicide rates fluctuated only slightly upward from 9.3 to 9.5 (per 100,000 population) between 1992 and 1993 (see Figure 4.1). (As of the writing of this book, the media are providing ample coverage of the declining crime rates. But there were years of delay between when the evidence of the decline began to appear in the official crime rates and when the news media began reporting the decline. They were obviously reluctant to report the decline because such news does not "sell" as well as news of increasing crime rates. When and if the crime trend reverses, it is doubtful that there will be any such delay.)

Most criminologists would agree that the best way to analyze the *Uniform Crime Reports* is in conjunction with *victimization surveys*. The largest and most renowned of these are conducted by the Bureau of Justice Statistics, in which tens of thousands of people are selected randomly every year and interviewed about whether they have been victimized by crime in the past year. Criminologists generally consider victimization surveys to be more accurate indicators of crime trends, because they take into account both crimes that are reported to the police and those that are *not* reported to the police. Consequently, these surveys show a good deal more crime occurs than is indicated by the *Uniform Crime Reports*. However, once again, they do not show that crime has been skyrocketing or increasing at an alarming rate, nor did they show this when the media were inundating the public with alarmist crime coverage in the mid-1990s. In 1997, Eric Lotke wrote about the perceived increase in crime despite declining victimization rates,

> The declining victimization rates may come as a surprise to Americans accustomed to hearing that crime is on the rise. Part of the misconception stems from relying on police records of arrests [the *Uniform Crime Reports*] to show crime trends. Police record keeping has improved over the years, as staffing has increased and file keeping has been computerized. Much of the supposed increase in crime is explained by changes in methodology rather than actual changes in victimization rates. For instance, between 1973 and 1992, police statistics showed a 120 percent *increase* in the rate of aggravated assault. Direct surveys of the American population, however, indicate that rates of aggravated assault *declined* 11 percent during that period.[14]

Images of Crime from the Media

While most people have little of no personal experience of serious criminal victimization,[15] they nevertheless are often very fearful and have some strong opinions about the nature of crime in the United States and what to do about it. If the fear of crime does not come from personal victimization, then it must come from other sources. It may be that those who are fearful know others who have been personally victimized or, more likely, that they have been exposed to a steady regimen of television news coverage, cop shows, and crime dramas.

It has long been recognized that crime news sells. Not only does it sell, but it is cheap to produce. Local news stations often make the most of crime news. Steven Beschloss writes, "Television stations, armed with polls that place drugs and crime at the top of people's fears, are feeding the perceived public appetite for these stories. And as the federal government has pushed its war on drugs, news organizations—hungry for ratings and determined to cover the news for less—often provide a willing outlet and heighten the fevered pitch."[16] All that is really needed is a camera on the scene; the gorier the images, the better they sell (as the old news adage goes, "If it bleeds, it leads"). Today, with the advent of the videocam and the help of a police scanner and perhaps a helicopter, news coverage of crime has become more and more immediate and graphic. The news emphasizes violent crime when, by far, the most frequent crimes are property offenses. With crime making up a steadily increasing amount of TV programing,[17] the viewer can easily get the sense that violent crime is skyrocketing and is taking place everywhere, all of the time. Combined with the often-times alarmist rhetoric of the newscasters, the public can come to feel that it is under siege by violent, ruthless criminals. In 1995, when rates of violent crime were actually decreasing, network news coverage of crime was unrelenting. For weeks, one major network started its news stories with the headline "America the Violent"; another started its stories with "America Under Siege."

News coverage is usually so immediate that the viewer has little chance to understand the context of the crime. The criminal incident *is* the news; the reasons for the crime are not newsworthy. A crime is news as, or shortly after, it occurs. An understanding of why the crime took place usually does not come about until after the crime has lost its newsworthiness. Random violence is emphasized, and a lack of context makes almost any violent crime seem like a random and senseless act—which makes it seem all the more threatening to the general public, and which makes a punitive response seem all the more appropriate.

A relatively recent television genre is the "reality-based" cop show, including programs such as *Cops, Top Cops, America's Most Wanted, American Detective,* and *Real Stories of the Highway Patrol.* Like the news broadcasts, these shows emphasize violent crime. And what many in the audience may not realize is that, despite their "reality," they depict inaccurate accounts of unrepresentative cases. The problem lies in their selectivity. It is best to think of what is portrayed in such shows as a *sample* of what goes on in the real world of crime. In fact, that is how these shows present themselves. However, all social scientists would agree that the most important feature of a sample is that it be *representative* of the world that it is supposed to represent. The best way to ensure a representative sample is through random selection. The images presented in these shows are far from randomly selected. They are selected, first, on the basis of their entertainment value. Another important consideration is that the images shown do not present the police in a bad light. These shows depend upon the cooperation of the authorities, and their producers must keep in mind that if the police are not presented in a positive light then they will not get their cooperation for future broadcasts.

The cases selected in "reality-based" crime shows do not represent the real world of crime, nor do the images even represent the cases that are selected. Much of the reality of crime is edited from "reality-based" shows. The following was written by Debra Seagal, a former "story analyst" for the show *American Detective*: "I'm developing a perverse fascination with the magic exercised in our TV production workshop. Once our supervising producer has picked the cases that might work for the show, the 'stories' are turned over to an editor. Within a few weeks, the finished videos emerge from the editing room with 'problems' fixed, chronologies reshuffled, and, when necessary, images and sound bites clipped and replaced by older filler footage from unrelated cases."[18] In an article entitled "Tales from the Cutting-Room Floor," Seagal describes some of the material edited out from the shows broadcast. "While an undercover pal negotiates with a drug dealer across the street, the three detectives survey an unsuspecting woman from behind their van's tinted windows," writes Seagal, footage includes the following conversation:

DETECTIVE 1: Check out those volumtuous [sic] breasts and that volumtuous [sic] ass.

DETECTIVE 2: Think she takes it up the butt!

DETECTIVE 1: Yep. It sticks out just enough so you can pull the cheeks apart and really plummet it. [Long pause] I believe that she's not beyond fellatio either.

[Zoom to close-up of Detective 1]

DETECTIVE 1: You don't have true domination over a woman until you spit on 'em and they don't say nothing.

[Zoom to close-up of Detective 3]

DETECTIVE 3: I know a hooker who will let you spit on her for twenty bucks. . . .

[Direct appeal to camera]

Can one of you guys edit this thing and make a big lump in my pants for me?

[Zoom to close-up of Detective 3's crotch, walkie-talkie between his legs.][19]

Needless to say, this footage was edited out. It shows the police in a negative light. The detectives' brazenness in the face of the camera also shows that the police *know* such negative images will be edited out. Seagal reports that it usually required the editing of fifty or sixty hours of "mundane and compromising" video footage in order to produce one episode. The result is a highly distorted image of crime and law enforcement.

Another problem with both news coverage of crime and "reality-based" programing is their emphasis on crimes committed by poor minorities. Many, if not most of the images of violent crime that are presented involve minorities. "The pictures we tend to show are white officers arresting black people," says one television news director in Texas, "it creates the impression that it's all black people who are using drugs." He goes on to explain, "The problem is that the police don't tend to raid white middle-class people and pull them out of their homes. Is that because it's not there—or the police are afraid of losing their jobs?"[20] Whatever the answer, the disproportionate representation of minorities in crime reports is sure to reinforce prejudices already rife in society, especially given the failure of the news and "reality-based" programs to provide context. Without a context—an explanation—for the crime being covered, viewers may come to attribute the crimes committed by a particular minority group to something inherent— or genetic—in that group rather than to their position and experiences within the social structure. This is a form of biological determinism that is the essence of racial bigotry.

In short, non-fictional accounts of crime that make up the almost daily regimen of millions of television viewers do very little to promote an understanding of crime. This is disturbing because, as voters, the viewing public can and does affect policy-making. "If people are operating with theories of crime that are derived from television," write Craig Haney and John Manzolati, "and these theories are *wrong*, then real world decisions will be made and actual consequences follow from these unreal perspectives."[21] To the extent that the public internalizes the misleading images of crime provided through television, appropriate solutions to the crime problem may be ignored, avoided, evaded, delayed, or outright condemned.

CRIME SCARES

Earlier, the point was made that, in contrast to public perceptions, crime and crime rates are not directly related. At certain times, crime in general, or certain types of crime, receives a great deal of attention from the media, politicians, and the public, though this attention is unwarranted, given the data. That is, suddenly crime, or certain types of crime, becomes a heated social problem, even though the evidence suggests that there has been no sudden surge in criminal activity. The media and the public are whipped into a frenzy; many come to think that social life is very dangerous and/or that society is on the verge of a moral breakdown. We might call this phenomenon a "crime scare." The infamous Salem witch trials provide a classic example of a crime scare. Following are some examples of crime scares that have taken place in recent history.

The Missing Children Scare

Beginning in the early 1980s, Americans were besieged by reports of missing children. While the phrase "missing children" actually includes runaways, children taken by a parent who lost legal custody, and abduction by strangers, the public was given the impression that stranger abductions represented the preponderance of the problem. This followed a couple of well-publicized stranger abductions that resulted in the child's death. Most notable was the case of Adam Walsh, who was abducted and whose dismembered body was later found on a riverbank. His father, John Walsh, subsequently became a leading activist for the cause of missing children, and he is now renowned as the television host of *America's Most Wanted*.

Activists and politicians began describing a social problem of immense proportions. Joel Best describes the situation,

The crusaders described a stranger-abduction problem of astonishing dimensions. Then U.S. Representative Paul Simon offered "the most conservative estimate you will get anywhere"—50,000 children abducted by strangers annually. Child Find, a leading child-search organization, estimated that parents recovered only 10 percent of these children, that another 10 percent were found dead, and that the remainder—40,000 cases per year—remained missing. In short, the crusaders described a large number of stranger abductions with very serious consequences.[22]

The social problems perspective defines a social problem as a phenomenon defined as such by a significant part of the population. By the mid-1980s, stranger abduction easily met this definition. The National Center for Missing and Exploited Children had been established, pictures of missing children were showing up on the sides of milk cartons, talk shows devoted considerable airtime to the issue, the estimate of 50,000 stranger abductions per year became popular wisdom (although some estimates went as high as 400,000), and the press played its role in perpetuating the scare. Best reports that ABC's first news story about the problem stated, "By conservative estimate, 50,000 children are abducted each year, not counting parental kidnappings and custody fights. Most are never found. Four to eight thousand a year are murdered."[23] Meanwhile, surveys showed a growing concern, some might say "paranoia," among parents and children.[24] Parents became ever more watchful of their children, sometimes going so far as to keep identification files with photographs and dental records (in case they should be needed to identify their children's dead bodies). And children were encouraged to be fearful of strangers.

In 1985, however, the 50,000 figure began to be questioned. *The Denver Post*, which later won a Pulitzer prize for its coverage of the issue, drew attention to the fact that the FBI investigated only 67 cases of stranger abductions in 1984. A *Post* editorial suggested that there are more "preschoolers who choke to death on food each year" than there are who are abducted by strangers.[25]

In actuality, the FBI figure is probably way too low (because they do not investigate all stranger abductions), and the 50,000 figure claimed by the crusaders is probably way too high. According to Best and extrapolations made by other researchers, the figure is probably in the neighborhood of 500 to 1,000 children abducted by strangers every year.[26] When confronted with the outrageousness of the 50,000 estimate, crusaders would often respond that "one missing child is too many."

As sociologists interested in social problems, we need to look more carefully at this statement. Yes, it is true, one missing child is a tragedy. But there are millions of tragedies that take place in the world each and every day; few of them are successfully constructed into "social problems." People have a limited amount of time and emotion to attach to social problems, and they cannot do this for the millions of tragedies that take place every day. Potential social problems compete for the public's attention. The public needs accurate information in order to set rational priorities with regard to social problems. Suppose there were "only one" missing-then-murdered child per year, but 15,000 deaths resulting from worker safety violations every year. More people might rationally assess worker safety to be a greater threat to themselves and their families. Then worker safety would become a heated social problem. And then public policy might be implemented that would improve the safety conditions of millions of workers. This rational prioritization of social problems is preempted by much of the heated rhetoric and inflated statistics that are often used by activists, capitalized on by politicians, and parroted by the media.

The Serial Murder Scare

In the 1970s and '80s, serial murder came to occupy the public imagination in a big way. This was thanks largely to some highly publicized cases (e.g., Ted Bundy, Henry Lee Lucas, John Wayne Gacy, and later, Jeffery Dahmer), as well as some very popular fictional books and movies (most notably, *Silence of the Lambs*). The FBI's Behavioral Sciences Unit was also highly instrumental in spreading fear of serial homicide. In the early 1980s, it estimated that approximately one-fifth of all American homicides were cases of serial murders; their estimates went as high as four or five thousand cases per year. These estimates were based on the assumption that when the police reported *unknown* circumstance in a homicide case, that case must have been the work of a serial killer. Phillip Jenkins writes,

> . . . this interpretation of the data is quite unwarranted. In effect, it suggests that an *unknown* circumstance equates to *no apparent motive*, which in turn means that the murder is *motiveless*, or "with no apparent rhyme, reason, or motivation." This is unpardonable. All that can be legitimately understood from an *unknown* circumstance is that, at the time of completing the form, the police agency in question either did not know the exact context of the crime, or did not trouble to fill in the forms correctly.[27]

Nevertheless, in 1983, the U.S. Justice Department held a news conference about the alarming increase in the serial murder phenomenon. At the conference, Justice Department officials reiterated that there were likely several thousand cases of serial murders each year and "that there might be thirty-five such killers active in the United States at any given time."[28] The juxtaposition of these two figures—4,000 victims and 35 serial killers—meant that the average serial killer must have been responsible for over 100 killings per year. Interestingly, there is no case on record in which a serial killer was responsible for so many murders. At least one of the two statistics was in need of serious readjustment.

According to Jenkins and, indeed, more recent FBI estimates, there may indeed be more than thirty-five serial killers operating in the United States at any given time, *but* the annual number of victims, rather than being in the range of 4,000, is more likely to be in the neighborhood of 50 to 70 per annum.[29] This latter estimate amounts to considerably less than 1 percent of all U.S. homicides. Writes Jenkins, "In reality, serial homicide accounts for a very small proportion of American murders, and the claims frequently made in the 1980s exaggerated the scale of victimization by a factor of at least twenty. Moreover, such offenses are far from new, and the volume of activity in recent years is little different from conditions in the early part of the present century, while the phenomenon is by no means distinctively American."[30]

Much as in the case of stranger abductions of children, discussed above, misleading statistics and images concerning serial murders captured the public's attention and fostered a deeply ingrained fear of strangers among millions of Americans even though, statistically, their chances of being murdered by an acquaintance or loved one were enormously greater than their chances of being murdered by a serial killer. In fact, seventy serial killings per year in a country of over 270 million people means that any person's chances of being murdered by a serial killer were infinitesimally small.

Thus, in the case of serial homicide, the perceived, or subjective, reality of the problem bore little resemblance to its objective reality. We can say, then, that serial homicide was a socially constructed problem. This leads us to the question: Why was this social problem so successfully constructed? Why were such misleading statistics accepted and internalized by so many? The answer, according to Jenkins's constructionist analysis, lies in the fact that a diverse number of interest groups found it to their advantage to perpetuate exaggerated statistics.

The FBI had an interest in perpetuating the myth that there were thousands of victims of crazed killers who roamed the country. They claimed part of the problem lay in the lack of communication between law enforcement agencies, as well as their inability to make the connections between similar crimes happening in very different locations. By exaggerating the extent of these crimes and the extent to which serial killers actually "roam," and by establishing themselves as the experts who could link these disparate killings, the FBI was able to enhance both its jurisdiction and its prestige. Prior to the serial homicide scare, the FBI's jurisdiction was quite limited, restricted only to federal crimes and/or crimes that involved the crossing of state lines. But thanks to the serial homicide scare, the Behavioral Sciences Unit managed to portray themselves as super-sleuths, and the public and other law enforcement agencies came to welcome their help rather than resent the intrusion of federal powers, as they might have prior to the scare.

Jenkins argues that the serial killer scare also fit neatly into the ideological framework of the conservative Reagan administration. Conservative ideology places blame for society's problems on weak, immoral, or depraved individuals rather than on the social structure. The serial homicide scare diverted attention away from other crimes—the vast majority of crimes—that can be more readily associated with the social structure. The vast majority of homicides, for example, occur within the lower class and can, therefore, arguably be linked with poverty and similar structural determinants. Serial homicides, on the other hand, are less readily linked to the social structure; they appear to occur randomly, and they seem to be committed by crazed, pathological, immoral individuals who are, quite simply, "evil." Consequently, by shifting society's focus on crime to serial killings, conservatives were able to perpetuate their view that crime has more to do with the moral breakdown of our society than with poverty, inequality, and the dismantling of social welfare programs.

Paradoxically, liberal groups also found an interest in perpetuating the inflated statistics. When the victims were black, as were many of Jeffery Dahmer's and John Wayne Gacy's victims, black leaders could blame the problem on a lack of concern on the part of law enforcement agencies and their neglect of cases involving missing African Americans. When the victims were gay, similar complaints could be lodged by gay activists. And when the victims were female, feminists could blame the patriarchal criminal justice system for its lack of concern for female victims, in which case, serial homicide could be "contextualized together with offenses such as rape, child molestation, and sexual harassment."[31]

In other words, the myths surrounding serial homicide were successfully constructed because many parties had an interest in perpetuating these myths, and few had an interest in uncovering the truth. Once again, we can see a connection between crime—in this case, perceptions of crime—and politics. Once again, different groups entered the political arena fighting for their interests and allowing certain misperceptions to reign because it suited them to do so.

The Drug Scare

Beginning in 1986 and continuing for several years, the American public was hit with a barrage of news stories about the problem of drugs, especially crack cocaine. Arnold Trebach refers to "The Scared Summer of '86," while Craig Reinerman and Harry G. Levine refer to the phenomenon as "The Crack Attack: America's Latest Drug Scare." Reinerman and Levine note that while there have been numerous drug scares in the United States, probably none have paralleled in intensity this latest "crack attack."[32] Goode and Ben-Yehuda write, "It is possible that in no other decade has the issue of drugs occupied such a huge and troubling space in the public consciousness."[33]

Powder cocaine is a stimulant that is usually inhaled through the nose (i.e., "snorted"); it is quite expensive, and the "high" that it induces is generally a subtle one. Crack cocaine, however, is crystalline; it is smoked; it is considerably less expensive; and the high it induces is quite intense, though fairly brief. Crack's effects are considerably harsher than those of powder cocaine, and its appeal seems, more or less, limited to residents of impoverished inner-city neighborhoods, the same people, note Reinerman and Levine, who have traditionally gravitated toward heroin.[34]

While a smokable and more intense form of cocaine (namely "freebase") had been around since the 1970s, crack did not appear on the scene until the mid-1980s. When it did appear, it was referred to by the media, politicians, and many in the drug treatment community as being one of the worst scourges ever to hit America. Numerous stories in the press referred to crack as "instantly addicting."[35] Terms such as "epidemic" and "plague" were popularly used to describe the phenomenon. Crack's popularity in the inner-city ghettos was usually noted, but then news stories went on to explain how the "epidemic" was spreading into middle-class high schools and suburbs. A full-page editorial in *Newsweek*, written by the editor-in-chief and entitled "The Plague Among Us," reported that "An epidemic is abroad in America, as pervasive and dangerous in its way as the plagues of medieval times. [The epidemic] has taken lives, wrecked careers, broken homes, invaded schools, incited crimes, tainted businesses, toppled heroes, corrupted policeman and politicians."[36] The CBS television weekly newsmagazine *48 Hours* aired an episode, entitled "48 Hours on Crack Street," which attracted the highest viewer audience for a show of its kind in five and a half years. "In July 1986 alone," write Craig Reinerman and Harry Levine, "the three major TV networks offered 74 evening news segments on drugs, half of these about crack. In the month leading up to the November elections, a handful of national newspapers and magazines produced roughly 1,000 stories discussing crack. Like the TV networks, leading newsmagazines like *Time* and *Newsweek* seemed determined not to be outdone; each devoted five cover stories to crack and the 'drug crisis' in 1986 alone."[37]

In 1987, a non-election year, drug coverage began to subside; then in 1988, it began to pick up again. On September 5, 1989, President George Bush went on the air with a speech from the Oval Office about the drug crisis in the United States. During the speech, he held up a plastic bag labeled "EVIDENCE" that contained crack, and he announced that it was "seized a few days ago in a park across the street from the White House." It was revealed a couple of weeks later by the *Washington Post* and by *National Public Radio* that the bag of crack President Bush held up was little more than a staged theatric. "A White House aid told the *Post* that the President 'liked the prop. . . . It drove the point home.' Bush and his advisors also decided that crack should be seized in Lafayette Park across from the White House or nearby so that the president could say that crack had become so pervasive that men were 'selling drugs in front of the White House.' "[38] White House and Justice Department operatives, however, found it quite difficult to find any drugs being sold in the vicinity of the White House. As a last resort, they had to entice an eighteen year old to come to the park and sell them the crack. Rather than "seizing" the crack, they bought it from him and sent him on his way. ("Seizure" implies that an arrest was made and if an arrest had been made, the White House might have had to answer some sticky questions about entrapment, and the whole "set-up" would have been brought more readily to the public's attention.)

The "bag of crack speech" provides a good example of how the public was being manipulated throughout the drug scare years. While reporting about the drug "epidemic" was skyrocketing, actual drug use was not. Reports of the "epidemic" rarely, if ever, referred to objective data. Surveys showed that *drug use was actually going down at the time of the scare.* These surveys did not distinguish between different types of cocaine use, but they did show cocaine use, in general, was dropping.[39] While the networks were reporting that crack was "flooding America" and that it had become "America's drug of choice," in 1986, report Reinerman and Levine, "*there were no prevalence statistics at all on crack*"[40] (authors' original emphasis). "The first official measures of the prevalence of crack began with [the] National Institute on Drug Abuse's 1986 high school survey. It found that 4.1 percent of high school seniors reported having *tried* crack (at least once) in the previous year. This figure dropped to 3.9 percent in 1987, and to 3.1 percent in 1988, a 25 percent decline. This means that at the peak of crack use, 96 percent of America's high school seniors had never tried crack, much less gone on to more regular use, abuse, or addiction."[41]

The objective data hardly indicated a plague or crack epidemic. And if those who touted the problem were so concerned about drug use's threat to our health, they might have mentioned that alcohol and tobacco are, by far, the most popular drugs among Americans, including teenagers, and that they account for far more deaths than do cocaine or crack.

While drug use was dropping, surveys indicated that the number of Americans who thought drugs to be the most serious problem facing the country went up dramatically. "The percentage reporting that drug abuse was the nation's most important problem," notes Katherine Beckett, "jumped from 3 percent in 1986 to 64 percent in 1987."[42] Since this dramatic change in the popular perception of drugs was not due to actual increases in drug use, it must have been related to the rhetoric of politicians and/or the intensified media coverage. According to Beckett, Reinerman, and Levine, the drug scare was largely the result of a political initiative.[43]

As with the serial homicide scare, the drug problem resonated with the conservative ideology that was very popular at the time. Liberal ideology had fallen from grace and social welfare programs were being defunded. Society's problems were seen not in terms of inequality and social structural arrangements, but as indicative of a moral breakdown. The solution, according to First Lady Nancy Reagan's antidrug crusade, was learning to "just say no." To the extent that it was recognized that crack was used disproportionately by poor, inner-city minorities, poverty was considered the *effect*, not the cause of drug abuse. Reinerman and Levine write, "Drug problems fit neatly onto this ideological agenda and allowed conservatives to engage in what might be called sociological denial—to scapegoat drugs for many social and economic problems. For Reagan-style conservatives, people did not so much abuse drugs because they were jobless, homeless, poor, depressed, or alienated; they were jobless, homeless, poor, depressed, or alienated because they were weak, immoral, or foolish enough to use illict drugs."[44]

Meanwhile, in Congress, this conservative ideology had become so popular that both Republicans and Democrats were jostling to demonstrate who could be tougher on crime. A "feeding frenzy" ensued, resulting in more and more media coverage of the issue and tougher and tougher legislation aimed at drug abuse. Lengthier and mandatory sentences were imposed, and rather than just focusing on sellers, the casual user became the target of stronger law enforcement measures. In the 1980s, the U.S. incarceration rate more than doubled, becoming one of the highest, if not the highest in the world. This expansion was due in large part to the "war on drugs."

From the perspective of critical constructionism, all of these crime scares diverted the public's attention away from other problems whose remedies might threaten elite interests.

STREET CRIME

While the media, politicians, and various activists may succeed in exaggerating the amount of crime, there is no denying that the United States has inordinately high rates of street crime, especially violent crime. In the words of Steven Messner and Richard Rosenfeld, "When it comes to lethal violence, America remains the undisputed leader in the modern world."[45] Using data from the World Health Organization and comparing the United States with fifteen other industrialized nations, they note that the U.S. has a homicide rate more than three times our nearest competitor, Finland, while it is almost nine times higher than Japan's. Regarding non-lethal violence, they examine data on robbery (defined as "threats accompanied by force or the threat of force") from the International Police Organization. Again, comparing the United States to the same fifteen industrialized nations, they found U.S. robbery rates to be more than twice as high as our nearest competitors (Canada and France), and 158 times higher than Japan's robbery rates.[46]

The reasons for such high incidence of violence in the United States are, of course, very complex and subject to debate, but they seem to be deeply rooted in our culture and social structure.

One often-heard explanation for our high rates of violence is the relative lack of gun control in the United States. Americans, both criminal and noncriminal, arm themselves at extraordinarily high rates, whereas in most other industrialized countries in the world, guns are very hard to come by. Japan, for example, with its extraordinarily low rates of violence, notes David Bayley, "has the toughest laws on the ownership of firearms, especially handguns, of any democratic country in the world. . . . No handguns are permitted in private hands, even registered, with the exception of people who participate in international shooting competitions."[47] While the availability of guns in the United States almost assuredly contributes to a significant proportion of violence, especially violent fatalities, the evidence indicates that American society would be relatively violent even without firearms. That is, according to Messner and Rosenfeld, "even if all of the gun-related homicides were eliminated from its homicide rate, the United States would still have a *nongun* homicide rate that is higher than the *total* homicide rates of other developed nations. . . . We simply want to call attention to the . . . sobering point that even if none of these weapons were ever used in another killing the United States would still have the highest rate of homicide of any advanced industrialized nation."[48]

It appears that violence in the United States is also not due to some fleeting or sudden changes in the culture, such as a breakdown in morality. While there have been surges in violent crime, namely in the 1920s and 1970s, during this century, even our lowest homicide rates exceed the highest rates in other industrialized countries.[49] In other words, it would appear that there are some enduring features of American culture and/or social structure that explain its violent nature.

Robert Merton and the American Dream

In perhaps the single most important theoretical formulation in the American sociology of crime and deviance, Robert Merton identified the "American Dream" as the feature of American culture that explains much of its crime problem.[50] All cultures define values for their members. One culture might be distinctive in the emphasis it places on the value of having a tight-knit family. Another culture might be distinctive in the emphasis it places on the value of military service. The United States is distinctive in the value it places on monetary success. A well-socialized American (that is, most of us) is one who is directed to the goal of financial success. This has long been the American Dream, and the value placed on it exceeds all other cultural values. While we may pay lip service to the preeminence of the values of family and/or education, most Americans judge themselves to be successful based on their ability to achieve the American Dream. Not only do cultures specify the goals for which their members are to strive, but they also specify the means. The culture directs us to strive for monetary success, and we are told to follow legitimate means to this success. That is, we are supposed to be ambitious, work hard, and be innovative. Unfortunately, the goal of success receives far more emphasis than do the means to achieve it. (Thus, it is far more important whether "you win or lose" than "how you play the game.") Consequently, people are tempted to resort to illegitimate means in order to attain the all-important goal of success.

The emphasis that our society places on the American Dream can be seen as beneficial in that it serves as the driving force of our capitalist economy and provides motivation to better oneself through hard work and innovation. However, it can also be problematic in that the social structure limits the ability of many, especially those in the lower class, to achieve success. Unlike the preeminent values defined by some societies, the goal of monetary success is not achievable by all. Though the American Dream is a virtually universal goal in our culture, the capitalist economy simply is not designed to provide monetary success to all members of society.

The American Dream presupposes equality of opportunity. Almost all Americans are brought up to believe that it is available to them. This belief suffuses our culture, pervading our political, economic, media, educational, and religious institutions. Yet, as mentioned in Chapter 2, it is much easier to stay rich in the United States if you are born rich than it is to get rich if you are born poor. Those born rich are likely to stay rich; those born poor are likely to stay poor. While individual motivation, hard work, and innovation are not irrelevant, the poor need far more of these qualities to achieve monetary success than do the rich. Consequently, there is not equality of opportunity in the United States.

To summarize Merton's theory, there is so much crime in the United States because of our culture's emphasis on the goal of monetary success. The emphasis on success is so great that it becomes the yardstick by which we measure our self-worth and the worth of others. The emphasis on success is so great, the emphasis on the legitimate means of achieving it pales in comparison. The goal of success propels and strains all of us, but people in the lower class are under considerably more strain because they have fewer avenues for attaining monetary success. They, therefore, experience greater temptation to pursue illegitimate means to achieve success—means such as violence, prostitution, drug dealing, etc.

At first glance, Merton's theory perhaps explains property crime as well or better than it explains violent crime. Property crime can be more easily seen as an illegitimate means of achieving the culturally defined value of monetary success. However, most violent crime is concentrated in the lower class, and Merton's theory helps us understand the frustration of living in the lower class in capitalist society, especially in the United States. Remember that when a society places so much emphasis on a goal for its members, the ability to achieve that goal becomes the yardstick by which people measure their self-worth and the worth of others. Those who have little regard for their own lives, as measured by this yardstick, will likely have little regard for the lives of others. Thus the violence that is endemic to the American lower class—both that which is oriented toward monetary gain and that which is not—should not be unexpected.

Other American Values and their Contributions to Crime

There are several important principles from the sociology of values that will help us understand the contribution of American values to the American crime problem. First, the more important values that define and are defined by a culture tend to permeate that culture, its social structure, and its institutions. For example, as mentioned above, the American Dream can be found in and is reinforced by most of society's institutions. The theme of the American Dream is reiterated by governmental leaders, religious leaders, industrial leaders, classroom teachers, athletic coaches, popular culture idols, and numerous other representatives of society's institutions. A second theme relative to our analysis represents one of Karl Marx's more important contributions to the sociology of values. Marx asserted that the dominant institution in any society is its economic institution and that the dominant values will support the prevailing economic arrangements in that society. Hence, as mentioned above, the American Dream is a critical component of American capitalism, providing us with the motivation to work hard and innovate—also providing us, inevitably, with winners and losers. A final principle from the sociology of values is that the more important values tend to be interrelated and to reinforce one another. Two such important and interrelated values often identified with the American "character" are *individualism* and *competition*.

Few would argue that the United States is among the most capitalistic countries in the world. Adam Smith enunciated the guiding principles of capitalism: namely, that if everybody pursues his or her own *individual* self-interests in a market of free *competition*, then the best quality products will be made available at the lowest possible prices, and the society will thrive. Individualism and competition are the foundation of our economic structure, and they are integral components of our value structure. (Americans are so fiercely individualistic that it is perhaps more difficult to teach sociology in the United States than in most other countries. That is, Americans are inclined to think of their destinies solely in terms of their individual efforts; in contrast, sociology emphasizes that so much of our life chances depend upon group influences and one's position in the social structure.) More so than people of other countries, Americans view life as a competition between individuals, with winners and losers, and losers have only themselves to blame. Again, this belief presumes the preexistence of equal opportunity, which can be easily refuted. But the tenacity with which so many Americans hold this view speaks volumes about the nature and importance of these values.

These values help to explain the problem of poverty in the United States, and the connection between street crime and poverty is inescapable. American individualism, combined with the premium that we place on competition, results in a form of *Social Darwinism*, or a "survival of the fittest" mentality. As seen in Chapter 2, in the U.S., more than in most other countries, the poor are blamed for their own poverty, for their lack of *individual* initiative. Rather than sympathy, contempt for the poor is not unusual. Consequently, the poor get very little help in the form of governmental assistance. As we have seen, the United States provides less in the way of welfare assistance than most other advanced industrialized countries in the world. While it is true that poverty itself does not *cause* crime (that is, all poor people do not commit crime), it could hardly be refuted as a *source* of crime. The vast majority of people of who commit the vast majority of street crimes—both violent and non-violent—are poor.

Independently of their contribution to poverty, the values of individualism, competition, and financial success provide powerful motivation to succeed by any means necessary. Criminologist Edwin Schur writes, "It is difficult not to conclude that American society has embraced an ideology of what might be termed capitalism with a vengeance—a reverence for the values of individualism, competition, and profit of such intensity as to provide incentives to crime that go well beyond a level that must be considered inevitable in a modern complex society, even a basically capitalist one."[51] Motivated by the same values that motivate us all, the drug pusher, the pimp, the burglar, and the robber are all entrepreneurs in neighborhoods that provide few opportunities for legitimate entrepreneurship. As Merton would argue, they are innovators in a country whose claim to fame is innovation.

Race and Street Crime

In examining the racial composition of our prisons today, we cannot help but be struck by the fact that African American males are disproportionately represented in our prison populations. A critical question that is difficult to answer conclusively is whether African Americans are disproportionately represented because they commit more crimes or because of biases operating in our criminal justice system. As with most difficult questions, the answer is most likely both.

There is certainly no dearth of evidence demonstrating racial bias in the criminal justice system. The highly publicized case in which Rodney King was severely beaten by Los Angeles police officers brought racial bias to the American consciousness, at least temporarily, in 1992. Probably most Americans would agree that this beating (accompanied by racial epithets) would have been far less likely to occur had Rodney King been white. But bias in the criminal justice system is usually far more subtle, and it has the potential to occur at any stage in the criminal justice process, from arrest to prosecution to conviction to sentencing.

One method of determining bias is by examining the ratio of African American males who are arrested versus the ratio incarcerated. Though this method neglects any bias that may lead to arrest, it does provide an indicator of subsequent bias in the criminal justice system. That is, if there were no bias operating, then we would expect the ratio of African Americans incarcerated to be the same as the ratio of African Americans arrested. Relative to their proportion of the population, African Americans are *five times* more likely to be arrested than whites for serious crimes such as murder, rape, and aggravated assault. And they are *three times* more likely to be arrested for less serious crimes. However, rather than being incarcerated at a rate of three to five times greater than whites, African Americans are *seven times* more likely to be incarcerated.[52] In short, African Americans who are arrested are more likely to be incarcerated than whites who are arrested. It is difficult to say exactly where and when this bias comes into play because it does so in different stages in different cases. For some, it may be in the charging process; in other cases it may be in the plea bargaining; in yet others it may be in the provision of services by a court-appointed attorney; sometimes there could be a racist jury; other times there may be bias on the part of the presiding judge; of course, in many cases, the process may be completely fair and unbiased. But the disparity between arrest ratios and incarceration ratios suggests a cumulative racial bias at work in our criminal justice system.

As mentioned, an examination of the difference between arrest ratios and incarceration ratios does not take into account biases that affect the decision to arrest in the first place—which may have an even greater impact than subsequent biases. A study published by the *Harvard Law Review* indicates that police officers will casually admit that race is an important factor in their decision of whether or not to put someone under surveillance, or to search or arrest that person.[53] Steven Donziger, writing for the National Criminal Justice Commission, asserts,

> Some police officers believe that race provides a legitimate and significant basis to suspect a person of criminal behavior. To justify the use of race in forming this suspicion, these officers might point to racial disparities in arrest patterns: if minorities get arrested more often, they argue, then minorities must be committing more crime. This is a self-fulfilling statistical prophecy: racial stereotypes influence police to arrest minorities, thereby creating the statistics needed to justify the racial stereotype.[54]

In our criminal justice system, in which a person is presumed innocent until proven guilty, the data suggest that African Americans are likely presumed less innocent from their very first contact with the system.

While African Americans are arrested at rates three to five times greater than whites relative to their representation in the population, given the biases evident in the criminal justice system, it is difficult to determine what proportion of street crime they do indeed commit. However, it is not likely that the differences in arrest rates are due solely to biases in the criminal justice system. As mentioned earlier, homicide rates are probably the most accurate crime statistics. Virtually all homicides are reported and, given the seriousness of the crime, the police are likely to use less discretion in making an arrest; that is, racial bias is less likely to come into play. Proportional to their representation in the population, African Americans are arrested *eight times* more frequently for homicide than whites. "This overrepresentation by African Americans in arrests for murder," writes criminologist Jay

Livingston, "cannot be a mere byproduct of police racism. Even if all the uncleared murders were committed by whites, African Americans would still account for 45 percent of all murders"[55] (even though they make up only about 13 percent of the population). Victimization surveys also indicate that African Americans are responsible for approximately 60 percent of robberies.[56] The disproportionate involvement of African Americans in street crime needs to be explained.

There are those who believe that crime is the result of moral deficiency. When attempting to explain why one sociodemographic group commits more crime than another, this explanation is *antisociological*. When attempting to explain why African Americans commit more street crime than whites, this explanation smacks of racism because, essentially, it asserts that blacks are less moral than whites. Is this because of their biological make-up (an explicitly racist assumption), or is it because of their position in the social structure and the prejudice, discrimination, and poverty that are likely to go along with it? If the latter, then it is not moral deficiency, but the social structure that requires examination.

One of the principal explanations for African American street crime is poverty. As we have seen, African Americans are far more likely to experience poverty than whites. Again, poverty does not itself cause crime; but the connection between poverty and crime can hardly be thought a coincidence. Rates of street crime are especially high among African Americans in the inner-city ghettos. As noted in Chapter 2, in the 1970s, job opportunities rushed out of these areas into the suburbs and, more importantly, into Third World countries where labor is cheaper. As job opportunities rapidly disappeared and the unemployment rate, especially among young African American men, climbed to new heights, these young men became less "marriageable" and less able to support a family, thus contributing to the rise of the single parent, female-headed household in the black community.[57] In addition to these forces, the inner-city African American community was further destabilized by the exodus of successful African Americans from the inner cities to the suburbs. Before desegregation, successful African Americans were more or less forced to live in the ghettos with their poor neighbors. As housing became less segregated, those who could afford to moved out. They took their jobs, their money, and their more affluent lifestyles with them, further contributing to the dilapidation of the ghettos. But more importantly, their presence had provided successful role models for their young, poor neighbors. When they left, according to William Julius Wilson, the role models left.[58] Poor, young African American males were almost exclusively surrounded by those who had failed to achieve the American Dream.

Being surrounded by "failure" does not temper one's desire to achieve the material comforts promised by the American Dream. The values propagated by the American Dream are nearly universal in our culture. These values became even more exaggerated in the 1980s and '90s. Notes Elliott

Currie, a "hypermaterialist culture" emerged that had been "fueled by the massive growth of consumer advertising and marketing and celebrated on television, on movie screens, and in popular music."[59]

Probably the most influential of these media has been television. "Television's capacity to reach into the privacy of all households," writes Carl Nightingale, "regardless of class and race boundaries, and the medium's consolidation of image, sound, movement, and color have firmly and inalterably established an intimate familiarity with mass-market America among the poor. Indeed, it appears that poor households and poor teenagers have been significantly more attached to TV than have more affluent kids."[60] In the first several decades of television, almost all commercials depicted the lifestyle of upper-middle-class whites, with all of its material accouterments. The contrast of this lifestyle with that of most African American viewers must have been frustrating, degrading, and cumulative. Today's television commercials are more or less the same, except that now there are more ads actually targeting poor, inner-city, African American youth. Their inclusion on commercial television represents a double-edged sword. On the one hand, it symbolizes a form of acceptance of African Americans into the culture of the American mass market. On the other hand, it increases material expectations and the frustration and humiliation of not having.

Young African American males experience another form of degradation in our society, with which few others can relate. That is, young African American maleness has come to symbolize a threat to the physical well-being of other Americans. Everywhere we turn, we are constantly being exposed to the image of the criminally violent African American male—especially on television: on local news, on television documentaries, and on "reality-based" crime shows. "[W]hen a violent crime occurs," writes Donziger, "the perpetrator who comes immediately to mind to white Americans tends to be a person of color."[61] The stereotype is pervasive, and there needs to be more research on how it affects the behavior and psyche of the young African American male. What we do know about stereotypes, however, is that they tend to be self-fulfilling. According to Nightingale, fulfilling the stereotype can serve as a means of dealing with pain and resentment.

> The unequal burden of proof the African American kids have to shoulder in their dealings with the white world is both a source of humiliation and resentment. But there is another way that kids, and particularly teenage boys, react to the linking of race with violence—or what the rap group Public Enemy has called whites "fear of a black planet." This is teenage inner-city boys' practice of mixing ridicule of white fear with a glorification of the stereotype of the violent black male to create a self-image that actually helps young black men to compensate for experiences of economic failure and racial insult.[62]

What is the cumulative effect of being eyed with suspicion, of being feared and avoided? According to Sykes, we have a basic need to be regarded as trustworthy. When one is regarded with distrust—that is, rejected—by most of society, one defense is to reject one's own rejectors.[63] As a way of fending off the pain of rejection, the rejected come to view their rejectors with disdain and contempt. To the extent that this occurs among young African American males, it further drives a wedge between them and white society, alienating them, and thereby contributing to the likelihood of criminal activity. Hence, the stereotype becomes a self-fulfilling prophecy.

THE AMERICAN PUNISHMENT FRENZY

In 1967, the federal courts placed a moratorium on all executions in the United States; the U.S. Supreme Court continued this ban in 1972, and the ban was lifted in 1976. Since then, there have been ever more executions. The United States is among a very few industrialized countries in the world that still makes use of the death penalty. Also, since the mid-1970s, the United States has escalated its rate of imprisonment at a pace that has seldom, if ever, been matched. Between 1975 and 1995, the prison population rose from just over 204,593 to 1,085,363 an increase of 430 percent. During the same period, the United States went from an incarceration rate of 111 to 411 inmates per 100,000 population, an increase of 270 percent. And this figure does not include the estimated 507,000 inmates in local jails in 1995 (up from roughly 257,000 in 1985).[64] Table 4.1 displays the incarceration rates from a survey of 59 nations; as indicated, the United States has the second highest incarceration rate in the world, exceeded only by Russia, and five to ten times the rate in most other industrialized nations.

Most notably, this escalation in the use of imprisonment in the United States has occurred despite the fact that there has been no substantial increase in crime. It is also important to note that states are continuing to build more and more prisons and that it appears the escalation will continue into the foreseeable future. In spite of incontrovertible cross-cultural evidence to the contrary, popular constructions still hold that our criminal justice system is "soft on crime."

The correctional system is growing at such a rapid pace that only in recent years have criminologists and social commentators become concerned with the political power of the correctional industry. In 1960, President Dwight D. Eisenhower alerted the public to the presence, or omnipresence, of the "military-industrial complex." He was concerned about the political power of the military and the alliances it had formed with private industry. Of course the problem with such power and such powerful alliances is that they often serve private interests better than they serve the public interest. Today, we need to turn our attention to the "prison-industrial complex." There are a number of interests, other than the public interest, that are served by correctional expansion.[65] For example, prison guards make up one of the more powerful unions in California. The union grew in membership from

Table 4.1 International Incarceration Rates
(Per 100,000 Population)

Russia	690	Spain	105
United States	600	Malaysia	104
Belarus	505	China	103
Ukraine	390	England/Wales	100
Latvia	375	France	95
Lithuania	360	Germany	85
Singapore	287	Italy	85
Moldavia	275	Austria	85
Estonia	270	Switzerland	80
South Africa	265	Turkey	80
Cook Islands	225	Belgium	75
Hong Kong	207	Sweden	65
Romania	200	Netherlands	65
Czech Republic	190	Denmark	65
Thailand	181	Finland	60
Poland	170	Greece	55
Slovakia	150	Norway	55
South Korea	137	Ireland	55
Kiribati	130	Croatia	55
New Zealand	127	Malta	55
Portugal	125	Solomon Islands	46
Fiji	123	Iceland	40
Hungary	120	Bangladesh	37
Canada	115	Japan	37
Luxembourg	115	Cyprus	30
Brunei Darussalam	110	Slovenia	30
Bulgaria	110	Cambodia	26
Scotland	110	Philippines	26
Macau	107	India	24
Northern Ireland	105		

Source: Marc Mauer, The Sentencing Project: Table 1 from "Americans Behind Bars:
U.S. and International Use of Incarceration," 1995.

4,000 to over 23,000 in one decade,[66] and it contributed more than $100,000
to the committee that pushed through California's punitive "three-strikes"
legislation.[67] Norwegian criminologist and prison critic, Nils Christie comments, "It is quite a fantastic situation when those who administer the pain-
delivery in our society have such a great say. It's as if the hangman's association got together to work for more hanging."[68]

Prison guards are not the only ones to benefit from the incarceration
boom. Of course, there is also a great deal of money to be made today in
prison construction. Many rural areas with depressed economies and high
unemployment rates have benefited and stand to benefit from prison construction. "Prisons have replaced factories as the economic center-piece of
many small towns."[69] In past decades, communities would fight to avoid

prison construction in their area. They feared that a criminal population nearby was too great a risk. Today, it is a very different story. For example, Donziger reports that fifty small towns in Texas recently lobbied for a new prison in their areas. Some even offered incentives, such as country club memberships for the wardens or longhorn cattle for the prison grounds. "A small town in Illinois put together a rap song and bought television time as part of a public relations blitz" to convince legislators to locate a prison in its vicinity.[70]

Compounding the problem, many prisons today are being run by private corporations whose only goal is generating a profit. "The goal of the industry is to keep prisons full. A successful company locks up as many people as possible for as long as possible," says Dr. Jerome Miller of the National Center on Institutions and Alternatives.[71] Electronics corporations are also enjoying the boom in prison construction. They make a generous profit wiring prisons and developing monitoring systems for prisoners inside the prison and for probationers outside. Phone companies charge inmates as much as six times the normal long distance rates. Food service, medical service, and transportation service companies are among others that profit from the incarceration boom. Thus, there are various interest groups, whose interests are not necessarily in the public interest, that have formed powerful political constituencies with the goal of continuing the incarceration boom.

There are a number of other factors that explain why the United States has gone on its punishment binge. Government leaders have found the topic of crime to be a rich source of political capital. Crime is politically expedient. It fits neatly with the American value of individualism, focusing attention away from the social structure and toward "evil" individuals. And few other social problems are as safe to attack as crime. Both liberal and conservative politicians have found it beneficial to their careers to advocate "get-tough" policies. Randy Shaw comments, "Even for progressive politicians, the label 'soft on crime' is the contemporary equivalent of the 'soft on communism' charge that doomed many a progressive political career in the post-World War II decades. In fact, progressives' response to crime closely resembles their response to communism, the bogeyman crime replaced. Conservatives have framed the crime issue as solvable only through expanding the criminal justice system, and progressives have swallowed this analysis hook, line, and sinker. . . ."[72]

Part of the appeal of the crime issue and of the punishment response comes from the fact that approaching so many other social problems involves much more political risk. Besides, crime is a popular issue, a popular problem, one that simplifies some of the more confounding and disturbing social problems in our society today, and one that most people can agree is bad. Political scientist Stuart Scheingold writes,

> To think of such problems as race, economic productivity, moral conflict, and poverty as street crime makes them *seem* much more familiar and much more manageable. This response is due to a powerful belief system, *the myth of crime*

and punishment. If the problem is street crime, we can readily identify the culprits and distance ourselves from them. They are unknown predators who seek out opportunities to prey upon us and disrupt our lives. This frightening image of crime is compelling because the myth of crime and punishment is paired with the resonance that punishment is an effective and virtuous response to crime (emphases in the original).[73]

Thus, according to Scheingold, some of the more serious and enduring social problems in our society—such as race relations and poverty—are subsumed under *the* problem of street crime. "A growing prison system," writes sociologist Elliott Currie, "was what we had instead of an antipoverty policy, instead of an employment policy, instead of a comprehensive drug-treatment or mental-health policy."[74] In a similar vein, activist and scholar Angela Davis writes, "Homelessness, unemployment, drug addiction, mental illness, and illiteracy are only a few of the problems that disappear from public view when the human beings contending with them are relegated to cages."[75] While these other problems are not so easily solved, Americans have *faith* in the appropriateness of punishment as a solution to wrongdoing.

Unfortunately, faith is based neither upon reason nor upon evidence. Indeed, if incarceration were an effective deterrent, then we might expect low or rapidly declining crime rates among African American males. They experience an incarceration rate of an astonishing 1,947 per 100,000 African American citizens (as compared with a rate of 306 for their white counterparts). Steven Donziger notes, "One out of every three African American men between the ages of 20 and 29 in the entire country—including suburban and rural areas—was under correctional supervision in 1994 . . . many inner-city areas are filled with people who have a criminal record . . . for many children, a trip to prison to visit relatives is more common than a school field trip."[76]

Some might argue that the recent decline in violent crime in the United States is the result of the increasing use of incarceration. But this decline did not occur until *twenty years after* the U.S. began its "imprisonment binge." The suggestion that the solution to the U.S. crime problem is to lock up the majority of the young black male population ignores the reasons why violent crime is disproportionately high among this population; it ignores the cross-cultural comparisons of crime rates and incarceration rates; it is quite likely motivated by racism; and it is unconscionable. Obviously, given the very high rates of crime still being committed by young African American males, wholesale imprisonment is having little deterrent effect. In fact, there is very little evidence indicating that imprisonment has any impact on crime rates. According to Joseph Dillon Davey, "despite extensive research on the subject, a direct link between increased incarceration and lower crime rates has never been empirically established."[77] Interestingly enough, many of the states with the highest incarceration rates also have the highest crime rates (for example, Florida), and many with the lowest incarceration rates have the lowest crime rates (for example, Minnesota). If incarceration were an effective and necessary deterrent, we would not expect to find such patterns.

Some believe that incarceration acts as a general deterrent; that is, it serves as an example of what happens to wrongdoers and deters would-be criminals. Others argue that it serves as a specific deterrent; that is, as long as a felon is incarcerated, he or she is deterred from committing further criminal acts. However, in an often-cited study, Isaac Erlich concluded that a 50 percent reduction in incarceration rates would result in only a 5 percent increase in crime rates. Conversely, Greenwood and Abrahamse found that increasing the prison population by 50 percent would lead to only a 4 percent drop in the crime rate.[78] Taken together, these two studies indicate that, as a general deterrent, incarceration has a very negligible effect and, to say the least, is not very cost-effective. In terms of specific deterrence, there is no denying that the felon is not committing street crime while he or she is incarcerated; however, the vast majority of felons will eventually be released. Davey writes, "[T]he truth is that almost all convicted criminals will be back on the streets just a few years after their convictions. And it is very likely that their experiences in prison will not succeed in improving their behavior. If we were to increase our prison budget by, say, 25 percent overnight, that would be enough to hold the average inmate for only a little while longer, but the costs would be staggering."[79] Thus, to achieve effective levels of specific deterrence, we would have to continue on our present course of prison escalation and basically "lock them up forever"—despite the fact that we already lock "them" up at higher rates and for longer sentences than almost every other country in the world. Yet, almost all of those countries have lower rates of street crime. In other words, contrary to popular belief, the causes of crime in the United States have less to do with the molly-coddling of criminals (because we do not molly-coddle criminals in the U.S.) and more to do with the other features of our culture and social structure.

The belief in the effectiveness of punishment is itself a product of culture. Most Americans began to learn the "value" of punishment at a very early age because most of them were physically punished for their wrongdoing as children. That is, most Americans have been programmed by their parents to automatically accept punishment as the appropriate response to wrongdoing. While Americans accept the rightfulness of spanking, and hit their children with considerable frequency, this is not the case in many other cultures throughout the world.[80]

As mentioned earlier in this chapter, while people may tend to think of crime and deviance as being inherently wrong, it is, in fact, culture that defines such things as wrong; and this is demonstrated by the cultural relativity of crime and deviance. Likewise, while people may tend to think that punishment is inherently right, it is, in fact, culture that defines such things as right. This, too, is demonstrated by the cultural relativity of punishment. While the American public tends to believe that we coddle criminals (based on their belief in the inherent rightfulness of punishment), a cross-cultural analysis indicates otherwise. It is worthwhile to note that, generally speaking, the countries that do impose more severe punishments than the United States are those that Americans would least like to emulate in all other political respects.

Societies More Punitive than the U.S.

Before we look at less punitive societies, we shall turn our attention to societies that are more punitive than the United States. There is an interesting contradiction regarding the American get-tough approach to crime. That is, *freedom* and *democracy* are two of the most powerful ideals in the American value system. Yet as the United States gets tougher on crime, its criminal justice system—a very important symbol of whether a country is free and democratic—begins to resemble the criminal justice systems of regimes that most Americans recognize to be repressive and authoritarian. As I have written earlier, "While the death penalty has been and continues to be associated with repressive regimes, the U.S. is using it more and more. While other nations that are making the transition from military or communist governments to democratic societies often immediately abolish capital punishment, the U.S. legislatures devise more and more crimes to which it should be applied."[81]

American criminology and criminal justice professors are often confronted by students who are upset about the molly-coddling of criminals in the United States, who say something to the effect, "Why don't we just cut off their hands like they do in Iran?!" It is true, some crimes in Iran are punishable by amputation. Some prisons are equipped with amputation devices. They also have the death penalty and sometimes order violators to be stoned to death.[82] But how many Americans would like to live in a society like Iran's? Most Americans would find Iran intolerably repressive, and its criminal justice system is a stark reflection of its repressiveness. If we look through history, those societies that inflict the worst punishments on their deviants and criminals are generally the most repressive in other political respects. Classical criminologist Cesare Beccaria made this point over 200 years ago and it still holds today.[83]

Get-tough proponents in the United States are concerned that criminals—the accused—have too many rights and that prison life is too comfortable; and they would like to see more executions. If they got what they wanted, how closely would the American criminal justice system resemble that in the People's Republic of China? There, the few rights enjoyed by the accused are easily abrogated by special "administrative sanctions," prison conditions are often miserable, and wholesale executions are common, perhaps as many as 20,000 per year (notes a report from the Lawyer's Committee for Human Rights, "the official number of death sentences is considered a 'state secret' and is not made public").[84]

Get-tough proponents in the United States would argue that the People's Republic of China has gone too far in its get-tough policies, that they do not wish for anything quite so draconian in the United States. But how do we in the U.S. know when we have gone too far? The answer to this question is a matter of opinion; but an informed opinion would, again, be aware of practices in other countries.

Societies Less Punitive than the U.S.

When a great many Americans trace their heritage they refer with pride to Western Europe. Interestingly, it is in Western European countries that we find perhaps the greatest tolerance of criminal wrongdoing and leniency in the treatment of criminal offenders. Among these, the Netherlands is probably the most famous among penologists and criminologists worldwide for its progressive criminal justice system. In democratic societies, such as the Netherlands or the United States, the treatment of criminal wrongdoers—whether lenient or harsh—depends largely on the public's attitudes toward them. In the Netherlands, public attitudes are far more forgiving, and there is an "active fostering of community tolerance and media support for broadly rehabilitative rather than punitive policies."[85] This stands in stark contrast to the situation in the United States. Heiner writes, "while the Dutch media are fostering tolerance, our media are constantly hammering us with exaggerated stories of skyrocketing crime rates, blood and gore, random acts of sadism, abused legal loopholes, and cushy prisons."[86]

The Dutch incarceration rate is roughly one-tenth the rate in the United States. Dutch prisons are considered among the most humane in the world. They are relatively small, housing only 80–120 inmates. Each inmate has his or her own cell. In contrast to the United States, prison administrators are allowed to accept new inmates only if they have a cell available.[87] There appears to be mutual respect between prisoners and their guards, and there is an elaborate grievance procedure that takes prisoners' complaints seriously. An Australian prison administrator who studied Dutch prison management comments,

> In the wings, the workshops and recreational and communal areas, there was a notable lack of tension. A number of social and physical factors contributed to this impression; the fact that prisoners and detainees wore ordinary clothing and subdued styling of the officers' "uniform", the use of standard fittings and furnishings in buildings that in Australia would bristle with locks, bars, and hardened glass, the intermingling of staff and inmates were some of the factors involved. Even more telling was the naturalness of the interactions observed between members of the staff as well as between staff and inmates. To say that the prisoners appeared "natural" in their relations with staff is not to imply that their interactions were always cordial. Prisoners expressed annoyance in our presence but their feelings were focused on specific grievances and the response they received from staff conveyed not a hint of questioning their

right to be angry. It should, however, be said that the social environment was generally friendly, robust and, as far as I could judge, devoid of the point-scoring that tends to characterize staff/inmate relations in Australian prisons.[88]

The Dutch are not alone in their humane treatment of criminal offenders. In Germany, for example, there is a women's prison called the *Mutter-Kind-Heim*, which allows its inmates to keep their young children with them. The prison is specially designed so that the children do not see bars and gates. The women live with their children in little apartments. The children spend the days with staff members who are responsible for their education and recreation. They may leave the prison to go to a museum or the zoo. Meanwhile their mothers are working either in the prison or at jobs outside of the prison. In the evening, mother and child reunite in the apartment where she cooks their dinner. Marie Douglas describes this as a very successful program with a zero percent recidivism rate (that is, none of its inmates reoffend after release).[89]

These are just a few examples of less punitive reactions to crime found in European societies. There are other examples: the Scandinavian countries are renowned for their progressive treatment of criminal offenders. And it should be noted that there are progressive, humane programs being tried in the United States. The decentralized nature of the U.S. criminal justice system allows for more flexibility and permits the testing of various treatment programs that may be difficult in the nationalized systems of most European countries. In spite of this flexibility and of the alternatives available, the United States continues its imprisonment binge—despite its costliness and the lack of evidence demonstrating its effectiveness. Nonetheless, in spite of their relative lack of punitiveness, European countries experience less homicide and less violent street crime than the United States. This, again, suggests that the explanation for crime in the United States lies in the culture and the social structure rather than in our "lenient" handling of criminal offenders.

APPLICATION: STREET VIOLENCE VS. CORPORATE VIOLENCE

While American levels of street violence are quite high, while street violence and exotic crimes (such as serial murder and child abduction) occupy the public imagination and fire its rage, and while public officials and law enforcement agencies expend a great deal of time and energy on these crimes, many sociologists who specialize in crime argue that corporate violence does more harm to society and deserves far more attention than it gets.

Ronald Kramer defines *corporate violence* as "corporate behavior which produces an unreasonable risk of physical harm to employees, the general public, and consumers, which is the result of deliberate decision-making by persons who occupy positions as corporate managers or executives, which is organizationally based, and which is intended to benefit the corporation itself."[90] Arguably, corporate violence injures and/or kills more people than street crime. Its victims include people whose lives and homes are wrecked by pollution, whose children are born with birth defects due to pollution, employees exposed to hazardous chemicals at work who develop cancers years later, consumers who buy dangerous products and are consequently injured or killed, farm workers in the Third World exposed to exported pesticides that have been banned in the U.S., and the list goes on. Depending on the estimates used, the number of victims ranges between hundreds of thousands and millions who are injured or killed every year. Many would argue that when corporate officials knowingly risk the life or health of the public, consumers, or its employees, they should be held criminally liable, prosecuted, and punished as much or more than any street criminal would be punished. Yet when such officials are held accountable for injuries they have caused, more often than not their cases are heard in civil or regulatory courts rather than criminal courts.

An often-cited example of corporate violence surfaced with the uncovering of the so-called "Pinto papers." The Pinto papers were internal memoranda at Ford Motor Company that reportedly demonstrated that officials at Ford knew the Pinto automobile was dangerous; they knew it tended to explode on rear-end collision; they estimated that about 180 people would die of burns incurred in such collisions and another 180 serious burn injuries could be expected. They also knew this problem in the Pinto could be fixed for about $11 per vehicle if they issued a recall. According to journalist Mark Dowie, to determine whether a recall was cost-effective, they proceeded to estimate the "cost" of a human life—that is, how much they could expect to settle with each victim's survivors—which came to just over $200,000. Using that figure, Ford officials determined that a recall would cost more than settling these cases and decided not to issue a recall for the Pinto. Mark Dowie, the author of the original article revealing Ford's alleged misconduct, quotes a critic of Ford as saying, "One wonders how long Ford Motor Company would continue to market lethal cars were Henry Ford II and Lee Iacocca [the top Ford officials at the time] serving twenty-year terms in Leavenworth for consumer homicide."[91] (A very similar internal memorandum from GM, with very similar calculations pertaining to burn deaths, surfaced in 1999.[92] Consistent with their pro-corporate bias, this memo received very little coverage on the networks' evening news broadcasts.)

As with the Pinto, corporate officials are sometimes in a position to make decisions that can result in large numbers of deaths or injuries. Sociologist Stuart Hills notes,

> The following examples are the result of such decision-making: the decision to continue to sell the deadly Ford Pinto and defective Firestone 500 radial tires; the midnight dumping of poisonous wastes; the cover-ups by Johns-Manville officials and company doctors of the hazards of working with asbestos, thereby subjecting thousands of workers to slow and painful deaths by

cancer; the Three Mile Island nuclear disaster; the horribly deformed thalido-
mide babies; the manufacturing of defective airplanes and cutbacks in airline
maintenance; and other hazards to life and limb brought on in large measure
by corporate negligence, the quest for profits, and deliberate violations of
health, safety, and environmental laws.[93]

Such examples of corporate disregard for human life and suffering
abound. As this book is being written, the tobacco industry is embroiled in
legal battles all over the United States. Tobacco has been linked to lung and
heart disease, which are linked to hundreds of thousands of deaths every
year. Beyond these harmful physical effects of tobacco, most experts would
agree that the nicotine it contains is addictive. For decades, however, tobacco companies have denied the connections between tobacco and lung
cancer and heart disease, and they have denied that nicotine is addictive.
Now internal memoranda and testimony from former employees are sur-
facing that cast serious doubt about what corporate officials have actually
known for many years and about what they have been hiding. In other
words, there is a strong case to be made that tobacco officials have been selling products they have long known to be deadly and that they have been
covering up evidence of its deadliness. If this is indeed true, then there is a
substantial argument to be made that the acts of corporate officials in the
tobacco industry *alone* cause more deaths and other physical and financial
harm to society than street crime.
  Why does street crime receive so much more attention relative to corporate violence? That is, why is street crime considered much more of a social
problem than corporate violence? Many would argue that street crime receives more attention because it is more threatening than corporate violence.
People choose to smoke cigarettes, knowing—whether tobacco companies
admit it or not—that it may be hazardous to their health. People, however,
do not choose to be robbed while walking down the street. Besides that, tobacco companies and their officials contribute to society by stimulating the
economy and providing tens of thousands of jobs to company employees
and tobacco farmers. Their economic activity cannot be compared to that of
a robber.
  However, the critical constructionist argues that the problem of crime is
socially constructed. We have been trained to see crime as being a problem
largely of lower class individuals wreaking havoc on each other and upon
the rest of society. The vast majority of the times we hear about crime, our
attention is drawn to the violent behavior of lower class individuals. However, politicians and the media, who are training us to view crime in this
manner, largely represent the interests of the corporate elite. The politicians
depend upon contributions from corporations for their campaigns, and the
media are themselves corporations depending upon other corporations for
their advertising dollars. Their interests and the interests of the corporate
world are one and the same. They do not want to focus our attention on
problems created by the corporate world; instead, they focus our attention

on the problems created by certain lower class individuals. The problem, they maintain, is not in the social and economic structure, but is in the moral breakdown of society and in certain pathological individuals. (As Senator Bob Dole stated in his acceptance speech for the 1996 Republican nomination for the presidency, "the root cause of crime [is] criminals, criminals, violent criminals.") Critical constructionism does *not* hold that there is a conspiracy among political, media, and corporate officials to divert attention away from their questionable activities, but due to their unity of interests, things work out *as if* there were a conspiracy.

SUMMARY

Crime and deviance are universal and unavoidable. Their presence in a society does not mean there is something wrong with that society. Crime and deviance are not only universal, occurring in all societies; but they are also relative to time and culture; that is, different societies define crime and deviance differently. Since definitions of crime and deviance vary, depending upon time and culture, this means that their definition depends upon things external to the behavior itself. That is, definitions of crime and deviance depend upon characteristics of social structure and culture, not upon the actual harm caused by the crime or deviance. Thus, for example, homosexuality was once defined as more deviant than it is currently. Changes in the deviant status of homosexuality were the result of (1) changes in the culture (changes in attitudes and beliefs about inequality, prejudice, and discrimination; and changes in values attributed to new sexual freedoms), and (2) changes in the social structure (different institutions acknowledging and giving way to the demands of oppressed minorities).

Since reactions to crime and deviance depend upon features external to the behavior, there is not a one-to-one correspondence between levels of public fear and the actual threat posed by a particular type of crime or deviance. The media, a critical institution affecting social problem construction, help to define which types of crimes and criminals are most threatening; and they tend to distort the real world of crime based upon their considerations of which types of images and stories "sell." Consequently, they opt for graphic depictions of violent street crimes because they are easy and inexpensive to cover; they appeal to the audience on a visceral level, their images are captivating even in the absence of a thoughtful explanation, and their perpetrators are most likely poor and in no position to fend off media coverage. The "reality-based" crime shows also have to consider their need for cooperation from law enforcement authorities. To ensure this cooperation, they have to depict law enforcement in a positive light.

"Crime scares" are another example of the way externalities affect the public's definition of criminal threats. The problems of missing children, serial murder, and drugs serve as examples of how particular types of crime and deviance can be exaggerated by the media, public officials, and various interest groups, and how these exaggerations can affect the public's perception of a threat. Again, factors external to the actual threat are critical to understanding why a particular type of crime or deviance comes to be recognized as problematic.

In general, the type of crime the American public views as most problematic is street crime, especially violent street crime. The United States does indeed have high levels of street violence relative to most other countries in the world. This is sometimes blamed on the availability of guns; however, even without access to guns, research indicates there would still be a disproportionately high incidence of violent crime in the United States. Nor would the high incidence of violence appear to be due to any recent changes in the American "moral fiber" because we have consistently had disproportionately high rates of violence throughout this century. The high incidence of violence in the United States must then be due to enduring features of the American culture and social structure. The most important feature of the American social structure that helps to explain street crime is its extremely capitalist economy; the most important features of its culture are the values placed on financial success (the American Dream), individualism, and competition. All of these combine to encourage a degree of ruthlessness among both winners and losers in the battle for success.

Political ideology is an important external factor that helps to define why certain social problems are defined as more threatening than others. Conservative ideologues, in particular, like to focus on crimes and especially on the individuals who commit them. Conservatives are more likely to view social problems as problems of moral breakdown or individual pathology, and not as problems of the economy or social structure. Hence in conservative times, the prescription for crime is not to change the social structure, the economy, and the poverty that it engenders, but to get increasingly punitive. The American punishment binge, however, does not appear to be a success. As measured by the implementation of the death penalty, and by incarceration rates, the United States is already one of the most punitive societies in the industrialized world, yet it has among the highest crime rates in the industrialized world also. The cause of the high rates of street crime in the United States, therefore, must be in the social structure and in the culture, and *not* in the criminal justice system's leniency. The solutions, then, must address changes in the social structure and/or the culture.

Street crime, in spite of the fact that it is relatively high in the United States, does not necessarily pose a more serious threat to society than crimes that receive less public attention. It is arguable that if the degree of public concern were to approximate the degree of threat to the public, more attention should be paid to corporate violence, which affects millions of Americans each year, either directly or indirectly, yet receives very little attention relative to street crime. Again, a critical constructionist analysis shows that factors external to the degree of threat explain not only the high levels of concern for street crime, but also the relatively low levels of concern for corporate violence.

Problems of the Environment

TECHNOLOGY AND THE ENVIRONMENT

It is technology that gives humans the ability to destroy virtually all life on Earth. It is technology that gives our species so much control over the natural environment. And it is technology that has impacted the environment so much over the last century that environmental issues have become of such concern to people throughout the world today. Technology allows us to extract and consume the earth's resources at ever-increasing rates, and extraction and consumption almost invariably produce waste. Technology threatens the environmental health of the planet, and many of us are planning to go on extracting and consuming at present rates, hoping that future technologies will restore the planet's health.

Technology has long been constructed in the Western mindset, especially the American mindset, as the solution to all problems vis-à-vis the environment. While there seems to be increasing recognition that the earth's resources are finite, historically we have tended to rely on technology as though it could stretch them forever. Technology, of course, has played a pivotal role in American history. Columbus's ships were the product of technology. Technology helped the settlers to wrest the land from the Native Americans. Technology made it possible for the United States to become first an agricultural leader, then an industrial leader, and now a leader in the postindustrial world. Our affinity for technology perhaps reached its zenith in what has been called the "Soaring '60s." In 1962, a committee of the National Academy of Sciences advised President Kennedy that science and technology would provide a future of abundance and that if natural resources—such as iron ore or petroleum—were depleted, better and cheaper substitutes could be developed. The committee predicted "dramatic increases" in food and energy and recommended a "shift away from a philosophy of conserving scarce resources," which had been recommended by the Paley Commission during the Truman administration. Then, in 1969, technology had its greatest public relations triumph with the lunar landing. President Nixon called it "the greatest week since the creation of the earth!"[1] Later, in 1973, referring to American technology's role in making the atomic bomb, as well as the lunar landing, Nixon launched Project Independence, the goal of which was to "free the United States from dependence on foreign oil" by 1980.[2]

This kind of optimism—expecting technology to free us from the limits of the earth's resources—while it may have been justified to some extent by past technological successes, has failed to play itself out as anticipated. In fact, the belief that technology has provided us with so many benefits in the past is itself, in part, a social construction. An alternative construction is that the past availability of natural resources accounted for technology's successes. The automobile and highway systems that have changed our lives and "solved" so many of our problems are important technological achievements, but they would not have had such powerful impacts on our society if it were not for the availability of petroleum. Likewise, many hail technological advances in agriculture and improvements brought about by mechanization, irrigation, and hi-tech pesticides, fertilizers, and herbicides. But once again, the availability of petroleum has made many of these advances possible by powering farm machines, providing electricity for irrigation pumps, and serving as an essential ingredient in many of the pesticides, fertilizers and herbicides. In this way and in so many other ways, *technology has not freed us from the limits of the earth's resources, but it has increased our reliance on these resources*; the greater our reliance, the more is at stake. In the words of former Secretary of the Interior Stewart Udall, "America has preened itself for three decades on the wizardry of its technologists. All the evidence suggests that we have consistently exaggerated the contributions of technological genius and underestimated the contributions of natural resources."[3]

SCIENTIFIC UNCERTAINTY

The role of the sociologist in the environmental debate is less than obvious at first glance. On the one hand, many of the issues that are part of the public discourse about the environment would not seem to fall within the domain of sociological inquiry. Is global warming taking place, how many people can the earth sustain, is the ozone hole indeed expanding—these are questions for the natural sciences. On the other hand, these occurrences and non-occurrences definitely can and do have profound effects on society, and society's responses to these problems (or potential problems) are of considerable sociological import. Sociology can help to clarify some of the issues in the environmental debate.

The essential questions in the debate are how serious is the damage being done by humans to the planet, how much do we know about this impact, and can we go on with business as usual. Unfortunately, the debate is riddled with uncertainty; but that uncertainty varies with the type of human impact under discussion. Generally speaking, we are more certain about some of the *local* effects of human impact than we are about the *global* effects. For example, it is quite certain that human sewage in the water supply can produce a local outbreak of cholera and other diseases. It is quite certain that the thousands of people who died in Bhopal, India after a gas leakage in a Union Carbide plant in 1984 died because of that leakage. It is quite certain that sharp increases in thyroid cancer among people living in the area of Chernobyl were in large part attributable to the accident at the nuclear power plant in 1986. However, local effects are not always that certain. If a factory is dumping toxic waste into a lake and the residents living in the area develop unusually high rates of leukemia, it may be quite likely that the toxins are linked to the leukemia, but it may also be difficult to prove and, therefore, less than certain.

For most of the history of environmental concern, most of the attention has been focused on local impacts. Then in the 1970s, attention was drawn to the fact that emissions from factories and automobiles were carrying acid across national borders and damaging crops and forests in other countries. "Acid rain" became one of the first environmental issues of international, though not global, concern. Scientists and government leaders were certain enough of the impacts of acid rain to hold international talks on the matter in Berlin in 1985. International agreements and regulations soon followed. In the 1980s, ozone depletion was among the first environmental issues to raise global concern. The ozone layer in the atmosphere serves to protect the earth from the more damaging effects of the sun's ultraviolet rays. Its depletion, caused by man-made pollutants (namely chlorofluorocarbons—CFCs), could possibly lead to increased rates of skin cancer, damage to marine life, and lower crop yields. In 1985, an ozone "hole" was discovered over Antarctica. Awareness of the problem has culminated in international treaties to phase out CFC production and use. The issue of ozone depletion was quickly followed by the issue of global warming. Gas pollutants, mostly from automobiles and factory emissions, are accumulating in the atmosphere, producing a "greenhouse" effect and allowing the sun's heat to warm the earth, but preventing that heat from escaping the atmosphere. Thus, the more greenhouse gases that accumulate, the warmer the earth's temperature. An average increase of just a few degrees could melt polar ice caps, raise ocean levels, flood coastal plains, change the world's climate and vegetation patterns, and, therefore, alter the conditions of life on earth. While the United States agreed to spear off ozone depletion, it has taken the lead in resisting measures to alleviate global warming.[4] This will be discussed later in the chapter.

It is important to note that problems associated with both ozone depletion and global warming are largely theoretical and, therefore, uncertain. The causes and the effects of such phenomena continue to be debated by scientists. If nothing were done, the worst effects of either might not be experienced for generations to come. Thus, a question of particular interest to the constructionist is why were publics and governments so much more responsive to the issue of ozone depletion than global warming? According to Ungar,[5] the imagery of a "hole" in the earth's protective shield is more evocative than any imagery associated with global warming. (There actually is no "hole" in the ozone layer, but an area that is considerably thinner than the rest.) During the 1980s, an era of *Star Trek* movies, the Cold War and Star Wars technology, the public was receptive to the notion of death rays penetrating faulty force shields. The "C-word"—cancer that could result from exposure to these rays—has been a particularly powerful motivation also. The issue of global climate change, on the other hand, without that kind of imagery, has failed to overcome the debate about scientific uncertainty that has surrounded it from the beginning.

The Intergovernmental Panel on Climate Change (IPCC), established by the United Nations in 1988 and made up of 2,500 scientists and other experts from around the world, concluded in 1995 that human activity is indeed having an impact on the earth's climate, and there is urgent need to cut back on greenhouse gas emissions. Earlier, in 1992, the Royal Society of London broke an official 300-year silence on public issues to join the U.S. National Academy of Sciences to issue a statement about population and climate change, warning that "if current predictions of population growth prove accurate and patterns of human activity on the planet remain unchanged, science and technology may not be able to prevent either irreversible degradation of the environment or continued poverty for much of the world."[6]

Even though the majority of climatologists who have weighed in on the issue agree that global warming is a threat,[7] skeptics are correct in arguing that the threat has not been conclusively demonstrated. They argue that there have always been fluctuations in the earth's temperature, and the earth has not been warm enough long enough to establish any long-term trends with scientific certainty.

In previous chapters, critical constructionism has shown us how often subtle elite interests have influenced the public debate concerning various social problems. With regard to global warming and other environmental issues, elite corporate interests are far less than subtle. Environmentalists claim that significant cutbacks in greenhouse emissions and other industrial pollutants would require substantial investments in environmental technology and/or substantial cutbacks in industrial production, either of which could present serious threats to corporate profits. In previous chapters, the case has been made that the resources that corporate interests can bring to bear in public debate often overwhelm the voice of social scientists who have studied the issues systematically. In the case of social problems dealing with the environment, the voice of both social and natural scientists who have weighed in on the debate have been frequently overwhelmed by an array of persuasive devices employed by corporate interests.

CORPORATE SUASION

Environmentalists are generally seeking government regulation and corporations, preferring to operate in the so-called "free market," are almost always opposed to regulation. In the 1970s, the environmental movement was at its peak, enjoying a great deal of public and political support throughout North America and Western Europe. In the United States, by the mid-1970s, ". . . 5.5 million people contributed financially to nineteen leading national organizations, and perhaps another 20 million to over 40,000 local groups. Environmentalism," write Faber and O'Connor, "had arrived as a mass-based movement."[8] Environmentalists were winning significant political victories and the corporate world was rocked by the passage of legislation such as the Clean Air Act, the Clean Water Act, and the establishment of the Environmental Protection Agency. In their "near-hysterical determination" to "put the environmental lobby out of business," according to Sharon Beder, corporations formed coalitions and alliances, established "public affairs" departments or increased the status of existing departments, and diverted increasing resources to lobbying Congress. In 1971, there were 175 firms represented by lobbyists in Washington; by 1982, the number had climbed to 2,445 firms.[9] Since college graduates were among those most supportive of the environmental movement, many corporations and conservative foundations pumped millions of dollars each year into establishing endowed chairs of "free enterprise," establishing the Institute of Educational Affairs, "which was conceived," writes Beder, ". . . to coordinate the flow of money from corporations into the production of conservative ideas," and funding scholars "whose views were compatible with the corporate view."[10] According to Beder, in her book, *Global Spin: The Corporate Assault on Environmentalism*, "In the late 1970s U.S. business was spending a billion dollars each year on propaganda of various sorts 'aimed at persuading the American public that their interests were the same as business's interests.' The result of all this expenditure showed in the polls when the percentage of people who thought there was too much regulation soared from twenty-two percent in 1975 to sixty percent in 1980."[11]

The corporate world succeeded throughout most of the 1980s in their battle against the environmentalists, and many environmental regulations were repealed or went unenforced during the Reagan administration. The problems of ozone depletion, global warming, and other environmental concerns attracted a great deal of public attention in the mid- to late-1980s, but this time the corporate world was ready for battle with the techniques they had learned earlier.

Exploiting Uncertainty

One of the corporate world's principal weapons in the battle against scientific findings that are unfavorable to their interests is to exploit the presence of scientific uncertainty. According to environmental sociologists Frederick Buttell and Peter Taylor, "Scientific uncertainty can be an enormously powerful tool and it is one that is often wielded against environmentalists with particular effectiveness."[12] As long as there is a shred of scientific uncertainty (and there almost always is), it can be exploited by skeptics. Most of us are familiar with this tactic as it was used by the tobacco companies. Despite the endless number of scientific studies linking cancer and cigarette smoking, the tobacco companies could always claim that it has not been *proven* that smoking *causes* cancer. Theoretically, they had a point; the link between smoking and cancer, after all, could be due to the possibility that people who are prone to cancer are more likely to smoke rather than smokers being more likely to contract cancer. The only scientific study that could determine which is the cause and which is the effect would require taking a random sample of newborn babies, randomly dividing them into two groups, later forcing one group to smoke incessantly, never allowing the other group near a cigarette, and then later examining which group developed higher rates of lung cancer. Obviously, for ethical reasons, such a study could never take place. The problem then with this type of research is one of *methodology,* and all scientific research encounters some sort of methodological difficulty. Few of us today, however, doubt there is a causative link between smoking and cancer.

Just as much of the research that once found tobacco to be a harmless substance was funded by tobacco companies themselves, much of the research that fails to find a link between various pollutants and environmental harm is funded by corporations. The corporation, of course, has an interest in producing findings that minimize the harm caused by its product or its emissions and, therefore, it is reasonable to suspect corporate-funded research is significantly biased. As with the tobacco companies, beyond using methodologies that are likely to produce desirable findings, corporations have been discovered on a number of occasions to have covered up findings that may lead to an increase in their production costs or a reduction in their profits. Environmental law requires that chemical companies have to turn over any research findings that indicate a substance may be harmful to people's health or to the environment. In 1991 and 1992, the Environmental Protection Agency offered an amnesty, allowing corporations who had not yet done so (who had been covering up) to turn such scientific documents over with impunity. Chemical manufacturers produced documents from over *10,000* studies indicating that their products produced substantial risks. "Until the amnesty was offered, until it was clear that they wouldn't be sanctioned, the manufacturers simply kept those studies to themselves, even though they were obligated by law to turn over the information."[13] In the name of profit, they had kept these documents secret, breaking the law, violating the ethical tenets of scientific discovery, and putting the environment and the public at risk. It is likely many documents were not turned over because their products were still turning profits.

Public Relations

Corporations have also been very successful in fending off regulation by hiring public relations (PR) firms to fight their battles against environmentalists. The PR industry is steadily becoming an increasingly powerful force in business and industry today. In 1991, the top 50 (out of more than 5,000) PR firms in the U.S. generated more than $1.7 billion in fees. In 1990, U.S. corporations were spending $500 million per year on environmental PR; in 1995, this figure had increased to about $1 billion. "Rather than substantially change business practices so as to earn a better reputation," writes Beder, "many firms are turning to PR professionals to create one for them. After all 'It is easier and less costly to change the way people think about reality than it is to change reality.' "[14]

Of course, one of the tactics employed by PR firms to protect their clients is to exploit the uncertainty surrounding so many environmental issues. For instance, when CFCs were implicated in ozone depletion, the $3 billion aerosol industry engaged the services of PR firms. The PR firms issued press releases emphasizing that the CFC link was theoretical, and they produced a handbook for their clients instructing them how to testify in hearings and respond to news journalists. When asked if aerosols should be banned, for example, the handbook suggested an appropriate response might be "There is slight risk that thousands of different products could be modifying the atmosphere to one degree or another. I do not think it is reasonable or proper to ban products at random to eliminate a threat that many qualified people doubt even exists."[15] US Gypsum, which was being sued for installing asbestos in public buildings, was advised by their PR firm that by "enlisting 'independent experts,' the issue of asbestos, instead of being a public health problem, could be redefined as 'a side issue that is being seized on by special interests and those out to further their own causes. . . .' The media and other audiences important to US Gypsum should ideally say, 'Why is all this furor being raised about this product? We have a non-story here.' "[16]

The best PR is that which is not recognized as such. In fact a good deal of PR output today passes as "news." To put it another way, much of today's newspaper and television news is generated by PR firms. It is estimated that "40 percent of all 'news' flows virtually unedited from public relations offices."[17] A former editor of the *Wall Street Journal* admitted that approximately half of their news stories were generated by press releases, but, he added, "In every case we try to go beyond the press release." *The Columbia Journalism Review*, however, upon examining the *Wall Street Journal*, found that more than half of its news stories were "based solely on press releases" often "almost verbatim or in paraphrase" even though those articles usually carried the by-line "By a *Wall Street Journal* Staff Reporter."[18] As mentioned above, the PR campaign for the aerosol industry involved sending out press releases emphasizing "knowledge gaps" rather than ozone holes, and its releases were often reprinted as news.[19]

A sophisticated and attractive alternative to the press release is the production and distribution of the VNR (video news release). PR firms are now producing video segments that are indistinguishable from—often better than—the segments produced in-house by television news staffs. Martin Lee and Norman Solomon, authors of the book *Unreliable Sources: A Guide to De-*

tecting Bias in News Media, report, "Every week, hundreds of local TV stations, beset by budget and staff cutbacks, air these free, ready-made news releases, which look increasingly realistic. Even veteran media observers often fail to distinguish between video PR spots and station-produced news."[20] A 1992 survey found that "eighty percent of U.S. news directors use VNRs a few times each month."[21] Together, the traditional press release and the VNR "ensure that much of the news people read or watch on television is manufactured by PR firms rather than discovered by journalists."[22] Thus, corporations, in addition to those actually owning the news agencies, are involved in the business of news production.

Another tactic employed by PR firms is the use of direct mail and phone-calling. In the early days of direct mail, PR firms generated lists of prospective sympathizers (in this case, antienvironmentalists) and sent them postcards, which the recipients could sign and then send on to their representatives in Congress, expressing their opposition to environmental regulation. Eventually, politicians became suspicious of frequent onslaughts of postcards and form letters, realizing that they might not actually represent a groundswell of public opinion. Today, PR firms have become more sophisticated in this technique. First, they often contact the sympathizers by phone, asking for permission to write a letter to Congress on their behalf; then, explains a person in the PR industry, "If they're close by we hand-deliver it. We hand-write it out on 'little kitty cat stationery' if it's a little old lady. If it's a business, we take it over to be photocopied on someone's letterhead. [We] use different stamps, different envelopes. . . . Getting a pile of personalized letters that have a different look to them is what you want to strive for."[23] Some PR firms with special phone connections can call potential supporters (in this case, opponents), talk them into calling their congressional representatives, and if the respondent agrees, they can switch them directly over to the politician's office before they can change their minds.

PR firms sometimes advise their corporate clients to establish or work through what are sometimes called "front groups." Front groups are organizations that are supported by corporate interests and are made up of citizens and/or "experts," which are mobilized to achieve particular political ends. Corporations that are often accused of environmental destruction frequently fund antienvironmental organizations such as the Wise Use Movement. If an organization that suits its cause does not already exist, the corporation can hire a PR firm to organize one. Lawyers for electric companies opposed to the Endangered Species Act advised their clients to "[i]ncorporate as a non-profit, develop easy-to-read information packets for Congress and the news media and woo members from virtually all walks of life. Members should include Native American entities, county and local governments, universities, school boards. . . ."[24] According to an article in *Consumer Reports,* PR firms organizing such groups often recruit with financial incentives, paying as much as $500 "for every citizen they mobilize for a corporate client's cause."[25]

Referring to the deceptive nature of industry front groups, the same article in *Consumer Reports*, entitled "Public-Interest Pretenders," observes,

> There was a time when one usually could tell what an advocacy group stood for—and who stood behind it—simply by its name. Today, "councils," "coalitions," "alliances," and groups with "citizens" and "consumers" in their names could as likely be fronts for corporations and trade associations as representatives of "citizens" or "consumers". . . . [Many industry front groups] use names that make them sound as if they represent the public interest, not a business interest. . . . Someone looking at the logo of the National Wetlands Coalition, which features a duck flying over a marsh, would have no clue that the coalition is made up mainly of oil drillers, developers, and natural gas companies that want national policy on wetlands use and development shaped for their industries' benefit.[26]

One might think the Global Climate Change Coalition is an organization concerned with the prevention of global warming; instead, it is a coalition of "fifty U.S. trade associations and private companies representing oil, gas, coal, automobile, and chemical interests" whose aims might be altogether different.[27]

PR firms have developed a vast array of tactics in addition to press releases, VNRs, and front groups. In the early 1990s, the PR firm representing the California raisin industry undertook a campaign to discredit David Steinman's book *Diet for a Poisoned Planet* even before it was published. In his book, Steinman recommended that people eat no fruits and vegetables other than those grown without pesticides. Ketchum, one of the largest public relations firms in the country, specializes in "crisis management," and apparently it was perceived that the publication of the Steinman book would precipitate a crisis for their clients. John Stauber and Sheldon Rampton detail Ketchum's campaign against the book in their exposé of the PR industry, entitled *Toxic Sludge is Good for You*. The campaign was carried out in the utmost secrecy. A memo from a senior vice-president at Ketchum warned, "All documents . . . are confidential . . . Make sure that everything—even notes to yourself—are so stamped. . . . Remember that we all have a shredder. . . . All conversations are confidential, too. Please be careful talking in the halls, in elevators, in restaurants, etc. . . ."[28] Using an informant at Steinman's publishing company, Ketchum managed to get an itinerary of his publicity tour, according to the vice-president's memo, "so that we can 'shadow' Steinman's appearances; best scenario: we will have our spokeman in town prior to or in conjunction with Steinman's appearances."[29] Then, according to Stauber and Rampton, Ketchum employees contacted newspapers and television shows, describing him as an "off-the-wall extremist without credibility" and/or demanding equal time to present opposing arguments.

The vice-president's memo also mentioned other "external ambassadors" who might be recruited in their campaign against the book. One such apparent "ambassador" was Elizabeth M. Whelan, a "prominent antienvironmentalist" and head of the American Council on Science and Health (ACSH). ACSH is funded largely by the chemical industry and happened also to have been a client at Ketchum. Whelan sent a letter to John Sununu, chief of staff at the White House, warning that Steinman and others "who specialize in terrifying consumers" and who "were threatening the U.S. standard of living and, indeed, may pose a future threat to national security." The introduction to Steinman's book had been written by Dr. William Marcus, senior science advisor to the U.S. Environmental Protection Agency. According to Stauber and Rampton, Marcus was pressured to have his introduction removed; he refused and was later fired. Since then government policy was changed to prohibit officials from writing book forewords.

Stauber and Rampton also detail PR firms' sabotaging other environmental books. In one case, the PR firm "hired an infiltrator to pose as a volunteer" in the author's office. After they obtained a copy of his publicity tour, the producers of the radio and television shows on which the author was to appear received phone calls from a woman falsely claiming to be the author's publicist and canceling his appearances.

While some of the techniques employed by PR firms are certainly legal and ethical, others might be legal and unethical, and others are certainly illegal. Further, there is no denying that environmental groups have sometimes resorted to similar tactics, some legal, some illegal. However, the financial resources that industry can use to sway popular constructions far outweigh those that are available to environmental groups. The PR firms might claim that they are just trying to expose the public to the truth or even to the uncertainty of environmental issues, and they are reasonable in their claim that both sides to an issue should be presented. Yet we should keep in mind that the PR firm is merely representing a paying client and has no interest in getting at the truth regarding their client's product or emissions that may cause harm. By using sometimes underhanded methods and by exploiting the uncertainty involved, PR firms are often very effective in preventing environmentalists' messages from reaching the public. Stauber and Rampton write,

> Neither Ketchum Public Relations nor the White House has any right to interfere with your access to good food or good reading materials. . . . You have never voted for a politician who campaigned on a pledge that he would work to limit your access to information about the food you eat. You have never voted for Ketchum PR, and, if you are like most people, you've never even *heard* of them. You never gave consent for them to be involved in your life, and in return, they have never bothered to *ask* for your consent. After all, they're not working for *you*. They are working for the California Raisin Board.[30]

SLAPPs

Another weapon in the corporate arsenal is the lawsuit. Oftentimes environmentalists and other activists are sued for defamation, nuisance, interference with contract, or a similar charge by the industry that feels threatened. The party initiating such a suit often has no intention of winning, but is instead attempting to tie the issue up in court, drain the financial resources of the activists, and intimidate others who were thinking of publicly criticizing their operations. Such lawsuits are called "SLAPPs," or "Strategic Lawsuits Against Public Participation." There have been thousands of such cases filed in the courts, with the plaintiffs often seeking millions of dollars in damages. In 1986, for example, a woman in Texas was sued for $5 million dollars for simply calling a landfill a "dump." The case dragged on for three years, costing the defendant thousands of dollars in legal fees. Finally the case was dropped and, following an investigation, the EPA ordered the site be cleaned up.

Critics, of course, argue that SLAPPs are a threat to activists' freedom of speech. Sharon Beder writes, "Multi-million dollar lawsuits are being filed against individual citizens and groups for circulating petitions, writing to public officials, speaking at, or even just attending, public meetings, organizing a boycott and engaging in peaceful demonstrations. Such activities are supposed to be protected by the First Amendment of the U.S. Constitution, but this has not stopped powerful organizations who want to silence their opponents."[31]

University of Denver professors George Pring and Penelope Canan were among the first to study this phenomenon, and they were the ones who coined the term "SLAPP." They found in their research that two-thirds of SLAPPs are dismissed before trial and, of those that are decided in favor of the plaintiff, most are overturned or dismissed on appeal.[32] Nonetheless, SLAPPs can be a traumatic ordeal for defendants, and they can be very effective in chilling the speech of those who might otherwise engage in protest. Pring and Canan write, "[T]ens of thousands have been SLAPPed, and still more have been muted or silenced by the threat."[33]

The Media

As discussed in earlier chapters, the media play a critical role in shaping popular constructions of social problems. The media are themselves run by corporations, and they are dependent upon the advertising revenue of other corporations. Consequently, corporate interests are highly influential in shaping the content of what we read in newspapers and see on television. In the early days of network television, presenting the news was seen largely as a public service, and news programs were not expected to bring in big profits. Small newspapers might be considered a success by their owners if they could simply produce enough revenue to pay the costs of overhead and salaries. Today, however, more and more media are being bought out by huge corporations. As this book is being written, ABC belongs to Disney, CBS belongs to Westinghouse, CNN belongs to Time Warner, and NBC belongs to General Electric. These are all multibillion dollar, transnational corporations that are heavily invested in a number of other businesses and industries. Meanwhile, both large and small newspapers are being bought up in a frenzy of corporate media acquisitions. "Gone is the owner-editor who purchased a press because, for better or worse, he had something to say."[34] Like their television counterparts, newspaper owners have one overriding goal—the same goal of almost all other corporate executives—profit. "Indeed," relates Calvin Exoo, author of *The Politics of the Mass Media*, "when GE took over NBC and installed one of its corporate lawyers as its president, he firmly declared that the network's overriding responsibility was to 'shareholders.' At that point, a member of the news division asked whether the network had another responsibility, whether the news was a 'public trust,' 'It isn't a public trust,' replied the boss. 'I can't understand that concept.' "[35]

Americans cherish the notion of a "free press" and loathe the notion of "censorship." The press, as it is popularly construed today, is considered to be free of censorship. But this construction only considers government censorship. Indeed, there is very little government censorship of U.S. media. *Corporate censorship*, on the other hand, guides so much of media content that it is hardly recognized as such. Beder writes, "Commercial television and radio [and newspapers] receive most if not all of their income from advertisers. Tens of billions of dollars are spent every year just on television advertising, and the media does its best to create a product that suits those advertisers."[36] The goal of both a news program or an entertainment program is to hold the audience's attention long enough to get them to the commercial, to "deliver the audience to the commercial." It is overwhelmingly in the media's best interest to present a pro-corporate bias in its program content. To do otherwise would compromise their ability to maximize their profits.

A survey of news editors found that 33 percent admitted they would not "feel free" to air a program that might harm the interests of their parent company.[37] (That is only the proportion who *admitted* that they might violate the ethics of news journalism in favor of corporate interests.) In the 1970s, *New York Times* editors were reportedly instructed to downplay the role played by the auto industry in air pollution because the auto industry was one of the paper's major advertisers.[38] Solomon and Lee write,

These days, no commercial TV executive in his right mind would produce a program without considering whether it will fly with the sponsors. Prospective shows are often discussed with major advertisers, who review script treatments and suggest changes when necessary. . . . Procter and Gamble, which spends over a billion dollars a year on advertising, once decreed in a memo on broadcast policy "There will be no material that will give offense, either directly or indirectly to any commercial organization of any sort." Ditto for Prudential Insurance: "A positive image of business and finance is important to sustain on the air."[39]

Solomon and Lee discuss in some detail a documentary aired by NBC about nuclear power plants in France, which "could have passed for an hour-long nuclear power commercial." The correspondent stated, "Looking at a foreign country where nuclear power is a fact of life may restore some reason to the discussion at home. . . . In most countries, especially the U.S., emotions drive the nuclear debate and that makes rational dialogue very difficult." The implication is that opposition to nuclear power in the United States is emotional, not rational. No mention was made that NBC's parent company, GE, was a major supplier of nuclear power, with 39 nuclear reactors in the United States. Nor was there mention of contentious debate among the French about nuclear power. Nor did NBC-TV later report the accidents injuring seven people in French nuclear power plants only one month after the airing of the special, accidents that received a good deal of coverage in the French media and some coverage in U.S. newspapers.[40]

When the major media outlets are owned by transnational corporations, and when they are dependent upon advertising revenue from corporations, they do not constitute a "free press." In the strictest sense, there probably is no such thing as a free press. Government controlled media is, of course, not free either. Both government controlled media and commercially controlled media are both inherently inclined to bias. But of interest to the critical constructionist is the popular perception of corporate controlled media as representing the opposite of government control and, therefore, representing the "free" alternative. This construction enables corporate interests to have immeasurable influence on social problem construction. According to David Edwards, "[T]he mass media system is not a medium for the 'free' discussion of ideas and viewpoints, but is deeply embedded in, and dependent on, the wider corporate status quo, and on the related capacity of corporate communications to boost facts, ideas, and political choices that are conducive to profit maximization, and to stifle those that are not."[41]

Irrespective of their ties to the corporate world, the status quo receives further nourishment from news journalists by their ostensible obsession with "impartiality." Though, as described above, their interests are aligned with corporate interests, news journalists are very careful not to appear to be taking sides. News journalists frequently boast about their objectivity, claiming to be impartial in obsessively covering "both" sides of the issues—even when there might be more than two sides to an issue, or when one of the two sides to an issue happens to represent a minority opinion or the lunatic fringe. In the realm of politics, one can either be for maintaining the status quo or for change. If one is not in favor of change then, *in effect*, one supports the status quo. In striving to maintain the appearance of objectivity, in failing to take sides, news journalists are thus supporting the status quo. "To give weight to both sides," writes Heiner, "as balance suggests, does not promote change; and if it does not promote change, then, by default, it promotes the status quo."[42] Those advocating change face an uphill battle trying to influence problem construction when the media can always be expected to give the opposing side "equal time." Environmental sociologist, John Hannigan writes, ". . . [R]eporters may turn to the 'equal time' technique whereby both environmental claims-makers and their opponents are quoted with no attempt to resolve who is right. In this case it becomes difficult for environmentalists to convince the public that an 'issue' is in fact a 'problem.' "[43]

The principle of impartiality in news journalism makes it very easy for corporations (and often their paid skeptics) to exploit the scientific uncertainty surrounding global warming. According to Paul Rauber, "In the pursuit of 'impartiality' the U.S. news media reflexively seek out the Two Sides to Every Question. . . . It happens more so when the topic is the least bit technical; most reporters don't know much about science, and are unable to distinguish legitimate scientific dispute from bogus posturing. Which is why there is still a 'debate' about global warming."[44] Though many of the scientists who are skeptical of global warming are sincere and not just "posturing," the skeptics do make up a small minority in the scientific community, and the tendency of news journalism to present both sides "equally" obscures their minority status, thereby weakening the argument of the majority. The public is left with the impression that "nobody knows what they are talking about," and therefore, there is no need for more regulations on industry or for them to change their patterns of consumption.

CONSUMERISM

To survive in a capitalist, free market economy, it is generally assumed, business competitors have to expand. Indeed, political commentators have argued that for capitalism to survive political challenges, it must provide for an ever-expanding economy. By its very nature, capitalism engenders inequality and, at least, relative poverty, if not absolute poverty. In order to quell those in poverty, rather than slicing up the pie differently, the poor are assured that the whole pie will expand and their lives will improve. "[C]apitalism's need for growth," writes Hertsgaard, "coincides with a broader political imperative: it keeps the peace. Without growth, the only way to satisfy the demands of the poor majority for a better life would be to share existing resources more equitably. Privileged classes throughout history have been less than keen on that idea. . . ."[45] In a similar vein, sociologist Juliet Schor writes, "Since the Second World War, growth has been the foundation of political consensus and stability in the North [i.e., the First World]. . . . The postwar regime was premised on steady increases in income and consumption, in that the Keynesian alliance between business, labour and government was essentially an agreement to avoid conflict over shares by ensuring higher absolute levels for all."[46] Thus, economically, capitalism requires individual competitors to grow to ensure *their* own survival; and politically, capitalism requires growth to ensure *its* own survival.

"Growth," in this context, is generally dependent on increasing the sale of commodities to a consuming public. Unfortunately such growth is responsible for a great deal of the environmental deterioration of the planet. The production of commodities is commonly connected with polluting emissions, and the consumption of commodities contributes to resource depletion and the generation of waste. In today's economy, growth depends upon consumption and consumption commonly results in environmental deterioration. Retailing analyst Victor Lebow summed up the relationship between growth and consumption, "Our enormously productive economy . . . demands that we make consumption our way of life, that we convert the buying and use of goods into rituals, that we seek our spiritual satisfaction, or ego satisfaction, in consumption. . . . We need things consumed, burned up, worn out, replaced and discarded at an ever increasing rate."[47] In this sense, capitalism and conservation may well be antithetical. Mary Mellor writes,

> Private ownership and profit-oriented economies within a system of nation-states are not conducive to seeing the natural heritage of the planet as a common resource for all humanity. . . . The commodified market economy quickly turns natural resources into cash. The seas are stripped of their fish, the hillsides of their trees, the rivers of their fresh water, and the land of its fertility. Under the logic of self-interest and survivalism, nothing will stop the fisher fishing the last fish, the logging company taking the last tree, or the dam withholding the last drop of water.[48]

As consumers, of course, we all play a pivotal role in resource depletion and waste production. In the United States, one's quality of life is, to a large extent, judged by one's capacity to consume. Consumption has become the principal measure of success, and most of us spend a great deal of our lives striving for it. " 'To go malling,' " comments Ynestra King, "has become a verb in American English—shopping has become our national pastime, as prosperous U.S. consumers seek to scratch an itch that can never be satisfied by consumers."[49] We are spending increasingly long hours making money, which enables us to spend more time shopping and consuming more plastics, lumber, petroleum and electricity. These activities take their toll on the environment. "The United States alone," writes Hertsgaard, "contains 5 percent of the world's population but accounts for 22 percent of fossil fuel consumption, 24 percent of carbon dioxide emissions, and 33 percent of paper and plastic use."[50]

Of course, our consumption is encouraged by a constant onslaught of corporate advertising. Advertising is everywhere today. More than $500 is spent for every man, woman, and child in the U.S. on "highly sophisticated and carefully targeted commercial messages" every year, with consumers "being bombarded by up to 3,000 marketing messages a day."[51] In 1994, $148 billion was spent on advertising, more than was spent on higher education in 1990, more than the government spent on Medicare, and more than the combined budgets of the Departments of Transportation, Justice, Interior, Labor, and Housing and Urban Development.[52] Notes James Twitchell, author of *Adcult USA*, "Almost every physical object now carries advertising, almost every human environment is suffused with advertising, almost every moment of time is calibrated by advertising."[53]

Among the most insidious forms of advertising are those ads shown on Channel One, broadcast in classrooms, introducing children to the value of consumption. Ruskin and Weissman address the issue,

> The best example of coercive techniques is Channel One, which uses compulsory school attendance laws to make eight million schoolchildren watch two minutes of ads in 12,000 schools each day. Channel One lends television and video equipment to schools in exchange for a guarantee that students will watch, every day, a 12-minute "news" show that includes two minutes of ads. Joel Babbitt, then-president of Channel One, explained in 1994 why advertisers like Channel One: "The biggest selling point to advertisers," he wrote, is that "we are forcing kids to watch two minutes of commercials."[54]

Outside of class, more and more children are watching more and more TV, to the point that they are watching approximately 40,000 TV commercials annually.[55] The overall impact is likely to be an increasingly consumerist culture. Ruskin and Weissman write, "[T]he overriding message of advertising is not to encourage people to buy particular products. Rather, the primary effect is to promote the ideology of buying: wants are good, and more possessions bring happiness, contentedness, love and fulfillment."[56]

To make matters worse, the U.S. appetite for consumption is being carefully propagated *throughout the world* by the "global integration" of capitalism and by corporate advertising. The first item on the "wants list" of so many Third World people is a television. Once they have a television, then they want so many of the other commodities they can see Americans consuming on the tube. (Their desire to have what Americans have is more than understandable, but this aspect of global integration poses serious ethical problems that will be discussed later in this chapter.) Global integration is helping to put a television in Third World homes, and television is helping to facilitate global integration. For this reason, First World corporations have an interest in propagating American television programs depicting First World lifestyles and habits of consumption. And many Third World countries are modeling their economies after American capitalism in the hopes of achieving American lifestyles. "Most, if not all, less developed countries," writes Lipietz, "have no other dream than to imitate the model of development that precisely led to the global crisis."[57] If Americans go on consuming at present rates, and if Third World countries are successful in their economic plans, then the burden on the planet will be enormous.

China, for example, is enjoying rapid economic expansion. Describing China's economic successes after its move to a free market economy, a *New*

York Times article exudes, "There is not an adjective that soars high enough or detonates with enough force to describe China's economic explosion or the promise of its future. . . . The Chinese are buying, building and consuming as if there were no tomorrow."[58] In the meantime, China is becoming one of the most polluted nations on earth. Farmland, increasingly critical for the expanding population, is being paved for roads and developed for housing. "Instead of conserving its resources," writes Tyler, "it is exhausting them with a vengeance. . . . [continuing] to squander farmland and water resources in its quest to catch up with consumption levels in the West. . . ."[59] Chinese leaders are reluctant to enact new environmental regulations or enforce existing regulations because that might slow economic development, create a restive public, and threaten their regime.[60] China is already one of the biggest polluters in the world, with only 1.8 million automobiles (1 percent as many as the U.S.; 1 automobile for every 670 people).[61] What happens to local and global pollution levels when and if this figure increases 50-fold? The number of registered automobiles in China has been growing at a rate of 12 to 14 percent per year for the past two decades.[62] In their first meeting in 1995, Bill Clinton reportedly told China's president, Jiang Zemin, that China's greatest security threat to the United States was not a nuclear, military, or trade threat, but an environmental threat. "Specifically, Clinton feared that China would copy America's bad example while developing its economy and end up causing terrible pollution and global warming."[63]

The Automobile

Easily, one of the most environmentally threatening consumables is the automobile. The United States ranks number one in the world for per capita car ownership. Automobiles account for half of the carbon dioxide emissions associated with global warming,[64] half of the world's oil consumption, and automobile exhaust is the principal cause of air pollution in many cities throughout the world.[65] A study by a team of Harvard University researchers found that 30,000 Americans die each year of respiratory illnesses related to automobile exhaust and another 120,000 lives are shortened due to such exhaust.[66]

Car ownership is necessary for millions of Americans because they live in the suburbs and must commute to work. Owning a car is necessary for millions of other Americans because public transportation in most cities in inadequate. These conditions—urban sprawl and poor public transportation—do not exist to such a degree in European countries, and it is not accidental that they came to exist in the United States. Once again, corporate interests are implicated.

Until the 1930s, railways and trolleys were the principal form of transport in the United States, and they posed a major stumbling block to their competitors in the auto and oil industries. Then in 1932, General Motors, Firestone Tire, Standard Oil (later to become Exxon), Mack Truck, and a number of other corporations secretly joined together to form a front company. In the name of National City Lines, they bought railways and trolleys throughout the country and proceeded to shut them down. They bought up and then closed almost 100 public transportation systems in 45 cities.[67] Between 1936 and 1955, the number of trolley cars operating in the U.S. declined from 40,000 to 5,000.[68] In the meantime, tax revenues were being diverted from public transport to road systems. Los Angeles, for example, which once boasted one of the finest public transit systems in the country, began building its freeway system. As public transportation began to decline, private transportation became more appealing. As public transportation began to decline, cities became less appealing. A costly highway system, paid for by public taxes, made it possible for people to escape the cities and move to the suburbs. People became auto-dependent, and the auto manufacturers and oil companies enjoyed tremendous profits. (Today, automobile manufacturing is the biggest industry in the world; the oil industry ranks second.[69]) Eventually GM and its co-conspirators were tried for the violation of antitrust laws. When found guilty of what Hertsgaard calls one of "the great corporate crimes of the century," GM was fined a mere $5,000; the GM executive who plotted the crime was fined $1.

Constructing the "Good Life"

If scientists are correct, people may not feel the full impact of the harm caused by global warming and the thinning of the ozone layer for generations to come. The only way to prevent the decline in the living standards of future generations caused by global warming, ozone thinning, and other forms of environmental deterioration may be to make drastic changes in our patterns of consumption today. While the well being of future generations resonates strongly in political and social discourse, what sacrifices are people willing to make to protect future generations from harm, especially given that the harm is at present theoretical? Even if it could be proven that our descendants living 50 or 100 years from now will experience marked increases in poverty and disease because of our lifestyles today, what proportion of the public would be willing to cut automobile and electricity usage and garbage output and shopping in half if that is what it would take to ensure the livelihoods of our distant descendants? The answer to that question depends in large part upon popular constructions of the "good life." One of the main messages in constructionism is that there are alternative ways of constructing perceptions, and perceptions of the "good life" can be and have been constructed so as not to center around consumption.

Of the people and interest groups that do not perceive environmental problems to be a threat to future generations, there are those who are not convinced by the majority of scientific opinions, and then there are those relying on the development of future technologies to thwart the threat. But relying on future technological solutions is risky business, especially when technology has had and continues to have so many negative impacts on the environment. Nor can we rely on political solutions (regulations) to work by themselves. If consumption is indeed a large part of the problem, then social solutions—lifestyle change—must be part of the equation. Finnish sociologist, Markku Wilenius, writes, "Prevailing ideas of how we ought to manage the global environment still largely refer to the Western notion of control over the environment, rather than the intelligent limitation of human action, and this bias may lead us to emphasize technological and political solutions rather than social solutions aimed at redirecting our ways of life."[70]

"Redirecting our ways of life" away from consumption does not necessarily mean lowering our standard of living. It means, literally, *changing* our standard. Constructions of economic growth, for example, rely on the GDP (Gross Domestic Product) as a standard of measurement. The GDP is a measure of the total amount of economic activity in a country. It is generally understood that the higher the GDP, the healthier the economy. That standard could be changed, and it should be changed, according to many critics. As mentioned in Chapter 2, the GDP does not distinguish between good and bad economic activity. When money changes hands, the GDP goes up. Thus, as noted earlier, when divorce rates increase, more money is paid to divorce lawyers and the GDP rises. When crime goes up, more people buy security devices, increasing the GDP. An earthquake or an environmental disaster will raise the GDP because of the money spent on funerals and rebuilding. Epidemics and surging rates of cancer can do wonders for the GDP. "[P]ollution," write Clifford Cobb and his colleagues, "shows up twice as a gain: once when the chemical factory, say, produces it as a by-product, and again when the nation spends billions of dollars to clean up the toxic superfund site that results. Furthermore, the extra costs that come as a consequence of that environmental depletion and degradation—such as medical bills arising from dirty air—also show up as growth in the GDP."[71]

Thus, the GDP can be a misleading indicator of "growth," especially when it is used to measure societal welfare. Though the GDP *may* bear a relationship to people's incomes, societal welfare, argue Ekin and Jacobs, also includes the "environment, employment, working conditions, leisure, income distribution, and the safety of the future."[72] Thus, while environmental regulations and reduced consumption might effect a reduction in GDP, as is often feared, societal welfare would not necessarily be adversely affected. There would be a trade-off: incomes may decline, but the environment would become more livable and "safety of the future" would be better assured.

If people consumed less, industrial production would have to decline, and there would be less strain on the environment. The GDP emphasizes *production*; but a decline in the country's productive output—while anathema to corporate interests and the constructions they propagate—could also enhance societal welfare by increasing the amount of leisure time that people have available to them. Increased productivity in the past could have led to decreased work hours, instead it led to increased wages, which could be spent on more commodities. Production increases at the cost of harder and longer work weeks. People are spending more time on the "treadmill of consumption."[73] with less and less leisure time to spend with family. Even though those long hours at work may have enabled them to buy more, they are not necessarily happier. Social scientists who have studied the issue have found very little evidence of a link between wealth (buying power) and happiness. In surveys, the percentage of Americans who identified themselves as "very happy" peaked in 1957, even though most are able to buy far more today. In 1960, a survey of people in fourteen countries found people were happiest in Cuba, Egypt, and the United States, three countries where the people have exceedingly different buying power.[74] In his classic essay, "The Original Affluent Society," anthropologist Marshall Sahlins argues that hunter-gatherer societies may be the most satisfied of all—even though they have very little in terms of material possessions. "Wants," Sahlins writes, "may be 'easily satisfied' either by producing much or desiring little. . . . [taking] the Zen road to affluence. . . a people can enjoy an unparalleled, material plenty—with a low standard of living."[75] The hunter-gatherer desires little, spends only a small part of his day working, eats well, and has a great deal of leisure time. Modern peoples, on the other hand, spend a enormous part of their lifetimes producing (i.e., working).

Juliet Schor describes what she calls "the work and spend cycle" that typifies modern life, "Employers set schedules and workers conform to them. When productivity rises, employers pass the gains along in the form of higher wages, rather than reduced worktime. Workers take the extra income and spend it. They become accustomed or habituated to the new level of spending and develop aversion to their previous, lower level of spending. Preferences adapt such that workers are unwilling to reduce current incomes in order to get more leisure."[76]

Schor, however, sees signs that the work and spend cycle can be broken. One sign is the growth of an anticonsumerist undercurrent in the United States, often going by the name of the "voluntary simplicity" or the "frugality" movement. The movement is made up of people "motivated by concern for the environment, a desire to be liberated from oppressive and meaningless work, and a traditional frugal attitude to money"[77] who often leave high-paying, high-stress jobs to accept lower-paid, lower-stress, often part-time, jobs. There is also a growing number of "downshifters" who spend less time at work so that they can spend more time with their families. While the 1985 Current Population Survey found only 8 percent of workers indicated they would prefer to work less for less pay, Schor believes the low response had to do with the wording of the question. A 1977 survey, for example, asked instead, "Would you like to spend less time working so that you could spend more time with your (husband/wife) and (children), even if it meant less money." This survey found 38 percent of fathers and 53 percent of mothers indicated they would want to work less. A 1991 survey asked if respondents would prefer to take one extra day off per week for one day's less pay; 70 percent of those earning $30,000 or more indicated they would and 48 percent earning $20,000 or less said they would.[78]

Increasing awareness of environmental problems may itself increase people's willingness to accept fewer work hours and consume less. In one recent survey, 77 percent of respondents either "strongly agree" or "somewhat agree" (37 and 40 percent, respectively) with the statement "Americans overuse of resources is a major global environmental problem that needs to be changed."[79] If the standard for "the good life" were to change, environmental problems might be averted and increased leisure time would be a bonus. "Difficult as it may be to tame northern appetites," writes Schor, "there may be no other choice if the planet is to escape environmental crisis. . ."[80]

INEQUALITY AND THE ENVIRONMENT

> Environmental externalities are not simply inflicted by identical agents upon each other; they are often what the rich and powerful do to the weak and hungry. They are what Union Carbide did to the people of Bhopal, what the Soviet State did to the people around Chernobyl, and what greenhouse gas emissions in the U.S. will do to the people of Bangladesh (V. Bhaskar and Andrew Glyn).[81]

Environmental Injustice

Soon after the environment was recognized as a problem, the environmental justice movement began to emerge. Representing a fusion of civil rights and environmental activism, the movement is concerned with the fact that environmental problems frequently have a greater impact upon minorities and the poor. The origin of the movement has been traced to an incident in 1967, when an eight-year-old girl drowned at a garbage dump in Houston, Texas. Students at a nearby, mostly-black college questioned why a garbage dump had been located in the middle of a mostly-black neighborhood. Similar questions have arisen ever since with regard to disproportionate exposure of minorities to environmental toxins. "They question," Carita Shanklin writes, "why communities of color and the poor breathe dirtier air, have higher blood lead levels, and host undesirable land uses such as landfills and incinerators."[82] In fact, from the 1920s until the late 1970s, all of Houston's municipal landfills and six out of eight of its incinerators, were located in neighborhoods that were mostly African American.[83]

Environmental justice activists are often critical of mainstream environmentalists for only attending to issues that are fairly abstract or that will not become serious matters for generations to come. The issue of wetlands preservation, for example, should not take attention away from the more pressing environmental concerns facing the minorities and the poor. Martin Lewis notes, "[E]nvironmentalism was often regarded with suspicion by civil rights activists, some of whom denounced it as little more than an elitist movement concerned primarily with preserving the amenities of prosperous suburbanites."[84] One major problem addressed by the environmental justice movement is the lack of minority representation in the upper echelons of state and local regulatory boards, in environmental organizations (e.g., the Audobon Society and the Sierra Club), and in the management of corporations that pollute.[85] For example, better minority representation might have prevented the National Institute for Environmental Sciences and the National Cancer Institute from excluding Hispanics from their ten-year epidemiological study of the effects of pesticides on farmers and their families, "even though demographic data on farmworkers reveal that 70 percent of seasonal workers and 91 percent of migrant farmworkers are Hispanic."[86]

In spite of the attention attracted by the environmental justice movement, minorities continue to suffer the brunt of pollution. In 1994, the National Wildlife Federation reviewed sixty-four studies that examined whether or not environmental discrimination was an issue; all but one "found environmental disparities either by race or income. . . ."[87] An often cited report, commissioned by the United Church of Christ and the NAACP, and entitled "Toxic Waste and Race in the United States," examined the racial composition in ZIP codes that contained a hazardous waste site. Updating their landmark 1987 report with the same name, the researchers found that people of color were disproportionately located in these areas and that the proportion of people of color living in these areas had actually increased between 1980 and 1993. Further, those areas with the higher number of hazardous waste sites, or the most hazardous sites, had the higher concentrations of people of color and experienced the greater increases in concentration between 1980 and 1993.[88] Similarly, a study of the location of hazardous waste dumps in the Southeast conducted by the U.S. Government Accounting Office found that three out of four facilities were located among majority African American populations.[89] "Garbage dumps," writes environmental sociologist Robert Bullard, "are not randomly scattered across the landscape. These facilities are often located in communities that have high percentages of poor, elderly, young, and minority residents."[90]

Exposure to lead poisoning at an early age is associated with poor mental development and lowered IQ, and such effects are permanent and can reduce a person's life chances. When the dangers of lead were discovered, it was banned from housepaint and gasoline. Today, children who are exposed to lead poisoning are likely to come into contact with it through the dust in their homes. House dust (which can be brought in from outside of the house) may contain the remnants of old, deteriorated lead-based paint;[91] hence, children living in neighborhoods with deteriorating housing are more susceptible to exposure. While some argue that the location of hazardous

sites is a function of socioeconomic status and not race, according to findings of research conducted by the federal Agency for Toxic Substances Disease Registry, lead poisoning disproportionately affects African American
children, irrespective of social class. "Even when income is held constant,"
writes Bullard, "African American children are two to three times more likely
than their white counterparts to suffer from lead poisoning." Bullard continues, "The ability of an individual to escape a health-threatening physical
environment usually correlates with income. However, racial barriers com-
plicate this process for millions of African Americans."[92]

Poor and minority children, especially, are at risk of environmental hazards. According to the *Journal of Environmental Health*, "Because children
breathe more air, drink more water, and consume more food relative to their
body weight than do adults, they receive higher doses of contaminants present in air, food, and water."[93] Children breathe twice as much air, relative
to their body weight, than adults, and the air they breathe is closer to the
ground, where there are higher concentrations of dust.[94] Children are further at risk because their organs and immune systems are in early stages of
development. The *Journal of Environmental Health* notes, "As a group, children of color are at greatest risk from environmental threats. More African-
American and Hispanic children than white children have unacceptable levels of lead in their blood. More African-American and Hispanic children
suffer from asthma and are therefore especially vulnerable to the effects of
air pollution. Children of farm workers are more likely to be exposed to pesticides because they may accompany their parents to work in the fields and
live in housing exposed to pesticide drift from nearby fields."[95]

Historically, Native Americans have been subjected to some of the worst
forms of environmental discrimination. It began with the confiscation and
clearing of their land for white settlers and continues today with the disposal of nuclear and toxic wastes. "The United States," writes King, "has
detonated all of its nuclear weapons in the lands of indigenous people; over
six hundred of those tests within property belonging to the Shoshone nation."[96] With a large proportion of North America's natural resources under their land, Native Americans will likely continue to suffer environmental discrimination.

In 1994, President Clinton signed Executive Order 12898, titled "Federal
Actions to Address Environmental Justice in Minority Populations and Low-
Income Populations." It instructed all federal agencies to "make achieving
environmental justice part of its mission by identifying and addressing, as
appropriate, disproportionately high and adverse health or environmental
effects of its programs, policies, and activities on minority and low-income
populations in the United States. . . ."[97] This is not a new law, "but it stresses
compliance with existing federal laws and regulations."[98]

It remains to be seen whether the executive order will have much impact
on environmental discrimination. It appeared that the first test case would
involve Shintech Corporation's attempt to locate its PVC (polyvinyl chlo-

ride) plant in a rural area of Louisiana. There are already so many hazardous waste facilities in the area that it is known as "Cancer Alley." Lawyers and activists, on behalf of the community, filed papers to stop the development. The state of Louisiana, however, rejected their arguments and decided to permit the plant to be built. The case was appealed to the EPA, citing Executive Order 12898. In the meantime, Shintech withdrew its application to build. Thus, as of the time of this writing, the order does appear to have had a chilling effect on the siting of hazardous facilities, but the EPA has not used its powers as directed by the order.[99]

However the order is applied, it is likely minorities and the poor will continue to bear a disproportionate share of environmental deterioration. Minorities and the poor have fewer resources to resist the location of hazardous sites in their neighborhoods. In that these cases are often fought in the courts and corporations usually have extensive financial and legal resources, undertaking such a fight can be very expensive. The Louisiana community described above was fortunate to have lawyers and activists volunteer their assistance, but not all poor communities can count on such help. "These are the people," write Hunt and Lunde, "who have least access to the legal tools to protect their rights and fend off would-be polluters."[100] Lacking economic resources, they also lack political resources. State and local boards that issue the permits for industrial sites are likely to give less weight to the concerns of these communities. "Since capital always seeks to pollute in ways that encounter the least political resistance," Faber and O'Connor note, "peoples and communities that have the least political power or social resources to defend themselves are the most vulnerable."[101]

Further, the impact of the executive order is doubtful because it does not address two problems. First, it does not provide for the correction of *past* environmental discrimination, which has left minorities and the poor with a disproportionate burden of pollution perhaps for generations to come. Second, it does not consider what might be considered *de facto* discrimination, referring to the fact that while a hazardous facility might be located in a racially and economically mixed neighborhood, those who can afford it will likely move away, leaving behind a neighborhood that is disproportionately minority and poor to suffer the effects.

GLOBAL INEQUALITY

In 1992, India's president, Indira Gandhi, stunned a conference on the environment in Stockholm with the statement, "Poverty is the worst form of pollution." Today, few familiar with pollution in the Third World would take issue with her statement. Though rarely acknowledged in the rhetoric of most American environmentalists, poor people in the Third World face the worst forms of pollution. Environmental problems faced by the poor in the Third World are immediate and certain, not uncertain or potential problems, as is global warming. There are millions of pollution-related deaths in the Third World every year. "All over the world," Geoffrey Lean writes, "the poor account for the most deaths from pollution, and are by far the greatest victims of the degradation of the natural world."[102] Besides living in more polluted areas, the poor are more vulnerable to various pollutants because of the lower immunity that results from malnutrition. Poor children are the most vulnerable, accounting for as much as two-thirds of preventable diseases associated with environmental conditions.[103]

One of the most serious ecological threats worldwide is the lack of potable water. About a billion people in the world have little or no access to clean water. Throughout most of the countries of the Third World, water that is available to the poor is likely to be contaminated, especially by human fecal matter; "human feces," according to the World Resources Institute, "remain one of the world's most hazardous pollutants."[104] Oral intake of fecal matter can lead to, among other things, often lethal bouts of diarrhea. According to the World Health Organization, diarrhea killed about 2.5 million people in 1996, most of whom were children under the age of five.[105] Frequently, the water that is available, contaminated or not, has to be carried more than a mile from its source back to the home. In such cases, only limited amounts of water can be used for washing, exacerbating already unsanitary conditions. Inadequate water supplies and the consequent inability to wash may be responsible for even more diarrheal diseases than contaminated water itself.[106] Increasingly, families in the Third World who can afford to, are resorting to buying clean water, often paying twelve times as much as it would cost to build the facilities to have clean water piped in. Water often accounts for as much as 20 percent of household expenses in parts of Nigeria and Haiti.[107]

Airborne contaminants are another form of pollution that exacts a high toll on Third World peoples of all financial means, but especially the poor. Although there have been incidents in which air pollution had been known to kill people, attention did not focus on the dangers of air pollution until almost 4,000 people were killed by smog in London in 1952. A more recent ecological disaster involving air pollution happened in Bhopal in 1984, which was mentioned earlier in this chapter. But even when localized disasters are not taking place, air pollution is still associated with millions of deaths. Acute respiratory infection (ARI) is the leading killer of children worldwide.[108] ARI is associated with, but not limited to, environmental pollution. Asthma attacks, for example, often increase when pollution levels are high. Interestingly, indoor air pollution poses a greater risk than outdoor pollution to the poor of the Third World, who often live in small, poorly ventilated homes and use traditional fuels, such as wood or coal, for heating and cooking. Data collected by the World Health Organization "suggest that many tens of millions of people in developing countries routinely encounter pollution levels reached during the infamous London killer smog of 1952, leading to a huge estimated toll in disease and premature death."[109] As many as two or three million people die as a result of indoor air pollution every year.[110] The World Bank ranks it among the most serious global environmental problems.

The poor of the Third World also suffer the most from many other forms of environmental degradation. The lives of numerous tribal peoples throughout the world have been devastated by the clear-cutting of rainforests and by industrial development. These once thriving hunter-gatherers are often forced to live in cities that are already teeming with millions of the poor and unemployed. Displaced, and living in an alien environment, they may suddenly find themselves living in absolute destitution.

The poor in Third World countries are those most vulnerable to any kind of ecological disturbance. Poor people are often the most dependent on the fish that they catch, the livestock they raise, or the crops they grow. Lacking any kind of financial buffer, their livelihoods are easily devastated by natural and not so natural disasters. Any ecological event that hinders or reduces global food production could eventually affect us all, but they affect the poor almost instantaneously. Overfishing, desertification, and soil erosion potentially threaten all of us in the future; but they can and do mean malnutrition and hunger for tens of millions of poor people in the Third World, who live just one step away from epidemics and famine.

Global Imbalance

The potential for global environmental problems, together with pollution and poverty in the Third World, pose serious moral and ethical questions for the First World. As mentioned in Chapter 2, much of the success of the First World has come from the exploitation of the Third World. "The industrialization and high levels of consumption in the North [i.e., the First World] have depended on access to the whole world's resources. But if the majority of the rest of the world industrializes," note Bhaskar and Glyn, "this shrinks the hinterland whose resources can be exploited for benefit elsewhere."[111] Given that resources are limited, if the Third World is unable to use its resources for its own development, then that development will be very problematic; if the First World is unable to continue exploiting the resources of the Third World, then First World economic expansion will become very problematic.

As mentioned earlier in this chapter, many peoples of the Third World and their political leaders are aspiring to First World standards of living, but environmentalists who examine the global situation are generally in agreement that the economies of the First World and the Third World cannot both expand without future environmental disaster, which will devastate the earth's natural resources and produce intolerable levels of pollution. So how should development in both the First World and the Third World proceed?

The answer frequently heard in environmental circles is "sustainable development," that is, if development is to proceed, it must be in a manner that can be sustained into future generations. Sustainable development emphasizes that the earth's resources are finite and that "we all share one world, and thus a common future."[112] Proponents frequently argue that development needs to be coordinated on a global basis and that there must be negotiations and a certain give-and-take between countries. All parties will have to make sacrifices. Frank Amalric expresses the essence of sustainable development,

> Since we all share the same world, we all have to make some efforts to save it, and thus, implicitly, we all have to make some sacrifices for it. This world we share is a world of limited natural resources, of limited global commons. In other words, what we share is a common problem, the global environmental crisis, because it may affect the lives of us all. Furthermore, through this crisis, we all become supposedly interdependent: each person's behavior and well-being is connected to other people's behaviors through the global biospheric system.[113]

Of course, when negotiations, give-and-take, and sacrifices are involved, the issue of fairness always comes into play. Representatives from First World countries say they already have enough environmental regulation and that the Third World needs to do more to control environmental degradation because, in their haste to industrialize, they have implemented virtually no controls over waste disposal, clear-cutting rainforests, and industrial and automotive emissions. Indeed, they have a point. On the other hand, the representatives from Third World countries say that the First World was able to achieve its level of industrial development without concern for environmental regulation, and it is now so far ahead in industrialization and material comfort that it has no moral right to ask the Third World to slow down its economic growth by way of environmental regulation. If anybody is going to make sacrifices, it is frequently heard, the First World should take the lead by cutting down on consumption.

Seventy-five percent of the world's carbon dioxide emissions are produced by industrialized countries. The average American produces 2.5 times more carbon dioxide emissions than the average European and 10 times more than the average African, South American, or Asian.[114] Notes Martin Khor Kok Peng, "[T]he North with 20 percent of the world's population uses 80 percent of the world's resources and has an average per capita income fifteen times higher than the South."[115] Given the extent of absolute poverty in the Third World, and with the average American producing waste and consuming resources at rates fifteen to thirty-five times greater than the average resident of the Third World, it may be argued that the Third World's emissions are largely a matter of survival. Further, at least from the Third World perspective, the emissions of the First World are largely a matter of maintaining luxury.[116] Thus, the First World's call for developing countries to implement costly environmental regulations often tends to ring hollow.

"It is easy for outsiders to warn against the long-term costs of damming Africa's rivers, ruining its scenery, or destroying its woodlands," says Hertsgaard, "but it is akin to a glutton admonishing a beggar to watch his carbohydrates."[117] And while Third World emissions are increasing by leaps and bounds, their "per capita emissions" are only a tiny fraction of per capita emissions in the First World. If the world is to be viewed as a "global commons," some argue, then perhaps the countries with the larger populations should be permitted to create more pollution.

The First World's contribution to global pollution levels is further exacerbated by efforts of multinational corporations to evade First World environmental regulations by building some of their more hazardous facilities in the Third World. Frequently, environmental regulations in the Third World are technically as stringent as those in the First World. However, they are far less likely to be enforced; Third World countries are well aware that if they enforce their environmental regulations, they will become less enticing to the multinational corporations. Until recently, it was also common practice for the First World to ship its toxic and nuclear wastes to the Third World for disposal. Many Third World countries (or their corrupt officials), desperate for First World monies, accepted this arrangement for a fee. In the late 1980s, it cost between $100 to $2,000 to dispose of a ton of hazardous waste in First World countries, but only between $2.50 and $50 in Africa.[118] In 1988, a load of polychlorinated biphenyls (PCBs) from Italy had been found dumped in a farmer's backyard in Nigeria. After this and a series of other internationally publicized "toxic cargoes" to the Third World, and realizing that poor countries were not properly disposing of these wastes, posing harm to both regional and global environments, in 1997, the Basel Convention on the Control of Transboundary Movements of Hazardous Wastes and their Disposal banned the shipment of hazardous wastes from developed to developing countries. Loopholes in the agreement, however, allow such practices to continue.

Since the issue of fairness often includes historical events, the Third World is not oblivious to the fact that so much of the material comfort of the First World was achieved and continues to be achieved at the expense of the Third World. Mellor writes, "The eco-economic chasm between rich and poor is created by a global market system that allows the over-consuming rich, white North, now joined by Japan, to scoop out the raw materials of the South, exploit its people as cheap labor, and use it as a dump for toxic waste."[119] It is not so difficult to understand the Third World's disdain for the First World's call for them to cut back on economic growth in favor of environmental regulation. "This," states Anil Agarwal, Director of the Center for Science and Environment in India, "is a very status quo approach in which the rich and powerful keep creating problems, and then the rest of the world, once those problems are created, must get together and try to solve them."[120]

APPLICATION: OVERPOPULATION

Many demographers argue that population growth is among the most, if not *the* most critical strain on the environment today. People, of course, need to expend resources in order to survive, and population growth has strained the earth's capacity to provide enough resources. A joint statement issued in 1993 by the national science academies of fifty-eight countries asserted that the more serious social, economic, and environmental problems of the world could not be successfully addressed without a stable global population.[121] Billions of dollars, for example, have been spent on improving the problems of water supplies to the poor countries of the Third World that were discussed earlier in this chapter. But many of these improvements have been overwhelmed or negated by the strains of population growth.

Despite declines in birth rates throughout most of the world, the human population is growing by approximately 85 million people a year, approximately the population of Mexico. Today, China and India both have populations of over one billion people. To make matters worse, the vast majority of the (almost quarter of a million) people born today are being born in the poorest countries, those least able to afford them. Throughout most of history and most of the world, birth rates have been highest among the poor. The poor are often dependent upon large numbers of children to help in producing more food for the family. In agricultural societies, for example, the more offspring a couple has, the more help there is in the field. Higher child and infant mortality rates among the poor also tend to push up their birth rates, in that parents have to produce more children to compensate for those who can be expected to die at an early age. Further, lacking any kind of security for old age, additional children help to provide for their elder parents. Value systems develop around these essential needs until high reproduction rates become part of the culture—sometimes even when the population becomes urbanized and large families become dysfunctional.

At the encouragement of the First World, and often with its financial assistance, many Third World countries are tackling the problem with aggressive population control programs. "[A]bout 61 percent of the people in the world live under a government that incites them to have fewer children," writes Amalric.[122] Such family planning programs bribe or entice women to use contraception. Birth control pills may be issued, IUDs (intrauterine devices) inserted, or Norplant implanted. (Norplant is a time-released birth control device implanted underneath the skin on the arm that can be effective for up to five years.) In the 1980s, the Dalkon Shield was banned in the United States, as it posed unacceptable risk of serious infection, but more than a million of them continued to be distributed in the Third World.[123] Women issued these and other forms of birth control were frequently not told of possible side effects, nor were they provided with the opportunity to have these devices and implants removed if complications developed.

As another means of birth control, Third World governments and their family planning agencies often encourage men and women—especially women—to undergo sterilization procedures. Fifteen percent of contraceptive use in the First World involves sterilization, whereas almost half (45 percent) of contraceptive use in the Third World involves sterilization, with rates as high as 86 percent in Nepal, 70 per cent in India, and 66 percent in Dominican Republic.[124] Although male sterilization is a simpler procedure, female sterilization is more common. In the First World, women are twice as likely to be sterilized than men, and in the Third World, they are almost three times more likely to be sterilized.[125] Reportedly, China, India, Bangladesh, and Indonesia have forced some women to be sterilized.[126] More often, however, Third World governments have offered women financial incentives or disincentives; but when financial incentives are offered to someone living on the brink of destitution, there is, of course, some question as to whether consent has been given voluntarily. Asoka Bandarage writes, "[C]oercion does not pertain simply to the outright use of force. More subtle forms of coercion arise when individual reproductive decisions are tied to sources of survival like the availability of food, shelter, employment, education, health care, and so on."[127]

A critical constructionist analysis recognizes that population growth strains the environment and that contraceptives should be made available to those who want them; however, such an analysis emphasizes, first, that in terms of per capita impact on the environment, First World populations do far more harm than Third World populations. The average per capita consumption of energy in the United States is more than 37 times greater than that of India and more than 55 times that of Nigeria.[128] Over the course of his or her lifetime, the average American has thirteen times more impact on the environment than the average Brazilian and thirty-five times that of the average Indian.[129] While poverty in Third World countries is often blamed on the fact that they are "overpopulated," they frequently have population densities considerably *lower* than their wealthy counterparts, such as Hong Kong and the Netherlands. Thus, the problem of population growth could be reconstructed as a problem relating to the distribution of resources. The First World, which consumes disproportionate amounts of resources and produces more than its share of waste, is rarely considered "overpopulated" because it can afford to consume and waste at present rates. In this sense, the problem of overpopulation boils down to the problem of poverty, and to blame poverty on overpopulation amounts to circular reasoning. The plight of the Third World poor is not so much due to "overpopulation" as it is to poverty itself. There is little doubt that if they had more money, they would have more food.

There is also little doubt that if they had more *land*, they would have more food. Much of the problem of poverty in the Third World stems from the inequitable distribution of land. This is especially the case in the former European colonies. When the Europeans took over these countries, they took the best lands for themselves. But when they gave their former colonies their "freedom" to become independent countries, they did not redistribute the land to the natives. Instead, the best land has remained in the hands of descendants of the European colonists, or descendants of those who collaborated with their European oppressors. In Guatemala, for example, 80 percent of agricultural land is owned by 2.1 percent of the landowners. Prior to land reform in El Salvador in 1980, less than 2 percent of the population owned almost all of the cultivatable land. In Nicaragua, before the Sandanista revolution, 23 percent of the arable land was owned by one family.[130] Many of these countries do indeed have the land resources to adequately feed their populations, but wealthy landowners, instead, use their lands to grow crops that can be exported to First World countries, such as coffee and bananas. Many of these countries, writes Bill Weinberg, "are producing massive quantities of luxury cash crops, such as coffee, for export. The beef from the livestock is not consumed domestically, but exported. It is not 'food' to feed 'their expanding populations.'"[131]

Given that the problem of overpopulation is as much or more a problem of resource distribution, critics often charge that the First World's involvement in birth control programs in the Third World amounts to little more than eugenics, with the mostly Caucasian First World demanding that the mostly non-Caucasian Third World limit its reproduction. Some critics also see it as a form of "population imperialism." Fearing that the teeming hordes of poor throughout the world will become a political threat to both regional and global stability, the elite have mounted a campaign to reduce their numbers. Uruguayan leftist Eduardo Galeano expressed these concerns in his classic book, *Open Veins of Latin America*,

In the eye of this hurricane 120 million children are stirring. Latin America's population grows as does no other; it has more than tripled in half a century. One child dies of disease or hunger every minute, but in the year 2000 there will be 650 million Latin Americans, half of whom will be under fifteen: a time bomb. . . .

The United States is more concerned than any other country with spreading and imposing family planning in the farthest outposts . . . [They] have nightmares about millions of children advancing like locusts over the horizon from the Third World. . . . [I]n our day this global offensive plays a well-defined role. Its aim is to justify the very unequal income distribution between countries and social classes, to convince the poor that poverty is the result of the children they don't avoid having, and to dam the rebellious advance of the masses. While intrauterine devices compete with bombs and machine-guns salvos to arrest the growth of the Vietnamese population, in Latin America it is more hygienic and effective to kill *guerrilleros* in the womb than in the mountains or the streets. . . . Most Latin American countries have no real surplus of people; on the contrary, they have too few. Brazil has thirty-eight times fewer inhabitants per square mile than Belgium, Paraguay has forty-nine times fewer than England. . . . Haiti and El Salvador, the human ant-heaps of Latin America, have lower population densities than Italy. The pretexts invoked are an insult to the intelligence; the real intentions anger us. . . .[132]

Blaming poverty in the Third World on overpopulation is, arguably, a form of "blaming the victim" and thereby serves as a means of diverting attention away from the problem of resource distribution. First World countries are able to deny any complicity and, thereby, deny any need to alter the status quo. Third World elites have similar motivation to subscribe to the theory of overpopulation and embrace sterilization and other contraceptive programs. Blaming the poor can be one of many means they have of preserving their privileged status.

Again, the critical constructionist does not deny that overpopulation may be a problem, but exposes alternative constructions and the possible interests of the elite who favor popular constructions. If overpopulation is indeed a problem, family planning/contraception is only one way of constructing a solution. It is a solution that does not threaten vested interests of the elite.

Another solution to the problem of overpopulation is the empowerment of women, which is, of course, a solution that threatens vested interests in patriarchal societies. Patriarchal arrangements, especially in poor countries, force women into a role in which they are valued primarily for childbearing. Poor women of the Third World are often forced by their husbands to produce large numbers of children, and they are provided few meaningful roles other than that of childbearer. Often, they are not allowed to have a formal education and are kept from jobs outside of the home. Frequently it is they who seek contraception, often without their husband's knowledge.

The first step in the empowerment of women is education. Educating women may impact population growth because an educated women is better at independent thinking and, therefore, better able to challenge notions about traditional gender roles. An educated woman is better able to get a job outside of the home and, spending her day outside of the home, she is more likely to be exposed to a variety of ideas about gender roles. Working outside of the home, she becomes less financially dependent on her husband and is able speak her own mind. Simply put, an educated woman is likely to have more options, other than childbearing, than a woman without an education. A study by the United Nations found that women who completed seven years of education were likely to have three fewer children than women with no education. The World Bank estimates that if the education of men and women had been equalized thirty years ago, population growth, today, would be nearly stable.[133] Writes Bandarage, "Economic and social empowerment of women is the key to breaking the cycle connecting women, population, and global crisis."[134] Unlike many of the contraception programs being foisted on poor women of the Third World, efforts to educate and empower women will, says Reed Boland, be "promoting human rights rather than compromising them."[135]

SUMMARY

Environmental problems can have both local and global impacts. Until fairly recently, only local impacts had been given much attention because they are more easily observed and understood. However, with the issues of ozone depletion and global warming, global environmental issues are receiving a good deal more attention today, sometimes at the risk of downplaying local problems. Global environmental issues tend to be very complicated both in terms of their causes and their effects. Global warming, if it continues at its present rate, is predicted to have disastrous effects on human society in coming generations. Such a prediction, while it is held by a large majority of climatologists, is hypothetical and cannot be definitively proven. Detractors of global warming theory argue that global temperature trends are always in flux and present warming trends do not represent anything out of the ordinary.

Scientists say that global warming is due in large part to industrial and automotive emissions. Preventing it will require cutting back on such emissions. Corporations that are responsible for a great deal of environmental pollution thus have an interest in delegitimating global warming theory, and they have a number of tools for doing so. First, with the help of hired scientists and PR firms, they do their best to highlight the uncertainty of global warming theory. Corporations, often through their PR firms, will clandestinely finance environmental front groups to fight their battles so that the corporation's true interests remain concealed. PR firms have also been known to use less than legitimate tactics to prevent environmentalists from getting their message to the public; for instance, figuratively "burning books," even before they are published. Another method for squelching environmental activists is to "SLAPP" them with a lawsuit when they complain about a particular corporation's contribution to the pollution problem. Such lawsuits are rarely successful in the courts, but they may succeed in intimidating activists and would-be activists because of the time and legal and financial resources required to respond to them.

If we are looking for an honest discussion of environmental issues, there is little sense in turning to the media. The media are, for the most part, owned by huge transnational corporations, and they are dependent upon other corporations for their advertising revenues. Their profits are dependent upon presenting the news with a corporate bias. Yet news journalists almost always claim to be objective and impartial. They offer as proof of their impartiality the fact that they always give equal time to both sides of an issue. Such a "balanced" approach does not favor change and, if it does not favor change, then, by default, it must favor the status quo—a status quo that favors corporate interests.

Irrespective of global warming theory, most agree that the earth's resources are finite. Per capita, First World countries consume resources and produce wastes at far greater rates than the more populous Third World countries. If the Third World comes close to achieving its goal of catching up with the First World, then resource depletion and waste production would reach levels that the earth probably could not sustain. One tentative solution to this problem would be for the First World to cut down on its rates of consumption. This would require altering constructions of "the good life" and a devaluing of consumption. Lowering consumption could be both the cause and the effect of a shorter work week. People might have less money to spend on commodities, but they would have a healthier environment, more leisure, and more time to spend with their family.

Like so many other resources discussed in previous chapters, healthy environments are not distributed equally, either within countries or between countries. Within the United States, minority and poor populations are more likely to be located near hazardous waste sites. Minority and poor children are more likely to be exposed to lead poisoning and are more vulnerable to other forms of pollution. These injustices gave rise to the environmental justice movement and, later, to a presidential executive order that outlaws environmental discrimination by federal agencies. The effectiveness of this executive order remains to be seen. There is concern, however, that its effect will be minimal.

Inequalities in the distribution of healthy environments are even more stark when we examine the differences between countries. The Third World faces far greater levels of pollution, and millions die as a result. Water pollution is perhaps the most serious environmental problem in the Third World, leading to millions of deaths from diarrheal diseases, especially among children. Air pollution levels in many areas of the Third World are also inordinately high; indoor air pollution, especially, is a very serious threat to poor residents of the Third World. Poor people of the Third World are more vulnerable to these and almost all other forms of pollution because of their poor diet and lowered immunity. Both global and regional environmental disasters would almost invariably affect them first.

Aware that the earth could not sustain six billion people living First World lifestyles, it is generally recognized, at least among environmentalists, that industrial development cannot proceed uncontrolled. Sacrifices will have to be made. But the First World wants to see the Third World make sacrifices in terms of tougher environmental regulations. The Third World responds that it cannot afford tougher environmental regulation, but the First World could afford to reduce its levels of consumption. Indeed, the average First World resident places many times more stress on the environment and enjoys a material lifestyle far greater than the average Third World resident. So when the First World countries ask the Third World countries to slow down development with environmental regulation, they may be seen as lacking a certain moral authority.

Concern about strains on the environment often focus on overpopulation. The poverty of the Third World poor and their unhealthy environments are often blamed on overpopulation. However, the critical constructionist notes that there are enough resources to feed, clothe, and shelter everyone in the world. Many rich countries that place more strain on the environment than their poor counterparts are rarely, if ever, considered "overpopulated." Many poor countries have population densities that are lower than some of their wealthier counterparts. Many poor countries that allegedly do not have enough resources to feed their own people are, nonetheless, able to grow luxury crops for export to the First World. The real problem of overpopulation, then, could easily be constructed as a problem of poverty and of resource distribution.

Yet rather than question a global economic system that leaves billions of people on the brink of disaster, the problem of overpopulation in poor countries is addressed with aggressive birth control programs that frequently compromise the rights of the people. If we indeed accept that overpopulation is a problem that needs to be addressed, an alternatively constructed solution could be the empowerment of women in the Third World. In these often fiercely patriarchal societies, women are often left with few options other than bearing children throughout their fertile years. Education and the empowerment of women would provide them with more alternatives, and there is evidence indicating that such an approach would reduce birth rates.

Like the other problems discussed in this book, many of the problems associated with the environment and overpopulation can be alternatively constructed as problems of inequality and can be addressed by examining the distribution of resources. In the case of poor women in the Third World, the resources that need to be redistributed include education, access to employment, and political power. And like so many other problems that were discussed in this book, if these kinds of resources were more equitably distributed, a multitude of other—often seemingly unrelated—problems might be alleviated.

6

Conclusions

While it is not the purpose of this book to provide solutions to all of the problems that are discussed in the preceding chapters, critical consrtuctionism, with its roots in conflict theory, does lend itself to certain policies that would alleviate many of the problems addressed herein.

First, we need to recognize the power of corporate interests in shaping social and economic policy, as well as our perceptions of what is right and what is wrong with our society. Political campaigns have become prohibitively expensive, often costing tens of millions of dollars. Candidates and politicians have become beholden to corporations for campaign contributions. If their campaign platforms or their legislative voting records do not suit the interests of their corporate contributors, they run the risk of not being elected or reelected. There needs to be campaign finance reform limiting the cost of a campaign, placing further restrictions on contributions, and requiring full disclosure of contributors. One of the reasons campaigns are so expensive is because of the exorbitant costs of running campaign ads on television. Legislation should be passed limiting these costs. Most of the public does not know that the airwaves belong to the public—through federal licensing agreements, the government has signed their use over to multibillion dollar corporations that use them to make more billions. In return for the use of those airwaves, the networks should be required to offer free prime-time spots to candidates who meet certain conditions (to be determined) for their campaign ads.

Keeping in mind the critical role played by the media in problem construction, for the use of those airwaves which earn them billions, the networks should also be required to provide us with an hour of prime-time, commercial-free news every night. While the news will still be tainted by the network's corporate interests, it might be slightly less influenced by the advertiser's corporate interests; moreover, the networks might feel less compelled to turn their news shows into "infotainment" if they are not worried about selling commercial air time during that hour. These would be but a few steps in the right direction; but there are more fundamental, global, and sweeping problems that need to be addressed.

The world is poised on the verge of a social, political, and economic revolution as profound and tumultuous as the Industrial Revolution. More and more countries are becoming more and more integrated into the global economy. Business and political leaders around the world are telling people that in order to compete in the global economy, they can no longer afford regulations restricting the behavior of corporations. Corporations, we are told, must be completely flexible (free of regulation) if they are to meet the demands of an ever-changing market. Less flexible businesses will be beaten out by more flexible businesses, and the countries that host the less flexible businesses will be beaten out by those that host the more flexible ones. But the regulations that are being sacrificed in the name of flexibility and competitiveness have everything to do with our quality of life. In the name of flexibility, corporate interests can disregard the need for families to have access to stable employment; they can disregard employees' needs for health benefits, time to be with their families, and a minimum standard of living; and they can disregard society's need for an environment that does not put health at risk. If government regulations force corporations to attend to such concerns, the argument goes, then they will lose their competitive edge and the economy will falter.

Corporations have always shunned government regulations, as they have always seen them as impeding their quest for profit. Profit is, after all, their one and only goal, their *raison d'etre*, not the welfare of society. In the United States, they have fought tooth and nail against government regulations throughout our history. Eventually, people came to realize that slavery is a bad thing, that child labor is wrong, that workers should not be required to work eighty-hour weeks in order to keep their jobs, that workers should be guaranteed a minimum wage, and that they should be allowed to organize to fight for their rights. Workers' rights have come a long way in American history. But now, we are told that, in the face of global integration, such concerns are too costly. Corporate leaders have always felt that way, but global integration has become their trump card.

Not only are wages, workers' rights, employee benefits, family stability, and the quality of the environment threatened by global integration, but so too are our democratic freedoms. Free trade agreements have given the World Trade Organization (WTO) the authority to undermine regulations that are the result of the democratic process. Democratically elected legislatures in the United States, Europe, Japan, and elsewhere have enacted policies to ensure workers' rights, employment stability, and national self-sufficiency. Government subsidies to farmers, for example, have been intended to protect agricultural workers and to protect nations from dependence on other countries for their food supply. Today, however, the WTO—made up of people who are not democratically elected—has the authority to sanction countries with such policies and regulations because they inhibit free markets.

Capitalism has always produced change. Production modes that are inefficient or targeting wrong markets must change or be wiped out by the competition. But the problem with today's form of global capitalism is that the change that it is producing is escalating at a pace that will inevitably produce more and more instability. Instability creates more need for change ("flexibility") and, therefore, more instability. Again, people of nations throughout the world are being told that government efforts to control the pace of change will only make their countries less competitive. Global capitalism is sweeping over the world like a juggernaut and we are told that it is uncontrollable.

A famous sociological principle is called the Thomas Theorem. Named after W. I. Thomas, it states that things perceived as real are real in their consequences. For example, if everybody thinks the stock market will crash, then there will be a huge sell-off and the stock market will indeed crash. Similarly and certainly, if the people of the world are convinced that global integration is uncontrollable, then it will not be controlled. Global capitalism, however, is a product of human action, and it can be influenced by further human action. Capitalism, unlike Frankenstein's monster, is not beyond the control of its human creators. We must maintain our sense of authorship over this awesome phenomenon.

If we are to control the pace of global capitalism and maintain a modicum of stability in our society and our lives, we must first keep in mind that our efforts do not amount to an all-or-nothing gamble. Critics of regulation would have us believe that any given employee benefit or environmental law could make the U.S. economy a non-competitive economy. Donald Barlett and James Steele, authors of the book *America: Who Stole the Dream* write,

> What has complicated the debate about the nation's economic course is that most policy issues are cast in either/or terms. Either you're for free trade, or you're a raving protectionist. . . . Either you want government off of business's back, or you favor shackling American companies with onerous regulations. . . . Because there is no middle ground, the doors have been flung open to products made around the world, often by workers whose wages have been counted in pennies—eliminating American jobs. Because there is no middle ground, the progressive income tax—designed so that the very rich would pay their appropriate share of the cost of government—has been gutted. And because there is no middle ground, the notion that government has a vital role in the economic direction of the country has been shoved aside. Either you believe in unfettered private enterprise or that the government should run the economy.[1]

An overregulated economy, such as that of the former Soviet Union, could certainly affect our lives more disastrously than the unregulated economy for which we are headed. But there *is* a middle ground.

If the pace of global capitalism is to be controlled, the United States must take the lead. The United States has led the industrialized world in opening markets, deregulating the economy, and failing to provide its citizens with safety nets. It must now take the lead in the opposite direction. The United States may well be the only country in a position to take the lead because it represents such a valuable block of consumers on the world trade scene. The

United States is the wealthiest country in the world and its citizens, as we have seen, have a taste for consumption. The economic health of our trading partners depends in large part upon trade with the United States.

If the United States adopted policies closing its markets to countries with certain labor practices, those countries would seriously have to reconsider their labor practices. In the past, the United States has threatened trade sanctions against countries that employed child labor or prison labor. Countries guilty of such labor practices rarely have to reconsider them seriously because the United States has rarely followed through on these threats. Powerful corporate interests and their lobbyists have persuaded government officials that such sanctions could cause us to lose our competitive edge. But such actions would be a step in the right direction. Proceeding in that direction, we could restrict access to our markets by countries that allowed their female workers to be subject to sexual intimidation and rape. We could restrict access to our markets by countries that did not provide a minimum wage, by those that do not allow their workers to unionize, or by those that do not provide a minimum of environmental regulation and enforcement.

Without such leadership, we will see a continual ratcheting down of global working conditions and environmental standards. As long as capital's only goal is profit, it will continue scouring the globe for the least expensive, least restrictive production conditions. First World wages—for both blue-collar and white-collar workers—will be competing with Third World wages. The costs of First World employee benefits will be competing with the costs of Third World employee benefits. The costs of First World environmental standards will be competing with the costs of Third World environmental standards. Without leadership, the First World will be under immense pressure to approximate the conditions of the Third World. If the United States took the lead, Third World countries would be pressured to adopt First World standards.

If the United States took the lead in controlling the pace of global capitalism, I doubt it would be alone. Western European countries, Canada, Japan, and others have been dragged kicking and screaming into the new global economy. To compete—mostly with the United States—they are having to ratchet down their ability to provide high wages, generous employee benefits, and job security. In addition, European countries have had to scale back government policies that were in place to ensure low unemployment rates. Further, they have had to give up a good part of their national identities to form the European Union and implement a common currency. Japan, long famous for job security and low unemployment, has had to ratchet down the policies that made these conditions possible. In the past, Japan has insisted on being self-sufficient in its rice production; now they have had to cut back on subsidies that made this self-sufficiency possible. The programs and policies that are now being scaled back in the face of global competition were highly cherished and are being given up only with a great deal of resistance. Further, these countries have neither historically nor culturally placed as high a value on market freedom as has the United States. Many, if not most, countries would breathe a sigh of relief if the United States took the lead in controlling the fierce competition and instability engendered by global capitalism. Together, with the United States, they would represent a powerful block that could indeed slow down global economic integration to a pace that would continue to assure a reasonable standard of living in the First World and improve standards in the Third World.

If, however, we succumb to the dictum that government regulation of the economy can only do us harm, then many of the social problems discussed in this book will only get worse.

NOTES

Chapter 1: An Introduction to the Sociology of Social Problems

1. *Sourcebook of Criminal Justice Statistics.* U.S. Department of Justice, Bureau of Justice Statistics, Washington, D.C., 1994.
2. Emile Durkheim, *The Rules of Sociological Method.* Translated by S. A. Solovay and J. H. Mueller, edited by G. E. G. Catlin. New York: Free Press, 1966.
3. Kai Ericson, *Wayward Puritans.* New York: Macmillan, 1966.
4. Daniel Bell, "Crime as an American Way of Life," *Antioch Review,* vol. 13, 1953, 131–154.
5. Lloyd de Mause, *The History of Childhood.* New York: Psychohistory Press, 1974.
6. Steven J. Pfohl, "The 'Discovery' of Child Abuse," in D. H. Kelly (ed) *Deviant Behavior,* 3rd ed. New York: St. Martin's, 1989, 40–51.
7. George Herbert Mead, *Mind, Self, and Society.* Edited by C. W. Morris. Chicago: University of Chicago Press, 1934.
8. Neil McInnes, "Antonio Gramsci," *Encyclopedia of Philosophy,* Vol. 3. New York: Macmillan and The Free Press, 1967, 376–377.
9. Antonio Gramsci, *Selections from the Prison Notebooks.* Translated and edited by Q. Hoare and G. N. Smith. New York: International Publishers, 1971.
10. Daniel Hallin, "Whatever Happened to the News?" *Media and Values* (Spring) no. 50, 1990, 2–4.
11. Calvin Exoo, *The Politics of the Mass Media.* St. Paul, MN: West Publishing, 1994.
12. David Croteau and William Hynes, *Media/Society: Industries, Images, and Audiences.* Thousand Oaks, CA: Pine Forge, 1997.

Chapter 2: Inequality

1. John Gray, *False Dawn: The Delusions of Global Capitalism.* New York, New Press, 1998, 114.
2. *Measuring 50 Years of Economic Change Using the March Current Population Survey.* P60–203. U.S. Bureau of the Census, Washington, D.C.: USGPO, 1998.
3. Marc Miringoff and Marque-Luisa Miringoff, *The Social Health of the Nation: How America Is Really Doing.* New York: Oxford University Press, 1999.
4. Gregory Mantsios, "Class in America: Myths and Realities," in T. Ore, (ed) *The Social Construction of Difference and Inequality: Race, Class, Gender, and Sexuality.* Mountain View, CA: Mayfield, 2000, 512–526.
5. Robert H. Frank and Philip J. Cook, *The Winner-Take-All Society.* New York: Free Press, 1995.
6. Holly Sklar, "Boom Times for Billionaires, Bust for Workers and Children," *Z Magazine,* (November) 1997. Aavailable online at http://www.lol.shareworld.com/zmag/articles/nov97sklar.htm.
7. William Julius Wilson, *The Bridge over the Racial Divide.* Russell Sage Foundation. Berkeley: University of California Press, 1999, 27.

8. Miringoff and Miringoff, *The Social Health of the Nation*.

9. Harold Kerbo, *Social Stratification and Inequality: Class Conflict in Historical. Comparative, and Global Perspective*, 4th ed. Boston: McGraw Hill, 2000.

10. Miringoff and Miringoff, *The Social Health of the Nation*, p. 108.

11. John Gray, *False Dawn*, p. 2.

12. Harold Kerbo, *Social Stratification and Inequality*.

13. Edward N. Wolff, *Top Heavy: The Increasing Inequality of Wealth in America and What Can Be Done About It*. New York: New Press, 1996, 1–2.

14. James Lardner, "The Rich Get Richer," *U.S. News and World Reports Online*, February 12, 2000. (Available online at wysiwyg://75/http://www.usnews.com/usnews/issue/000221/rich.htm.

15. Richard Leone's introduction to Wolff, *Top Heavy*.

16. Cited in Kim Clark and Margaret Mannix, "Show Me the Money! Debunking the Myth that Everybody But You is Rich," *U.S. News and World Reports Online*, May 24, 1999. (Available online at wysiwyg://119/http://www.usnews.com/usnews/issue/990524/24mill.htm.

17. Wolff, *Top Heavy*, p. 21.

18. Quoted in Anthony Platt, "End Game: The Rise and Fall of Affirmative Action in Higher Education. Reconfiguring Power: Challenges for the 21st Century," in A. Aguirre, Jr. and D. Baker (ed) *Structured Inequality in the United States*. Upper Saddle River, NJ: Prentice Hall, 2000, 320.

19. Harold Kerbo, *Social Stratification and Inequality*, p. 355.

20. Mantsios, "Class in America," p. 523.

21. Sklar, "Boom Times for Billionaires."

22. Jeff Faux, "You Are Not Alone," in S.B. Greenberg and T. Skocpol (ed) *The New Majority: Toward a Popular Progressive Politics*. New Haven: Yale University Press, 1997, 23–41, at 24 (emphasis in the original).

23. Miringoff and Miringoff, *The Social Health of the Nation*.

24. Faux, "You Are Not Alone."

25. Lester C. Thurow, "Rise in Women's Earnings Mask Deterioration in Men's Pay: Family Income Stagnates," *The Boston Globe*, June 15, 1999 (online).

26. Juliet Schor, *The Overworked American: The Unexpected Decline of Leisure*. New York: Basic Books, 1992.

27. Miringoff and Miringoff, *The Social Health of the Nation*.

28. Wilson, *The Bridge Over the Racial Divide*, p. 30.

29. Beth A. Rubin, *Shifts in the Social Contract: Understanding Change in American Society*. Thousand Oaks, CA: Pine Forge, 1996, 61.

30. Louis Uchitelle, "Survey Finds Layoffs Slowed in Last Three Years," *The New York Times*, August 20, 1998 (online).

31. Noam Chomsky, "How Free is the Free Market?" A speech given in London, England, 1994. Available online at http://www.oneworld.org/second_opinion/chomsky.html.

32. Edward Luttwak, *Turbo-Capitalism: Winners and Losers in the Global Economy*. New York: Harper Collins, 1999, 45.

33. Katherine S. Newman, *Falling from Grace: Downward Mobility in the Age of Affluence*. Berkeley: University of California Press, 1999.

34. Ibid., p. 35.

35. Luttwak, *Turbo-Capitalism*, p. 59.

36. Newman, *Falling from Grace*, p. 242.

37. Lawrence Mishel, Jared Bernstein, and John Schmitt, *The State of Working America, 1998–99.* Economic Policy Institute, Ithaca: Cornell University Press, 1999.
38. Research cited in Newman, *Falling from Grace*, p. 28.
39. Ibid.
40. "Few Recover Totally from Downsizing," *USA Today* (*Magazine*) vol. 127, no. 2639, August, 1998 (online).
41. Rubin, *Shifts in the Social Contract*, p. 79.
42. Ibid.
43. Paul Osterman, "New Rules for the New Economy," *The Boston Globe*, Sept. 5, 1999 (online).
44. Steven Greenhouse, "Joe Hill in High Tech: Unions Need Not Apply," *The New York Times*, July 26, 1999 (online).
45. Rubin, *Shifts in the Social Contract*, p. 179.
46. Luttwak, *Turbo-Capitalism*, p. 60.
47. Newman, *Falling from Grace*.
48. Ibid., p. 8.
49. Sarah Ramsay, "'Downsizing' Takes its Toll on UK Professionals." *The Lancet*, vol. 354, no. 9181, Sept. 4, 1999, p. 843. Available online: Infotrac: Expanded Academic Index.
50. Wilson, *Bridge Over the Racial Divide*, p. 31.
51. Donald Barlett and James B. Steele, *America: Who Stole the Dream?* Kansas City, MO: Andrews and McNeel, 1996, 43.
52. Gray, *False Dawn*, p. 111.
53. Kerbo, *Social Stratification and Inequality*.
54. Holly Sklar, "Imagine a Country," in P. S. Rothenberg (ed) *Race, Class and Gender in the United States: an Integrated Study*. New York: St. Martin's Press, (2000), 192–201.
55. Phineas Baxandall, "Jobs Vs. Wages: The Phony Trade-Off," in D. S. Eitzen and C. S. Leedham (eds) *Solutions to Social Problems: Lessons from other Societies*. Needham Heights, MA: Allyn and Bacon, (1998), 136–140.
56. Ibid.
57. Elliott Currie. *Crime and Punishment in America*. New York: Owl Books, 1998.
58. Newman, *Falling from Grace*, p. 30.
59. Sylvia Nasar, "Where Joblessness Is a Way of Making a Living," *The New York Times*, May 9, 1999 (online).
60. Gray, *False Dawn*.
61. Thomas W. Haines, "French Workers Rally for Additional Time Off: Employers Chafe at 35-hour Workweek," *The Boston Globe*, Oct. 17, 1999, p. A16.
62. Kerbo, *Social Stratification and Inequality*, p. 272.
63. Gray, *False Dawn*, 93.
64. Quoted in Haines, "French Workers Rally," (emphasis added).
65. Luttwak, *Turbo-Capitalism, p. 40.*
66. See Luttwak, Turbo-Capitalism; Gray, *False Dawn*; and Barlett and Steele, *Who Stole the Dream?*
67. Kerbo, *Social Stratification and Inequality*.
68. Ibid.
69. *Household Food Security in the United States, 1995–1998 (Summary)*. United States Department of Agriculture, USDA, Washington, D.C., 2000. Available online at http://fns1.usda.gov:80/OANE/MENU/Published/FSP/FILES/fsecsum.htm.

70. *Statistical Abstract of the United States,* Bureau of Statistics, Treasury Department, Washington, D.C.: G.P.O., 1999.
71. John E.Schwarz, "The Hidden Side of the Clinton Economy," in T. Ore (ed) *The Social Construction of Difference and Inequality: Race, Class, Gender, and Sexuality.* Mountain View, CA: Mayfield, 2000, 67–70.
72. Jessie Willis, "How We Measure Poverty: A History and Brief Overview," Paper from the Oregon Center for Public Policy, February 2000. Available online at http://www.ocpp.org/poverty/how.htm.
73. Schwarz, "The Hidden Side of the Clinton Economy."
74. Ibid., p. 69.
75. Quoted in Louis Uchitelle, "Devising New Math to Define Poverty," *The New York Times,* October 18, 1999 (online).
76. Mishel et al., *The State of Working America.*
77. Joseph Dillon Davey, *The New Social Contract: America's Journey from Welfare State to Police State.* Westport, CT: Praeger, 1995, 41.
78. Ralph Nunez and Cybelle Fox, "A Snapshot of Family Homelessness Across America," *Political Science Quarterly,* (Summer) vol. 114, no. 2, 1999. Available online: Infotrac: Expanded Academic Index.
79. Gregory Weiss and Lynne E. Lonnquist, *The Sociology of Health, Healing, and Illness,* 3rd ed. Upper Saddle River, NJ: Prentice Hall, 2000.
80. Kerbo, *Social Stratification and Inequality.*
81. Mantsios, "Class in America."
82. Weiss and Lonnquist, *The Sociology of Health, Healing, and Illness.*
83. World Health Organization, "Press Release: World Health Report 2000." Available online at http://www.who.int/why/2000/en/press_release.htm.
84. Miringoff and Miringoff, *The Social Health of the Nation.*
85. World Health Organization, "Press Release: World Health Report 2000."
86. Weiss and Lonnquist, *The Sociology of Health, Healing, and Illness.*
87. Miringoff and Miringoff, *The Social Health of the Nation.*
88. Reported in Miringoff and Miringoff, *The Social Health of the Nation.*
89. World Resources Institute, *World Resources 1996–97: A Guide to the Global Environment; The Urban Environment.* New York: Oxford University Press, 1998.
90. Dennis Cauchon and Kathy Kiely, "Prescription Imports Get Big Approval," *USA Today,* July 20, 2000, p. 13A.
91. Ibid.
92. Theodore R. Marmor and Jerry L. Mashaw, "Canada's Health Insurance and Ours: The Real Lessons, the Big Choices," in R. Heiner (ed) *Social Problems and Social Solutions: A Cross-Cultural Perspective.* Needham Heights, MA: Allyn and Bacon, 1999, 185–195.
93. Kerbo, *Social Stratification and Inequality,* p. 281 (emphasis in the original).
94. Quoted in John Pease and Lee Martin, "Want Ads and Jobs for the Poor: A Glaring Mismatch," *Sociological Forum,* vol. 12, no. 4, 1997, 546.
95. Ibid., p. 545.
96. Kerbo, *Social Stratification and Inequality.*
97. Mishel et al., *The State of Working America.*
98. Donald L. Barlett and James B. Steele, *America: Who Really Pays the Taxes?* New York: Touchstone, 1994, 26.
99. Ibid.

100. Donald L. Barlett and James B. Steele, "Corporate Welfare," *Time*, vol. 152, no. 19, November 9, 1998, 38.
101. Ibid.
102. Ibid.
103. Ibid.
104. Mark Zepezauer and Arthur Naiman, *Take the Rich Off Welfare*. Tucson: Odonian Press, 1996, 8.
105. Prince Brown, Jr., "Biology and the Social Construction of the 'Race' Concept," in J. Ferrante and P. Brown (ed) *The Social Construction of Race and Ethnicity in the United States*. New York: Longman, 1998, 136.
106. Dalton Conley, *Being Black and Living in the Red: Race, Wealth, and Social Policy in America*. Berkeley: University of California Press, 1999, 10.
107. Blaine Friedlander, Jr., "Poverty Touches 91% of African Americans During Adult Years," *Cornell Chronicle*, vol. 30, no. 29, April 8, 1999. Available online at http://www.news.cornell.edu/Chronicles/4.8.99/poverty_study.html.
108. Martin Marger, *Social Inequality: Patterns and Processes*. Mountain View, CA: Mayfield, 1999, 281.
109. Ibid.
110. Quoted in Wilson, *Bridge Over the Racial Divide*, p. 19.
111. Katherine S. Newman, "Job Availability: Achilles Heel of Welfare Reform," in R. Heiner (ed) *Social Problems and Social Solutions: A Cross-Cultural Perspective*. Needham Heights, MA: Allyn and Bacon, 1999, 144.
112. Conley, *Being Black and Living in the Red*.
113. Isabelle Wilkerson, "Middle Class Blacks Try to Grip a Ladder While Lending a Hand," in P. S. Rothenberg (ed) *Race, Class, and Gender in the United States*, 4th ed. New York: St. Martin's, 1998, 226.
114. Conley, *Being Black and Living in the Red*, 6.
115. Platt, "End Game: The Rise and Fall of Affirmative Action," p. 322.
116. Wilson, *Bridge Over the Racial Divide*, p. 23.
117. Deborah L. Rhode, "Affirmative Action," in R. Heiner (ed) *Social Problems and Social Solutions: A Cross-Cultural Perspective*, p. 69.
118. Ibid., p. 70.
119. Ibid.
120. Michael Parenti, "Imperialism 101," in R. Heiner (ed) *Social Problems and Social Solutions: A Cross-Cultural Perspective*, p. 32.
121. Ibid., p. 34.
122. Ibid.
123. Ibid.
124. Walden Bello, "Global Economic Counterrevolution: The Dynamics of Impoverishment and Marginalization," in R. Hofrichter (ed) *Toxic Struggles: The Theory and Practice of Environmental Justice*. Philadelphia: New Society Publishers, (1993), 197–208.
125. Dennis Pirages, "The Global Environment: Megaproblem or Not?" *The Futurist*, (March-April) vol. 31, no. 2, 1997. Available online: Infotrac: Expanded Academic Index.
126. Paul Lewis, "World Bank Says Poverty Is Increasing," *The New York Times*, June 3, 1999 (online).

127. Hazel Henderson, "The Global Environment: Megaproblem or Not?" *The Futurist* (March–April), vol. 31, no. 2, 1997. Available online: Infotrac: Expanded Academic Index.

128. Frederick H. Buttel and Peter J. Taylor, "Environmental Sociology and Global Environmental Change: A Critical Assessment," *Society and Natural Resources*, vol. 5, 1992, 225.

129. Robert Weissman, "Corporate Plundering of the Third World," in R. Hofrichter (ed) *Toxic Struggles: The Theory and Practice of Environmental Justice*. Philadelphia: New Society Publishers, (1993), 186–196.

130. Ibid.

131. Richard W. Stevenson, "Debt Relief Promised, But Who Pays the Bill?" *The New York Times*, September 19, 1999 (online).

132. Jonathan Rowe and Judith Silverstein, "The GDP Myth: Why Growth Isn't Always a Good Thing," *The Washington Monthly*, March, 1999, 17–21.

133. Ibid., p. 17.

134. Michael Jacobs and The Real World Coalition, "The Politics of the Real World: Hope, Fear, and the New Century," in R. Heiner (ed) *Social Problems and Social Solutions: a Cross-Cultural Perspective*, p. 24.

135. Robert Heiner, *Social Problems and Social Solutions: A Cross-Cultural Perspective*. Needham Heights, MA: Allyn and Bacon, 1999, 368.

136. Quoted in Jacobs, "The Politics of the Real World," p. 25.

Chapter 3: Problems of the Family

1. Mary Ann Mason, Arlene Skolnick, and Stephen D. Sugarman, *All Our Families: New Policies for a New Century*. New York: Oxford, 1998.

2. Arlene Skolnick, *Embattled Paradise: The American Family in an Age of Uncertainty*. New York: Basic Books, 1991, 8.

3. John Demos, "Myths and Realities in the History of American Family Life," in H. Grunebaum and J. Christ (eds) *Contemporary Marriage: Structure, Dynamics and Therapy*. Boston: Little, Brown, and Co., 1976, 9.

4. Skolnick, *Embattled Paradise*.

5. Demos, "Myths and Realities," p. 29.

6. Ibid., p. 29.

7. Stephanie Coontz, *The Way We Never Were: American Families and the Nostalgia Trap*. New York: Basic Books, (1992), 15.

8. Ibid., p. 43.

9. Cited in Skolnick, *Embattled Paradise*, p. 11.

10. Coontz, *The Way We Never Were*, p. 11.

11. Demos, "Myths and Realities."

12. Ibid., p. 24.

13. Ibid.

14. Ibid., p. 25.

15. Mason et al., *All Our Families*, p. 2.

16. Skolnick, *Embattled Paradise*, p. 8.

17. Coontz, *The Way We Never Were*, p. 25.

18. Quoted in Coontz, *The Way We Never Were*, p. 26.

19. Skolnick, *Embattled Paradise*, p. 53.

20. Ibid., p. 52.
21. Coontz, *The Way We Never Were*, p. 9.
22. Carol Warren, *Madwives: Schizophrenic Women in the 1950s*. New Brunswick: Rutgers University Press, 1987.
23. *The Fifties*. "Let's Play House," television series broadcast on The History Channel, written and directed by Alex Gibney, The Fifties, Inc., 1997.
24. Coontz, *The Way We Never Were*.
25. Murray Straus, Richard Gelles, and Suzanne Steinmetz, *Behind Closed Doors*. New York: Anchor Books, 1980.
26. Coontz, *The Way We Never Were*.
27. Steven J. Pfohl, "The 'Discovery' of Child Abuse," in D.H. Kelly (ed) *Deviant Behavior*, 3rd ed. New York: St. Martin's Press, 1989, 40–51.
28. Coontz, *The Way We Never Were*.
29. Ibid., p. 30.
30. Ibid., p. 30.
31. Sylvia Ann Hewlett and Cornel West, *The War Against Parents: What We Can Do for America's Beleaguered Moms and Dads*. Boston: Houghton Mifflin, 1998, 97–98.
32. Julie Matthaei, *An Economic History of Women in America*. New York: Schocken Books, 1982, 213.
33. *Statistical Abstract of the United States*, Bureau of Statistics, Treasury Department, Washington, D.C.: G.P.O., 1997.
34. Hewlett and West, *The War Against Parents*.
35. Michael Wallace, "Downsizing the American Dream: Work and Family at Century's End," in D. Vannoy and P. J. Dubeck (eds) *Challenges for Work and Family in the Twenty-first Century*. New York: Aldine deGruyter, 1998, 23–38.
36. Children's Defense Fund, *Yearbook 1998*. CDF, Washington, D.C., 1998.
37. W. Norton Grubb and Marvin Lazerson, *Broken Promises: How Americans Fail Their Children*. New York: Basic Books, 1982, 248.
38. Philip Cowan and Carolyn Pape Cowan, "New Families: Modern Couples as New Pioneers," in M. A. Mason, A. Skolnick, and S. D. Sugarman (eds) *All Our Families: New Policies for a New*. New York: Oxford Univ. Press, 1998, 169–192, at 172.
39. Arlie Hochschild, with A. Machung, *The Second Shift: Working Parents and the Revolution at Home*. New York: Viking, 1989.
40. Maxine Baca Zinn and D. Stanley Eitzen, *Diversity in Families*, 4th ed., New York: Harper Collins, 1996.
41. Cowan and Cowan, "New Families; Modern Couples," p. 184.
42. Bryan Strong, Christine DeVault, and Barbara W. Sayad, *The Marriage and Family Experience: Intimate Relationships in a Changing Society*, 7th ed., Belmont, CA: Wadsworth, 1998.
43. Cowan and Cowan, "New Families; Modern Couples," p. 179.
44. Ibid., p. 171.
45. Ibid.
46. Ibid.
47. David Elkind, *The Ties That Stress: The New Family Imbalance*. Cambridge, MA: Harvard University Press, 1994, 4.
48. Juliet Schor, *The Overworked American: The Unexpected Decline of Leisure*. New York: Basic Books, 1992. Schor's estimate dates to 1992. A more recent estimate

from the Economic Policy Institute (July 24, 2000) indicates that "the typical married-couple family with children . . . worked 256 more hours per year in 1997 than in 1989." Report available online at http://www.epinet.org/briefing-papers/labor99.html.

49. Quoted in Lucia Hodgson, *Raised in Captivity: Why Does America Fail its Children?* St. Paul, MN: Graywolf, 1997, 210.

50. Ruth Sidel, "Family Policy in Sweden: Lessons for the United States," in R. Heiner (ed) *Social Problems and Social Solutions: A Cross-Cultural Perspective.* Needham Heights, MA: Allyn and Bacon, 1999, 112.

51. Josh Chetwynd, "Day Care Gets a Muted Cheer," *U.S. News and World Report,* (April) vol. 122, no. 14, 1997, p. 38.

52. Sidel, "Family Policy in Sweden."

53. Sheila B. Kamerman and Alfred J. Kahn, *Starting Right: How America Neglects its Youngest Children and What to Do About It.* New York: Oxford Univ. Press, 1995, 136.

54. David Whitman, "Waiting for Mary Poppins," *U.S. News and World Report,* (November 24) vol. 123, no. 20, 1997, p. 10.

55. Cost, Quality, and Outcomes Study Team "Cost, Quality, and Outcomes in Child Care Centers: Key Findings and Recommendations," *Young Children,* (May) 1995, 40–41.

56. Kamerman and Kahn, *Starting Right,* p. 198.

57. Paul Wellstone, "The Quiet Crisis," *The Nation,* vol. 264, no. 23, 1997. Available online: Infotrac: Expanded Academic Index.

58. National Center for Children in Poverty "Young Children in Poverty: A Statistical Update." Press release. Columbia University School of Public Health, 1998. Available online at http://cpmcnet.columbia.edu/dept/nccp/98Upress.html.

59. Arloc Sherman, *Poverty Matters: The Cost of Child Poverty in America.* Children's Defense Fund, Washington, D.C., 1997, 7.

60. Timothy M. Smeeding, "Why the U.S. Anti-Poverty System Doesn't Work Very Well," in D. S. Eitzen and C. S. Leedham (eds) *Solutions to Social Problems: Lessons from Other Societies.* Needham Heights, MA: Allyn and Bacon, 1998, 35.

61. National Center for Children in Poverty, "Young Children in Poverty."

62. Kamerman and Kahn, *Starting Right,* p. 9.

63. Dr. David Hamburg, head of the Carnegie Corporation, a foundation dedicated to the study of children's well-being, quoted in Kamerman and Kahn, *Starting Right,* pp. 4–5.

64. Children's Defense Fund, *The State of America's Children.*

65. Ibid.

66. Kamerman and Kahn, *Starting Right.*

67. National Center for Children in Poverty, "Young Children in Poverty."

68. Hewlett and West, *The War Against Parents,* p. 66.

69. Judith Chafel, *Child Poverty and Public Policy.* Washington, D.C.: Urban Institute Press, 1993.

70. Rebecca Blank, "Poverty and Policy: the Many Faces of the Poor," C. R. Strain (ed) *Prophetic Visions and Economic Realities.* Grand Rapids, MI: Erdman, 1989, 160.

71. Grubb and Lazerson, *Broken Promises.*

72. Sherman, *Poverty Matters.*

73. Cited in Sherman, *Poverty Matters.*

74. Ibid., p. 1.
75. Greg Duncan, Jeanne Brooks-Gunn, and Pamela Kato Klebanov, "Economic Deprivation and Early Childhood Development," *Child Development*, vol. 65, no. 2, 1994, 296–318.
76. Sherman, *Poverty Matters*, p. 15.
77. Ibid., p. 34.
78. Kamerman and Kahn, *Starting Right*, p. 20.
79. William H. Scarborough, "Who Are the Poor? A Demographic Perspective," in J. A. Chafel (ed) *Child Poverty and Public Policy*. Washington, D.C.: Urban Institute Press, 1993, 55–90.
80. Sherman, *Poverty Matters*.
81. Hewlett and West, *The War Against Parents*.
82. Children's Defense Fund, *The State of America's Children*, p. xvii.
83. Wellstone, "The Quiet Crisis."
84. Children's Defense Fund, *The State of America's Children*, p. xvii.
85. Kamerman and Kahn, *Starting Right*, p. 44.
86. Sidel, "Family Policy in Sweden," p. 116.
87. Kamerman and Kahn, *Starting Right*, p. 26.
88. Smeeding, "Why the U.S. Anti-Poverty System Doesn't Work Very Well."
89. Hewlett and West, *The War Against Parents*, p. 92.
90. Edward Luttwak, "Turbo-Charged Capitalism Is the Enemy of Family Values," *New Perspectives Quarterly*, (Spring) vol. 12, no. 2, 1995. Available online: Introtrac: Expanded Academic Index.
91. Sally MacIntyre and Sarah Cunningham-Burley, "Teenage Pregnancy as a Social Problem: A Perspective from the United Kingdom," in A. Lawson and D. L. Rhode (eds) *The Politics of Pregnancy: Adolescent Sexuality and Public Policy*. New Haven: Yale University Press, 1993, 61.
92. Jane Mauldon, "Families Started by Teenagers," in M. A. Mason, A. Skolnick, and S. D. Sugarman (eds) *All Our Families: New Policies for a New Century*. New York: Oxford Univ. Press, 1998, 39–65.
93. Deborah L. Rhode, "Adolescent Pregnancy and Public Policy," in A. Lawson and D. L. Rhode (eds) *The Politics of Pregnancy: Adolescent Sexuality and Public Policy*. New Haven: Yale University Press, 1993, 301–336.
94. Annette Lawson and Deborah L. Rhode, *The Politics of Pregnancy: Adolescent Sexuality and Public Policy*. New Haven: Yale University Press, 1993, 3.
95. Susan E. Harari and Maris A. Vinovskis "Adolescent Sexuality, Pregnancy, and Childbearing in the Past," in A. Lawson and D. L. Rhode (eds) *The Politics of Pregnancy*, pp. 23–45.
96. Rhode, "Adolescent Pregnancy and Public Policy."
97. Ibid.
98. Ibid., p. 301.
99. Diane M. Pearce "'Children Having Children': Teenage Pregnancy and Public Policy from the Woman's Perspective," in A. Lawson and D. L. Rhode (eds) *The Politics of Pregnancy*, p. 47.
100. Guttmacher Institute, *Sex and America's Teenagers*. New York and Washington, D.C.: The Alan Guttmacher Institute, 1994.
101. Ibid.
102. MacIntyre and Cunningham-Burley, "Teenage Pregnancy as a Social Problem: A Perspective from the United Kingdom," p. 59.

103. Ibid., p. 65–66.
104. Ann Phoenix, "The Social Construction of Teenage Motherhood: A Black and White Issue," in A. Lawson and D. L. Rhode (eds) *The Politics of Pregnancy*, pp. 74–97.
105. Ibid., p. 74.
106. Mauldon, "Families Started by Teenagers."
107. Phoenix, "The Social Construction of Teenage Motherhood."
108. Elliott Currie and Jerome Skolnick, *America's Problems: Social Issues and Public Policy*. New York: Longman, 1997.
109. Mauldon, "Families Started by Teenagers."
110. Rhode, "Adolescent Pregnancy and Public Policy;" Mauldon, "Families Started by Teenagers."
111. Ibid.
112. Joseph V. Hotz, Susan Williams McElroy, and Seth G. Sanders, "Mothers: Effects of Early Childbearing on the Lives of the Mothers," in R. Maynard (ed) *Kids Having Kids: Economic Costs and Social Consequences of Teenage Pregnancy*. Washington, D.C.: Urban Institute Press, 1997, 55–94.
113. Mauldon, "Families Started by Teenagers," p. 51.
114. Quoted in Phoenix, "The Social Construction of Teenage Motherhood."

Chapter 4: Crime and Deviance

1. Emile Durkheim, *The Rules of Sociological Method*. Translated by S.A Solovay and J.H. Mueller, edited by G.E.G. Catlin. New York: Free Press, 1966.
2. See Jack P. Gibbs, "Conceptions of Deviant Behavior: The Old and the New," in D.H. Kelly (ed) *Deviant Behavior*, 5th ed. New York: St. Martin's Press, 1996.
3. Clellan S. Ford and Frank A. Beach, *Patterns of Sexual Behavior*. New York: Harper, 1951.
4. J. M. Carrier, "Homosexual Behavior in Cross-Cultural Perspective," in J. Marmor (ed) *Homosexual Behavior: A Modern Reappraisal*. New York: Basic Books, 1980, 100–122. See also Roger N. Lancaster, *Life Is Hard : Machismo, Danger, and the Intimacy of Power in Nicaragua*. Berkeley: University of California Press, 1992.
5. David F. Musto, *The American Disease: Origins of Narcotic Control*. New York: Oxford, 1987. See also Troy Duster, "The Legislation of Morality: Creating Drug Laws," in D. H. Kelly (ed) *Deviant Behavior*, 3rd ed. New York: Saint Martin's, 1989, 29–39.
6. James A. Inciardi, *The War on Drugs II: The Continuing Epic of Heroin, Cocaince, Crack, Crime Aids, and Public Policy*. Mountain View. CA: Mayfield Publishing, 1992.
7. Duster, "The Legislation of Morality."
8. For a discussion of cross-cultural variability in drug consumption, see Ed Knipe, *Culture, Society, and Drugs: The Social Science Approach to Drug Use*. Prospect Heights, IL: Waveland Press, 1995.
9. Stuart A. Kirk and Herb Kutchins, *The Selling of DSM: The Rhetoric of Science in Psychiatry*. New York: Aldine de Gruyter, 1992, 88.
10. Patricia A. Morgan, "The Legislation of Drug Law: Economic Crisis and Social Control," in J. D. Orcutt (ed) *Analyzing Deviance*. Homewood, IL: Dorsey Press, 1983, 358–371.

11. Musto, *An American Disease*, p. 244.
12. Craig Reinerman and Harry Levine, "The Crack Attack: America's Latest Drug Scare, 1986–1992," in J. Best (ed) *Images of Issues: Typifying Contemporary Social Problems*. New York: Aldine de Gruyter, 1995, 147–186. See also Arnold S. Trebach, *The Great Drug War: And Radical Proposals That Could Make America Safe Again*. New York: Macmillan, 1987.
13. Gary W. Potter and Victor E. Kappeler, *Constructing Crime: Perspectives on Making News and Social Problems*. Prospect Heights, IL: Waveland, 1998.
14. Eric Lotke, "Youth Homicide: Keeping Perspective on How Many Children Kill," *Valparaiso Law Review*, (Spring) vol. 31, no. 2, 1997.
15. Potter and Kappeler, *Constructing Crime*.
16. Steven Beschloss, "TV's Life of Crime," *Channels*, September 24, 1990.
17. Piers Beirne and James Messerschmidt, *Criminology*, 2nd ed. Fort Worth, TX: Harcourt Brace, 1995.
18. Debra Seagal, "Tales from the Cutting-room Floor: The Reality of 'Reality-based' Television," *Harper's Magazine*, (November) vol. 287, no. 1722, 1993, 52.
19. Ibid., p. 51.
20. Quoted in Beschloss, "TV's Life of Crime," p. 14.
21. Craig Haney and John Manzolati "Television Criminology: Network Illusions of Criminal Justice Realities," in E. Aronson (ed) *The Social Animal*. New York: W.H. Freeman, 1988, 125.
22. Joel Best, "Missing Children, Misleading Statistics," in W. Feigelman (ed) *Readings on Social Problems: Probing the Extent, Causes, and Remedies of America's Social Problems*. Fort Worth, TX: Holt, Rinehart and Winston, 1990, 11–16, at 11.
23. Ibid., p. 12.
24. Ibid.
25. Quoted in Best, "Missing Children," p. 12.
26. Ibid.
27. Phillip Jenkins, *Using Murder: The Social Construction of Serial Homicide*. New York: Aldine de Gruyter, 1994, 61.
28. Ibid., p. 64.
29. Ibid.
30. Ibid., 22.
31. Ibid., p. 17.
32. Trebach, *The Great Drug War*; Reinerman and Levine, "Crack Attack."
33. Erich Goode and Nachman Ben-Yehuda, *Moral Panics: The Social Construction of Deviance*. Cambridge, MA: Blackwell Publishers, 1994, 205.
34. Reinerman and Levine, "Crack Attack."
35. See Trebach, *The Great Drug War*; Reinerman and Levine, "Crack Attack."
36. Richard Smith, "The Plague Among Us," *Newsweek*, June 16, 1986, 15.
37. Reinerman and Levine, "Crack Attack," p. 152.
38. Ibid., p. 155.
39. Ibid.
40. Ibid., p. 164.
41. Ibid., p. 164.
42. Katherine Beckett, "Setting the Public Agenda: 'Street Crime' and Drug use in American Politics," *Social Problems*, vol. 41 no. 3, 1994. Available online: Infotrac: Expanded Academic Index.
43. Beckett, "Setting the Public Agenda"; Reinerman and Levine, "Crack Attack."
44. Reinerman and Levine, "Crack Attack," p. 170.

45. Steven F. Messner and Richard Rosenfeld, *Crime and the American Dream*, 2nd ed. Belmont, CA: Wadsworth, 1997, 22.

46. Ibid.

47. David H. Bayley, "Lessons in Order," in R. Heiner (ed) *Criminology: A Cross-Cultural Perspective*. St. Paul, MN: West, 1996, 3–14, at 6.

48. Messner and Rosenfeld, *Crime and the American Dream*, pp. 24, 25.

49. Ibid.

50. Robert K. Merton, "Social Structure and Anomie," *American Sociological Review*, vol. 3, 1938, 672–682.

51. Edwin M. Schur, *Our Criminal Society: The Social and Legal Sources of Crime in America*. Englewood Cliffs, NJ: Prentice-Hall, 1969, 187.

52. Steven R. Donziger, *The Real War on Crime: The Report of the National Criminal Justice Commission*. New York: Harper Collins, 1996.

53. "Developments in the Law—Race and the Criminal Process." *Harvard Law Review*, vol. 101, no. 7, 1988, 1473–1641.

54. Donziger, *The Real War on Crime*, p. 109.

55. Jay Livingston, *Crime and Criminology*, 2nd ed. Upper Saddle River, NJ: Simon and Schuster, 1996, 123.

56. Ibid.

57. William Julius Wilson, *The Truly Disadvantaged: The Inner City, The Underclass, and Public Policy*. Chicago: University of Chicago Press, 1987.

58. Ibid.

59. Elliott Currie, *Crime and Punishment in America*. New York: Owl Books, 1998, 32.

60. Carl Husemoller Nightingale, *On the Edge: A History of Poor Black Children and Their American Dreams*. New York: Basic Books, 1993, 137.

61. Donziger, *The Real War on Crime*, p. 101.

62. Nightingale, *On the Edge*, p. 130.

63. Gresham M. Sykes, *The Society of Captives: A Study of Maximum Security Prison*, Princeton: Princeton University Press, 1958.

64. *Sourcebook of Criminal Justice Statistics*, U.S. Department of Justice, Bureau of Justice Statistics, Washington, D.C., 1996.

65. For a detailed discussion, see Nils Christie, *Crime Control as Industry: Towards Gulags, Western Style*. London: Routledge, 1993.

66. Eric Lotke, "The Prison-Industrial Complex," *Multinational Monitor*, (November) vol. 17, no. 11, November, 1996. Available online: Infotrac: Expanded Academic Index.

67. Richard Swift, "Crime and Civilization," an interview with Nils Christie, *The New Internationalist*, no. 282, August, 1996.

68. Ibid., p. 11.

69. Lotke, "The Prison-Industrial Complex."

70. Donziger, *The Real War on Crime*, p. 95.

71. Quoted in Lotke, "The Prison-Industrial Complex."

72. Randy Shaw, *The Activist's Handbook: A Primer for the 1990s and Beyond*. Berkeley: University of California Press, 1996, 28.

73. Stuart A. Scheingold, *The Politics of Street Crime: Criminal Process and Cultural Obsession*. Philadelphia: Temple University Press, 1991, 21.

74. Currie, *Crime and Punishment in America*, p. 32.

75. Angela Y. Davis, "Masked Racism: Reflections on the Prison Industrial Complex." *Color Lines*, (Fall) 1998. Available online at http://www.corpwatch.org/trac/feature/prisons/a-davis.html.

76. Donziger, *The Real War on Crime*, pp. 102, 128.
77. Joseph Dillon Davey, *The New Social Contract: America's Journey from Welfare State to Police State*. Westport, CT: Praeger, 1995, 63.
78. Isaac Erlich, "Participation in Illegitimate Activities: An Economic Analysis," in C.S. Becer and W.M. Landes (eds) *Essays in the Economics of Crime and Punishment*. New York: National Bureau of Economic Research, 1974; Peter Greenwood and Allan Abrahamse, *Selective Incapacitation*. Santa Monica, CA: The Rand Corporation, 1982.
79. Davey, *The New Social Contract*, p. 60.
80. David Levinson, "Physical Punishment of Children and Wife-beating in Cross-cultural Perspective," in R. Heiner (ed) *Criminology: A Cross-Cultural Perspective*. St. Paul, MN: West, 1996, 39–43.
81. Robert Heiner, *Criminology: A Cross-Cultural Perspective*. St. Paul, MN: West, 1996, 197.
82. Nader Entessar, "Criminal Law and the Legal System in Iran," in R. Heiner (ed) *Criminology: A Cross-Cultural Perspective*. St. Paul, MN: West, 1996, 163–171.
83. Cesare Beccaria, *On Crime and Punishments*. Translated by H. Paolucci, facsimile edition. Upper Saddle River, NJ: Prentice-Hall, 1998 (originally published, 1764).
84. Lawyers Committee for Human Rights, "Criminal Justice with Chinese Characteristics," in R. Heiner (ed) *Criminology: A Cross-Cultural Perspective*, pp. 172–181, at 178.
85. David Downes, "The Case for Going Dutch: The Lessons of Post-war Penal Policy," in R. Heiner (ed) *Criminology: A Cross-Cultural Perspective*, pp. 243–253, at 245.
86. Heiner, *Criminology*, p. 243.
87. Downes, "The Case for Going Dutch."
88. Quoted in Downes, "The Case for Going Dutch," p. 248.
89. Marie C. Douglas, "The Mutter-Kind-Heim at Frankfurt am Main: Come Together—Go Together," in R. Heiner (ed) *Criminology: A Cross-Cultural Perspective*, pp. 254–260.
90. Ronald C. Kramer, "A Prolegomenon to the Study of Corporate Violence," *Humanity and Society*, May, 1983, 166.
91. Mark Dowie, "Pinto Madness," in J.H. Skolnick and E. Currie (eds) *Crisis in American Institutions*, 9th ed. New York: Harper Collins, 1994, 23–38, at 37.
92. Frederic Tulsky, "Shades of Pinto," *MOJO Wire*, 2000. Available online at http://bsd.mojones.com/mother_jones/JF94/tulsky.html.
93. Stuart L. Hills, *Corporate Violence: Injury and Death for Profit*. Totowa, NJ: Rowman and Littlefield, 1987, 5.

Chapter 5: Problems of the Environment

1. Stewart Udall, Foreword to William R. Catton, Jr., *Overshoot: The Ecological Basis of Revolutionary Change*. Urbana: University of Illinois Press, 1980, xiv.
2. Terrence R. Fehner and Jack M. Holl, *The United States Department of Energy, 1977–1994: A Summary History*, Washington, D.C.: DOE/HR, 1994.
3. From foreword to Catton, *Overshoot*, p. xv.
4. Sheldon Ungar, "Bringing the Issue Back In: Comparing the Marketability of the Ozone Hole and Global Warming," *Social Problems*, vol. 45, no. 4, 1998. Available online: Infotrac: Expanded Academic Index.

5. Ibid.
6. Quoted in Mark Hertsgaard, *Earth Odyssey: Around the World in Search of Our Environmental Future.* New York: Broadway Books, 1998, 13.
7. See Markku Wilenius, "From Science to Politics: The Menace of Global Environmental Change," *Acta Sociologica,* vol. 39, no. 1, 1995, 5–30. See also, Hertsgaard, *Earth Odyssey.*
8. Daniel Faber and James O'Connor, "Capitalism and the Crisis of Environmentalism," in R. Hofrichter (ed) *Toxic Struggles: The Theory and Practice of Environmental Justice.* Philadelphia: New Society Publishers, 1993, 14.
9. Sharon Beder, *Global Spin: The Corporate Assault on Environmentalism.* White River Junction, VT: Chelsea Green Publishing, 1997, 17.
10. Ibid., p. 19.
11. Ibid., p. 21.
12. Frederick H. Buttel and Peter J. Taylor, "Environmental Sociology and Global Environmental Change: A Critical Assessment," *Society and Natural Resources,* vol. 5, 1992, 223.
13. "Toxic Deception: An Interview with Dan Fagin," *Multinational Monitor,* vol. 20, no. 3, March, 1999, 3. Available online: Infotrac: Expanded Academic Index.
14. Beder, *Global Spin,* p. 109.
15. Ibid., p. 114.
16. Ibid., p. 115.
17. John Stauber and Sheldon Rampton, *Toxic Sludge is Good for You: Lies, Damn Lies and the Public Relations Industry.* Monroe, ME: Common Courage Press, 1995, 2.
18. Martin A. Lee and Norman Solomon, *Unreliable Sources: A Guide to Detecting Bias in News Media.* New York: Carol Publishing Group, 1992, 66.
19. Ibid.
20. Ibid., p. 65.
21. Beder, *Global Spin,* p. 116.
22. Ibid., p. 112.
23. Quoted in Beder, *Global Spin,* p. 36.
24. Quoted in Beder, *Global Spin,* p. 32.
25. "Public Interest Pretenders," *Consumer Reports,* vol. 59, no. 5, 1994, 318.
26. Ibid., p. 316.
27. Beder, *Global Spin,* p. 29.
28. Quoted in Stauber and Rampton, *Toxic Sludge,* p. 5.
29. Ibid., p. 8.
30. Ibid., p. 10.
31. Beder, *Global Spin,* p. 63.
32. George Pring and Penelope Canan, *SLAPPS: Getting Sued for Speaking Out.* Philadelphia: Temple University Press, 1996.
33. Ibid., p. xi.
34. Calvin Exoo, *The Politics of the Mass Media.* St. Paul, MN: West, 1994, 88.
35. Quoted in Exoo, *The Politics of the Mass Media,* p. 88.
36. Beder, *Global Spin,* p. 180.
37. Exoo, *The Politics of the Mass Media.*
38. Michael Parenti, *Inventing Reality: The Politics of News Media,* 2nd ed., New York: St Martin's Press, 1993.
39. Solomon and Lee, *Unreliable Sources,* p. 60.
40. Ibid., p. 78.

41. From foreword to Beder, *Global Spin*, p. 9.
42. Robert Heiner, *Social Problems and Social Solutions: A Cross-Cultural Perspective.* Needham Heights, MA: Allyn and Bacon, 1999, xv.
43. John Hannigan, *Environmental Sociology: A Social Constructionist Perspective.* London: Routledge, 1995, 68.
44. Paul Rauber, "The Uncertainty Principle," *Sierra*, (Sept./Oct.) vol. 81, 1996, 20.
45. Hertsgaard, *Earth Odyssey*, p. 274.
46. Juliet Schor, "Can the North Stop Consumption Growth? Escaping the Cycle of Work and Spend," in V. Bhaskar and A. Glyn (eds) *The North, the South and the Environment: Ecological Constraints and the Global Economy.* New York: St. Martin's, 1995, 70.
47. Quoted in Richard Smith, "Creative Destruction: Capitalist Development and China's Environment," in R. Heiner (ed) *Social Problems and Social Solutions*, p. 355.
48. Mellor, Mary, "Building a New Vision: Feminist, Green Socialism." in R. Hofrichter (ed) *Toxic Struggles: The Theory and Practice of Environmental Justice.* Philadelphia: New Society Publishers, 1993, 41.
49. Ynestra King, "Feminism and Ecology." in R. Hofrichter (ed) *Toxic Struggles*, p. 77.
50. Hertsgaard, *Earth Odyssey*, p. 196.
51. Michael F. Jacobson and Laurie Ann Mazur, *Marketing Madness: A Survival Guide for a Consumer Society.* Boulder, CO: Westview Press, 1995, 13.
52. Ibid.
53. Quoted in Gary Ruskin and Robert Weissman, "The Cost of Commercialism," *Multinational Monitor*, vol. 20, no. 1–2, Jan.–Feb., 1999. Available online: Infotrac: Expanded Academic Index.
54. Ibid.
55. Jacobson and Mazur, *Marketing Madness.*
56. Ruskin and Weissman, "The Cost of Commercialism."
57. Alain Lipietz, "Enclosing the Global Commons: Global Environmental Negotiations in a North-South Conflictual Approach," in V. Bhaskar and A. Glyn (eds) *The North, the South and the Environment*, p. 119.
58. Patrick Tyler, "The Dynamic New China Still Races Against Time," *The New York Times*, January 2, 1994, p. 4E.
59. Ibid.
60. Hertsgaard, *Earth Odyssey;* Smith, "Creative Destruction."
61. Smith, "Creative Destruction."
62. Daniel Litvin, "Dirt Poor," *The Economist*, vol. 346, no. 8060, March 21, 1998. Available online: Infotrac: Expanded Academic Index.
63. Hertsgaard, *Earth Odyssey*, p. 186.
64. Jane Holtz Kay, "Cars Cloud Kyoto," *The Nation*, vol. 265, no. 19. Available online: Infotrac: Expanded Academic Index.
65. Smith, "Creative Destruction."
66. Cited in Kay, "Cars Cloud Kyoto."
67. Hertsgaard, *Earth Odyssey.*
68. D. Stanley Eitzen and Maxine Baca Zinn, *Social Problems*, 8th ed. Needham Heights, MA: Allyn and Bacon, 2000.
69. Hertsgaard, *Earth Odyssey.*
70. Wilenius, "From Science to Politics," p. 26.

71. Clifford Cobb, Ted Halstead, and Jonathan Rowe "If the GDP Is Up, Why Is America Down?" in R. Heiner (ed) *Social Problems and Social Solutions,* p. 372.

72. Paul Ekins and Michael Jacobs, "Environmental Sustainability and the Growth of GDP: Conditions for Compatibility," in V. Bhaskar and A. Glyn (eds) *The North, the South and the Environment,* p. 23.

73. Michael M. Bell, *An Invitation to Environmental Sociology.* Thousand Oaks, CA: Pine Forge Press, 1998.

74. Ibid.

75. Marshall Sahlins, *Stone Age Economics.* Chicago: Aldine-Atherton, 1972, 1–2.

76. Schor, "Can the North Stop Consumption Growth?"

77. Ibid., p. 81.

78. Ibid.

79. Quoted in Schor, "Can the North Stop Consumption Growth?" p. 70.

80. Ibid., p. 71.

81. V. Bhaskar and Andrew Glyn, *The North, the South and the Environment,* p. 4.

82. Carita Shanklin, "Pathfinder: Environmental Justice." *Ecology Law Quarterly,* vol. 24, no. 2, May, 1997, 333–376. Available online: Infotrac: Expanded Academic Index.

83. Robert D. Bullard, "Anatomy of Environmental Racism," in R. Hofrichter (ed) *Toxic Struggles,* pp. 25–35.

84. Martin Lewis, "The Promise and Peril of Environmental Justice" (book review), *Issues in Science and Technology,* vol. 15, no. 3. Available online: Infotrac: Expanded Academic Index.

85. Scott Kuhn, "Expanding Public Participation Is Essential to Environmental Justice and the Democratic Decisionmaking Process," *Ecology Law Quarterly,* vol. 25, no. 4, 1999. Available online: Infotrac: Expanded Academic Index.

86. *COSSMHO Reporter,* "NIH Omits Hispanics in Farmworker Study," The National Coalition of Hispanic Health and Human Services Organizations, vol. 18, no. 2, 1993.

87. Christopher Foreman, Jr., "A Winning Hand? The Uncertain Future of Environmental Justice," *Brookings Review,* vol. 18, no. 2, 1996. Available online: Infotrac: Expanded Academic Index.

88. Benjamin A. Goldman and Laura Fitton, *Toxic Wastes and Race Revisited: An Update of the 1987 Report on the Racial and Socioeconomic Characteristics of Communities with Hazardous Waste Sites.* Washington, D.C.: Center for Policy Alternatives, 1994.

89. Foreman, "The Uncertain Future of Environmental Justice."

90. Bullard, "Anatomy of Environmental Racism," p. 28.

91. "Ongoing Efforts to Prevent Childhood Lead Exposure," *Journal of Environmental Health,* vol. 61, no. 10, June, 1999. Available online: Infotrac: Expanded Academic Index.

92. Bullard, "Anatomy of Environmental Racism," pp. 26–27.

93. "The Five Worst Environmental Threats to Children's Health," *Journal of Environmental Health,* vol. 60, no. 9, May, 1999. Available online: Infotrac: Expanded Academic Index.

94. World Resources Institute, *World Resources 1996–97: A Guide to the Global Environment; The Urban Environment.* New York: Oxford University Press, 1998.

95. "The Five Worst Environmental Threats," *Journal of Environmental Health.*

96. King, "Feminism and Ecology."

97. Quoted in Stephen Huebner, "Storm Clouds over the Environmental Horizon," *Society*, vol. 36, no. 3. Available online: Infotrac: Expanded Academic Index.

98. Robert D. Bullard, "Just Transportation: New Solutions for Old Problems," *Environmental Action Magazine*, vol. 28, no. 1–2, Spring-Summer, 1996. Available online: Infotrac: Expanded Academic Index.

99. Gerald Markowitz and David Rosner, "Pollute the Poor," *The Nation*, vol. 267, no. 1, July 6, 1998. Available online: Infotrac: Expanded Academic Index; and James Worsham, "Business Loses First Round in Environmental Justice Fight," *Nation's Business*, November 1, 1998. Available online: Infotrac: Expanded Academic Index.

100. Tam Hunt and Kevin Lunde, "The Stanford Committee on Law and Human Rights and the International Environmental Legal Consortium's 1998 Global Challenges Forum: Access to Justice and Environmental Protection," *Journal of Environment and Development*, December, 1998. Available online: Infotrac: Expanded Academic Index.

101. Faber and O'Connor, "Capitalism and the Crisis of Environmentalism," p. 18.

102. Geoffrey Lean, "It's the Poor That Do the Suffering . . . While the Rich Do All the Protesting." *New Statesman*, vol. 127, no. 4407, 1998. Available online: Infotrac: Expanded Academic Index.

103. World Resources Institute, *World Resources 1996–97*.

104. Ibid.

105. Ibid.

106. Ibid.

107. Litvin, "Dirt Poor."

108. World Resources Institute, *World Resources 1996–97*.

109. Ibid., p. 66.

110. World Resources Institute, *World Resources 1996–97*; and Lean, "It's the Poor That Do the Suffering."

111. Bhaskar and Glyn, *The North, the South and the Environment*, p. 2.

112. Frank Amalric, "Population Growth and the Environmental Crisis: Beyond the 'Obvious,'" in V. Bhaskar and A. Glyn (eds) *The North, the South and the Environment*, p. 99.

113. Ibid.

114. Wilenius, "From Science to Politics."

115. Martin Khor Kok Peng, "Economics and Environmental Justice: Rethinking North-South Relations," in R. Hofrichter (ed) *Toxic Struggles*, p. 221.

116. Buttel and Taylor, "Environmental Sociology and Global Environmental Change."

117. Hertsgaard, *Earth Odyssey*, p. 77.

118. Jonathan Krueger, "The Basel Convention on Transboundary Movements of Hazardous Waste," Energy and Environment Programme Briefing No. 45, The Royal Institute of International Affairs, May 1998. (Available online at http://www.riia.org/briefingpapers/bp45.html.

119. Mellor, "Feminist, Green Socialism," p. 37.

120. "Local Control or Global Plunder" (interview with Anil Agarwal), *Multinational Monitor*, vol. 15, no. 9, September, 1994. Available online: Infotrac: Expanded Academic Index.

121. Population Summit, Population Summit of the World's Scientific Academies, Washington, D.C.: National Academy Press, 1994.

122. Amalric, "Population Growth and the Environmental Crisis," p. 88.
123. Asoaka Bandarage, *Women, Population and Global Crisis: A Political-Economic Analysis*. London: Zed, 1997.
124. Ibid. (Figures rounded to the nearest percent.)
125. Ibid.
126. Ibid.
127. Ibid., p. 71.
128. *Statistical Abstract of the United States,* Bureau of Statistics, Treasury Department, Washington, D.C.: G.P.O., 1997.
129. Hertsgaard, *Earth Odyssey*.
130. Bill Weinberg, "Population as a Propaganda Device," in R. Heiner (ed) *Social Problems and Social Solutions*, pp. 340–348.
131. Ibid., p. 345.
132. Eduardo Galeano, *Open Veins of Latin America: Five Centuries of the Pillage of a Continent*. Translated by C. Belfrage. New York: Monthly Review Press, 1973, 14.
133. Reed Boland, "The Environment, Population, and Women's Human Rights," *Environmental Law*, vol. 27, no. 4, Winter, 1997. Available online: Infotrac: Expanded Academic Index.
134. Bandarage, *Women, Population and Global Crisis*.
135. Boland, "The Environment, Population, and Women's Human Rights."

Chapter 6: Conclusions

1. Donald L. Barlett and James B. Steele, *America: Who Stole the Dream?* Kansas City, MO: Andrews and McNeel, 1996, 30–31.

INDEX